Sarah,

So glad we are together.

Welcom to Dentsu

[signature]

The
Dentsu
Way

Secrets of
Cross Switch Marketing
from the World's
MOST INNOVATIVE
ADVERTISING AGENCY

The
Dentsu
Way

KOTARO SUGIYAMA
TIM ANDREE

AND THE DENTSU CROSS SWITCH TEAM

New York   Chicago   San Francisco   Lisbon
London   Madrid   Mexico City   Milan   New Delhi
San Juan   Seoul   Singapore   Sydney   Toronto

2 3 4 5 6 7 8 9 10 QFR/QFR 1 9 8 7 6 5 4 3 2 1

ISBN: 978-0-07-174812-4
MHID: 0-07-174812-1

e-ISBN: 978-0-07-175278-7
e-MHID: 0-07-175278-1

This publication is designed to provide accurate and authoritative information in regard to the subject matter covered. It is sold with the understanding that neither the author nor the publisher is engaged in rendering legal, accounting, securities trading, or other professional services. If legal advice or other expert assistance is required, the services of a competent professional person should be sought.
—From a Declaration of Principles jointly adopted by a Committee of the American Bar Association and a Committee of Publishers and Associations

Library of Congress Cataloging-in-Publication Data
Sugiyama, Kotaro.
  The Dentsu way : 9 lessons for innovation in marketing from the world's leading advertising agency / by Kotaro Sugiyama and Tim Andree.
     p. cm.
  ISBN 978-0-07-174812-4 (alk. paper)
  1. Dentsu. 2. Advertising agencies--Japan--Management. 3. Marketing--Management. 4. Advertising. I. Andree, Tim. II. Title.
  HF6181.D4S84 2011
  658.8--dc22
                                                           2010025379

McGraw-Hill books are available at special quantity discounts to use as premiums and sales promotions or for use in corporate training programs. To contact a representative, please e-mail us at bulksales@mcgraw-hill.com.

This book is printed on acid-free paper.

CONTENTS

FOREWORD

There is a fundamental difference in the way marketing communications developed and evolved in Western markets and in Japan. In the West, the various marketing disciplines—advertising, direct marketing, public relations, promotion, design, events, sports marketing, and, more recently, digital advertising—were the province of "focused" agencies. In the 1970s, when advertising companies began to acquire or build these capabilities, they tended to leave them as freestanding entities. Integration was promised, but not often realized, as management teams competed for revenue and corporate attention. In the 1980s and 1990s, this model was replicated for media services, which were unbundled from the advertising agencies.

The Japanese agencies, led by Dentsu Inc., followed a completely different path. From its founding in 1901, integrated marketing and communications design have been at the heart of Dentsu's offerings to its clients. Dentsu never unbundled its services. Today, Dentsu enjoys a 22 percent share of the marketing communications business in the world's second-largest market. This is proof of the validity and efficacy of Dentsu's approach to integrated marketing and communications design.

That approach was revealed for the first time in the book, *Cross Switch*, which was published in Japan in 2008 and instantly became a business bestseller. It is an approach that addresses the enormous complexity of today's media and branding environments. The Cross Switch approach deftly combines deep consumer insight, sophisticated quantitative modeling, and smart innovation to deliver solutions that have been tested in one of the world's most intensively competitive markets.

Having proven the Cross Switch approach in Japan, Dentsu is now bringing it to global markets. The time is right. As the media landscape continues to fragment and consumer purchase behavior changes dramatically, marketers cannot rely on old methodologies. Innovation is now a necessity. Cross Switch not only promotes a different way of thinking about marketing communications, but it helps take the guesswork out of the decision-making process with rigorous analytics.

A decade ago, one might have questioned the relevance of a Japanese marketing methodology to international markets. Today, we live in a truly global market, where consumer homogenization is propelled by instant access to a common information stream. The Cross Switch approach is not Japanese; it is universal. We share it in the hope that it will help marketers be more confident and successful at making decisions in an increasingly complex and challenging world. Furthermore, as Dentsu builds its operations outside Japan, we are infusing them with this unique set of abilities to make Cross Switch methods an integral part of our global offering to clients.

Tim Andree

ACKNOWLEDGMENTS

I am fortunate to be part of a company that attracts the best and brightest talent in Japan. Cross Switch is the product of more than 100 years of day-to-day experience, but pulling it all together has been a labor of love for the Dentsu Cross Switch team:

Shun-ichi Akai: Planning Director, Dentsu Inc.
Hideaki Haruta: Chief Analyst, Dentsu Inc.
Yasushi Hidaka: Chief Planner, Dentsu Inc.
Naoto Ichimaru: Chief Planner, Dentsu Inc.
Satoshi Ishigai: Chief Planner/Team Leader, Dentsu Inc.
Mamoru Nishiyama: Chief Planner, Dentsu Inc.
Kenzo Setoguchi: Senior Director, Media and Marketing, Dentsu
    Network West
Takaharu Tokunaga: Planning Supervisor, Dentsu Inc.

This book could not have been published without the understanding, cooperation, and assistance of countless individuals. I would like to take this opportunity to express our deep appreciation to all who contributed.

At Dentsu, everything revolves around our clients, and we are deeply indebted to each of them every day for their trust and confidence. Special thanks are due to those companies that gave their permission to share successful case studies: Coca-Cola (Japan) Co., Ltd.; East Japan Railway Company; Japan Dairy Council; Japan Tobacco Inc.; Nissin Food Products Co., Ltd.; Rocket Co., Ltd.; Shueisha Inc.; Toyota Motor Corporation; and Warner Entertainment Japan Inc.

We also give special thanks to Mr. Satoshi Takamatsu, the representative of creative agency "ground," for accepting our request.

Finally, I want to recognize our company President and CEO, Tatsuyoshi Takashima, for his leadership and vision in calling for the globalization of Dentsu, and I want to offer thanks to my co-author, Kotaro Sugiyama, Senior Vice President of Dentsu Inc., for whom the publication of *Cross Switch* in English for "western" consumption as *The Dentsu Way* has been a long-held dream.

Tim Andree

INTRODUCTION

D entsu might surprise you.

Picture yourself traveling to Tokyo, Japan. You get off the plane. You clear passport control. You pick up your luggage. You pass through baggage inspection. You declare that you're in the country on business. The agent asks, "Where do you plan to do business in Tokyo?" You reply, "Dentsu." He looks up deferentially and says with relief, "Ahhh, Dentsu." You can see how Dentsu is trusted in this country.

You might be surprised to learn that, by total annual revenue, Dentsu Inc. is the world's largest single-agency brand in the advertising and communications business and the fifth-largest agency company. Not just in Japan, but in the world.

You might be surprised about several other Dentsu facts.

The employees who enter Dentsu must join an expedition to the top of Japan's 12,388-foot Mount Fuji as a demonstration of determination and teamwork. Such expeditions have been a hallmark of "The Dentsu Way" since 1925.

Dentsu has been actively participating in the financing and distribution of filmed entertainment, including *Departures* (Academy Award winner for best foreign language film) and *Spirited Away* (Academy Award winner for best animated feature film).

Dentsu owns the award-winning office building located in Shiodome (pronounced "she-oh-doe-may"), adjacent to the world-famous Ginza shopping district and within walking distance of Tokyo Bay. Designed by the French architect Jean Nouvel and completed in 2002, at 48 floors and 700 feet, it is a "green" building, featuring roof rainwater collectors and special computer-controlled ceramic dots on the windows to control the climate, among other features.

Dentsu's Shiodome office building houses over 6,000 employees (as of March 31, 2010), all working together to serve the needs of their thousands of clients. No converted warehouse loft offices and networks of freelancers—Dentsu is a true corporate enterprise.

Dentsu's employees get a lot of freedom. To meet their clients' needs, and to express themselves, even on their business cards, each employee gets to choose his or her own business card color out of a palette of one hundred colors, and that's just a start.

Dentsu's employees have this kind of freedom. But does it start and end with creativity? Hardly. As you would expect in Japan, Dentsu people are single-mindedly and irrevocably focused on their clients. Dentsu's employees work hard to apply the precision, discipline, rigor, and holistic thinking of a Japanese organization to something as nuanced, behavioral, and intangible as advertising and communications.

It is a best-of-both-worlds combination, and the results are stunning. It is the foundation of "The Dentsu Way."

What Is "The Dentsu Way"?

What is "The Dentsu Way," and what do we mean by a company "Way," anyway? And why do we bother?

Like many of its brethren—"The Toyota Way" and "The Disney Way" for example—"The Dentsu Way" is a pervasive combination of culture and philosophy, consumer experience, and specific tenets that influence individuals in the organization as well as the organization as a whole. With "The Dentsu Way," as with others, we believe there is value in defining a way of doing business, in our case the agency marketing business. There is value in letting our clients, industry professionals, and even our competitors know more about it. In short, defining and explaining "The Dentsu Way" is our way of making a contribution to our field.

Before examining *The Dentsu Way* and getting into the more specific messages of the book, however, an introduction is in order.

About the Authors

I am Kotaro Sugiyama, Senior Vice President and Chief Creative Officer of Dentsu. I have been with the company for 36 years in many roles, primarily in the direction of creative, interactive, and digital media solutions. I come to you along with Tim Andree, Executive Officer and President and CEO of Dentsu Network West.

Together we assembled *The Dentsu Way* with the indispensible help of a special team known as the "Dentsu Cross Switch Team" to share our view of "The Dentsu Way"—the philosophy and the many strategies, tactics, and tools that support it. The names and roles of these individual professionals are highlighted in the Acknowledgments section.

Different Approaches to the Same Idea

Here's an interesting exercise. Get some Dentsu employees together in a room, or even in an elevator or a hallway. Ask them the question: "What is 'The Dentsu Way'?" Will you get the same answer? Another Dentsu surprise, and probably contrary to your notions of Japanese business culture—you'll probably get a lot of different answers. For that matter, you'll get different answers from clients and outside observers, too.

Here are some of the answers you might hear (and were recently heard during a Dentsu meeting to develop this book):

- It is a blend of ideas, technology, and entrepreneurship applied to marketing.
- It is a full range of marketing communications services for clients.
- It is a varied expertise leading to creative marketing solutions.
- It is a meeting of traditional and new digital media.

- It is a mix of precision technique and creativity.

- It is "Plan-Do-Check-Act," or PDCA, applied to marketing.

- It is "east-meets-west" in marketing and communications.

- It is right-brain-meets-left-brain applied to communications.

- It is complete and holistic; a "tea ceremony."

- It is about "Good Innovation."

- It is "Cross Switch."

While these answers are presented in random order, it's probably clear that some of these answers come from management, some come from employees, and some come from clients and outsiders. We'll leave it to your imagination to decide which ones are which!

We do realize that some of these answers beg for further explanation. By the time you finish reading *The Dentsu Way*, all of the answers you just looked at will make sense. We'll explain the "Good Innovation." philosophy a little bit later.

"Cross Switch," as we'll learn later, is our strategy and toolbox for Cross Communication. Cross Switch is a core strategy and a good example of the application of The Dentsu Way. It is important enough to merit coverage by three-quarters of this book.

It might sound like a bad thing in the corporate world that no two employees can articulate a company's vision or foundation consistently. But we actually think it's a good thing. As we'll describe shortly, Dentsu—again somewhat in denial of its traditional Japanese business roots—promotes freedom and creativity. Two different views of the same thing are actually helpful in understanding and defining it—and working toward a solution if that's the job at hand. Remember, if two employees think the same thing, you don't need one of them!

We sometimes think of "The Dentsu Way" as a meeting of right-brained, or creative, and left-brained, or analytical, thinking in a way that draws the most positives from both. It will be surprising for many to see such a thorough left-brained approach to something as typically right-brained as marketing communications. Dentsu doesn't produce tangible products like cars, televisions, or digital cameras. Our product is more abstract than that. But you will get the same rigor and thoroughness in process design, quality, and quality measurement as you would if the product came in a box with a power cord. It's effective. It gets the right customer attention at the right time in the right place at the right price.

We really like to think of The Dentsu Way as "Good Innovation.," and also as an intersection of ideas, technology, and entrepreneurship, ideas which we'll proceed to describe now.

Dentsu's Core Idea: "Good Innovation."

As much as anything, The Dentsu Way is really a mind-set. It is a mind-set that uses "Good Innovation." to apply a sophisticated set of integrated communication tools to a specific consumer's needs. But "Good Innovation." is really more than a mind-set. As Figure I.1 shows, it is a corporate philosophy about applying innovation in new and creative ways using new and creative technologies to deliver consumer and social value.

The best way to explain Dentsu's corporate philosophy is to share the message of our current President and CEO, Tatsuyoshi Takashima, as he announced the "Good Innovation." philosophy in January 2009.

Figure I.1 Corporate philosophy: "Good Innovation."

A MESSAGE FROM OUR PRESIDENT

The Dentsu Group established a new corporate philosophy articulated as a "Message from the Management" in January 2009 to the media and shareholders of Dentsu. Here it is, as articulated by **Tatsuyoshi Takashima**, President and CEO of Dentsu Inc., on the corporate Web site (http://www.dentsu .com/vision/message.html).

The slogan that best embodies our new philosophy is "Good Innovation."

By "innovation" we are not talking about just technological innovation. We mean reforming our organization and business model to create new, socially significant value, and drawing on new ideas that give form to our vision of being a business group that can help create a brighter, happier future for society.

We believe our new slogan will guide our business in the communications domain and beyond, such as helping our clients with corporate management issues or challenges in their business operations. We will always look at the situation our clients are facing, define each core issue, and deliver solutions for them.

To achieve this kind of innovation we must gather the three sources of our strength which are defined in our new corporate philosophy: ideas that reach beyond the imaginable, technology that crosses the bounds of possibilities, and entrepreneurship that surpasses the expected. The Dentsu Group's mission is to bring positive change to society, which in turn will lead to increased value for all stakeholders of the Dentsu Group.

Under our new slogan of "Good Innovation." we will look ahead to the future as a partner to our clients, media companies, and contents holders by offering "Integrated Communication Design."

Up until now, we have defined our business domain as "Total Communications Services." However, we must now have keener insight into the essence of changes in consumer behavior and branding challenges so that we can offer high-quality services which are integrated and concrete. We believe that the phrase "Integrated Communication Design" best expresses the current business domain and the strength of the Dentsu Group. We aim to evolve into a group that as a whole is capable of designing, proposing, and implementing communications that provide true solutions in an integrated way.

Guided by the Dentsu Group's new corporate philosophy, we will bring about innovation through various activities beginning in the fields of Digitization, Globalization, and Solutions.

—Tatsuyoshi Takashima, January 2009

The Intersection of Ideas, Technology, and Entrepreneurship

There are two Core Ideas contained within the "Good Innovation." philosophy that merit further explanation. The first is that "Good Innovation." lies at the intersection of Ideas, Technology, and Entrepreneurship. The second is what we call "Integrated Communication Design."

When one hears a phrase like "Good Innovation." it's natural to think that it applies to technology alone. But in The Dentsu Way, "Good Innovation." is not just about technology. As Tatsuyoshi Takashima states in his "Good Innovation." message, our corporate philosophy is based on three "pillars" of strength: Ideas, Technology, and Entrepreneurship. We go a step further to share a slogan combining the three elements:

- "Ideas that reach beyond the imaginable"
- "Technology that crosses the bounds of possibilities"
- "Entrepreneurship that surpasses the expected"

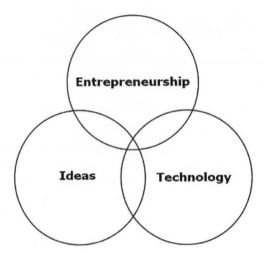

Figure I.2 The three elements of "Good Innovation."

The new "Good Innovation." philosophy stresses a new, fresh look at every possibility in every campaign, unconstrained by the standards of the past. Figure I.2 illustrates the triad.

Such an open, spirited way of doing business is very empowering and brings the kind of energy required to deliver a Dentsu solution. We know that Japanese companies are viewed as very structured and hierarchical, and not very accommodating to individual freedoms to create new ideas or new ways of doing things. With that in mind, it might surprise you that Dentsu is very entrepreneurial. Our employees are free. They're independent, free to think, free to act, and free to create. We may have 6,000 employees, but the way we look at it, we're really like 6,000 little boutiques. We have good ideas, and we have good technology. But it's the entrepreneurial spirit, and particularly the engagement among the entrepreneurial spirit, ideas, and technology, that make The Dentsu Way work so well.

Integrated Communication Design

In his statement on "Good Innovation." President Takashima noted that under our new slogan of "Good Innovation." we will look ahead to the future as a partner to our clients, media companies, and content holders by offering "Integrated Communication Design."

What does that really mean? For years, since the mid-1980s, we have recognized ourselves as a supplier of "Total Communications Services"—that is, a holistic blend of strategic planning, branding, marketing research, traditional media advertising, media buying and planning, creative design, sales promotion, public relations, and other marketing services. That vision was accurate then, and it still is now.

But today's marketing challenges have simultaneously become more global, more technology based, and spread across many more contact points with consumers. We now have technologies like point-of-purchase (POP) marketing and social networking services (SNS) that allow continuous real-time contact with consumers far beyond the traditional media advertising campaign. Those same technologies allow consumers to interact with us; these communications are no longer one-way. The potential "breadth" and "depth" of consumer involvement with a brand or a company is far greater than it once was, and the need to understand consumer behavior in this new environment and to adapt campaigns to it properly is obvious.

As a result, we at Dentsu believe that the phrase "Integrated Communication Design" better describes where we are today. To navigate this more complex maze of consumer interactions, we must now have keener insight into the essence of changes in consumer behavior and branding challenges so that we can offer high-quality services, which are integrated and concrete. We aim to evolve into a group that as a whole is capable of designing, proposing, and implementing communications that provide true solutions in an integrated way.

With our resources and experience all under one corporate roof, Integrated Communication Design isn't just a buzzword. We at Dentsu feel that we offer the sort of integrated solutions consumers really need today. These solutions blend consumer insight and research with a full set of creative and technology tools to pull them off in real time across all forms of media and consumer contact, including new ones as they evolve. We've done this for years, as you'll read in Chapter 1 with our involvement with the early days of television.

The Cross Communication solutions, which constitute most of the rest of this book, are an excellent example of how we bring ideas, technology, and entrepreneurship together to achieve Integrated Communication Design.

Cross Communication and Cross Switch

Throughout history, wars were said to be fought and won or lost depending on which side had the tactics that best kept pace with the technology–that is, the weapons–of the times. Marketing works in much the same way; it's imperative to keep up with and use new technologies to connect with consumers, or else the competition will get ahead and you'll have to invest heavily in playing catch up while also throwing money into gradually less effective campaigns and placements.

Technology gave us the Internet 15 years ago, and those who chose to embrace the Internet stayed ahead. The use of the Internet as a marketing tool is now almost universal.

Today, the Internet has matured, and we find ourselves in a new world where elevators, vending machines, and gas pumps are starting to talk to us. The mobile phone is becoming a "smart" rich media tool also capable of searching and making purchase transactions. Even more importantly, social networking services like Facebook and Twitter are adding a whole new dimension to the dissemination, and especially the sharing, of information about products and brand experiences. The possibilities are almost endless, and they're coming at us faster than the marketing profession can learn how to use them, particularly in an efficient, effective, and coordinated way.

It was around the year 2004 when the term "Cross Communication" began to gain popularity in the fields of communications and media. In this rapidly changing space many clichés and buzzwords came and went, but the term "Cross Communication" remains alive and well today, and Dentsu considers it to be an important and lasting concept in communication planning. That said, the term "Cross Communication" has been subject to a wide range of interpretations, likely because it is still in its early phases and really is still being defined.

Dentsu's "Cross Communication Development Project"

To address the possibilities of Cross Communication, Dentsu initiated a companywide "Cross Communication Development Project" in 2006 and has invested in a wide range of development activities. The formation of the cross-functional team to investigate and invest in the development of a complete set of Cross Communication strategies and tools is reminiscent of a similar commitment, made by Dentsu in the 1950s, undertaken to explore and capitalize on the possibilities of television. By now Dentsu has accumulated considerable know-how in this field, and has put this know-how into practice in order to resolve the issues faced by its clients.

The "Dentsu Cross Switch Team" is a cross-functional team composed of Dentsu employees with diverse specialties and experience in fields ranging from marketing and creative advertising to media, promotions, interactive advertising, and research and development (R&D).

New elements of Cross Communication, including approaches, know-how, success stories, and analysis methods, are being created every day through discussions among team members and extensive planning activities on the front lines of the advertising world. Parts 2 and 3 of this book are devoted to the specific premises and techniques of what we call Cross Switch, our Cross Communication solution and the brainchild of the Cross Communication Development Project. These sections will explain why Cross Communication is important, offer examples of why it works, and show you how to put it into play for your organization.

Dentsu's Cross Communication campaigns have won awards at a number of prestigious overseas advertising festivals such as the Asia Pacific Advertising Festival, or ADFEST, and the Cannes Lions International Advertising Festival. This book will share these success stories and introduce nine of Dentsu's latest methods and tools that will be useful in the creation of new advertising campaigns and ideas, and in the evaluation of results.

Flipping the Switch

By now you are probably wondering what Cross Switch is and where the term came from. In the early stages of the Cross Communication project, the team settled on a core strategy for Cross Communication: to "use Cross Communication to 'flip a switch' in the consumer's mind." See Figure I.3. The point is that it is no longer enough to simply use multiple forms of media to deliver the same message or campaign over and over. It's easy for consumers to filter that out, and likewise it fails to take advantage of the power of some forms of media, especially digital media.

"Cross Switch" is an approach—including strategies, tactics, and tools—to get through barriers put up by the consumer and maximize the

Figure I.3 Use Cross Communication to flip a switch in the consumer's mind.

results of a marketing campaign, especially the search, the action, and the sharing that consumers will do if they really respond to the campaign—that is, if their switch is flipped. Once that switch is flipped, consumer engagement and purchase action increase dramatically.

Dentsu recrafted the conventional "AIDMA" model for consumer response into a more twenty-first century approach called "AISAS" (which we'll cover in Chapter 3), which plays a very important role in Cross Switch. From there, Dentsu redesigned the campaign-planning process and created a set of new tools to accomplish the Cross Communication design. Cross Switch strategies, concepts, and case studies are covered in Part 2, while specific Cross Switch processes and tools are examined in Part 3. At this point, it's just important to know what Cross Switch is and where it came from.

SEEKING THE FIRST EDITION?

If you want a true first edition of *The Dentsu Way*, you'll have to find it in a Japanese bookstore. The book, titled *Cross Switch: How to Create Cross Communication by The Dentsu Way*, was published for the Japanese market in August 2008. It became a bestseller in the advertisement marketing category. The book has also been published in Korea and is also to be published in China.

Why Did We Write *The Dentsu Way*?

So why did we take the time and trouble to write *The Dentsu Way*? It was not to become a superstar in the publishing business, or to create an international bestseller (although if these things happened, we'd certainly be pleased.)

Simply, we at Dentsu felt we have a story to tell as we emerge onto the global stage. We have led the way in integrated marketing and communications design in Japan since the beginning of marketing as an "agency" profession. We have continued to develop this expertise to achieve excellence in today's complex branding and media environments. We now have the skills, the know-how, the technologies, and the insight to apply them to very complex marketing challenges. So far we have applied them mainly in Japan, but we feel our story is a compelling one, and we wish to share it with the worldwide marketing community, as well as others interested in Japan and Japanese business practices. We also consider *The Dentsu Way* as a medium to communicate our change in global strategy, from a company that affiliates with worldwide marketing companies to serve global needs to a fully integrated global enterprise ready to do business, with anyone and anywhere, applying Dentsu's methods.

We hope you gain and enjoy the insights from *The Dentsu Way* and that you can incorporate them into your own "Way" where it makes sense.

Mapping the Dentsu Way

To summarize what we've introduced so far: "Good Innovation." is the core philosophy of *The Dentsu Way*, while Integrated Communication Design is the principal service we provide. Within Integrated Communication Design, Cross Communication is a strategy for integrating communication, while the Dentsu application called Cross Switch is Dentsu's original approach to designing and providing Cross Communication. This will all become clearer in the chapters that follow.

The Dentsu Way is presented in three parts.

Part 1: Dentsu Comes of Age sets the stage by describing Dentsu's ascendance from its beginnings in 1901 to the "breadth and depth" of today's Dentsu.

- Chapter 1: The Origins of the Dentsu Way

- Chapter 2: Breadth and Depth: An Overview of Dentsu's Scope and Services

Part 2: The Cross Communication Imperative describes the emerging importance of Cross Communication as part of Integrated Communication Design. This section lays out our new "AISAS" consumer response model and the key elements of Cross Communication marketing campaigns.

- Chapter 3: From AIDMA to AISAS: The Growing Importance of Cross Communication

- Chapter 4: Cross Communication: A Look at What Makes It Work

- Chapter 5: Creating Scenarios for Cross Communication

Part 3: Putting Cross Switch into Play describes in more detail the strategic and tactical design of Cross Communication, including numerous examples and tools used to design, deliver, and measure the effectiveness of our Cross Switch campaigns.

- Chapter 6: Case Studies of the Cross Switch Way

- Chapter 7: The Cross Switch Design Process

- Chapter 8: From Insight to Scenario Creation

- Chapter 9: Structure Design and Measurement for Cross Switch

Cross Switch Online

For those who want to follow or expand their knowledge of the Cross Switch story, please refer to the Dentsu Cross Switch Web site at *www.dentsu.com/crossswitch.*

PART 1

DENTSU COMES OF AGE

CHAPTER 1

THE ORIGINS OF THE DENTSU WAY

Dentsu Inc., founded in 1901, is the largest advertising company brand and the fifth largest marketing and communications organization in the world. With overseas branches and subsidiaries on four continents, whether measured as a single agency brand or as a holding company, Dentsu routinely ranks among the top companies of the world in terms of revenue. For the fiscal year ended March 31, 2010, Dentsu's consolidated net sales totaled $18,041,897,000 (US $). These figures will be explored further in Chapter 2. We are the largest advertising agency in Japan, the world's second-largest advertising market after the United States. Our share of the mass media (newspaper, magazine, radio and television) advertising market is around 22 percent, almost twice that of our nearest competitor. Dentsu operates in 27 countries worldwide, and our portfolio of more than 6,000 clients includes multinationals in established markets such as the Unites States and the countries of Europe, as well as companies from the emerging economies in Asia and South Africa. That said, less than 10 percent of Dentsu's revenue comes from outside Japan. In fact, only $363,070,000 (US $), or 2 percent of Dentsu's total revenue for fiscal 2009, came from the United States.

Not only does one marvel at Dentsu's size, but also the breadth and depth of our offering. As mentioned in the Introduction, we operate within a framework of "Integrated Communication Design," which extends beyond the traditional parameters of the advertising business. Beyond the core of print and broadcast media advertising, the company does market research, branding, corporate image design, new product planning, publicity, and even major event planning and design for sports and expositions. We have traded on the Tokyo Stock Exchange since 2001. Chapter 2 will also examine some of the services and "Business Domains" in which Dentsu operates.

The company has undergone a major strategic transformation under the policy of "Good Innovation." toward digital marketing and to Integrated Communication Design. This strategic shift is targeted to help us grow in pace with—really ahead of the pace of—the digital world. It is also aimed to strengthen the offering, and bring growth, outside of Japan; that in fact is a lot of what *The Dentsu Way* is all about.

We have kept our traditional values, based on our long history, but on the other hand, we also have the most innovative minds and technology at the same time. This is just like the beauty of Japan, which has traditional values, represented by Kyoto and many other historical centers of culture, and also has one of the most high-tech industries in the world at the same time.

So how did we get so big? How did we start? Where are we going? This chapter tells the story.

The Early Story: 1901–1945

Most view the United States as the birthplace of advertising, and it is still the leader, both in size and development, of the advertising and marketing industry. While the United States leads the way, Asian advertising and marketing practices have not been far behind and, in fact, have tended to keep up well with the development of the industry in their societies.

Japan was hardly considered an industrialized country in 1901 when a journalist by the name of Hoshiro Mitsunaga, shown in Figure 1.1, set up a news agency called "Dempo Tsushin-Sha," or "Telegraphic Service Company," and an advertising firm called "Nippon Koukoku KK," or "Japan Advertising Ltd." He no doubt had a vision at the time to create and distribute the news and advertising to go with it.

Figure 1.1 First president Hoshiro Mitsunaga.

The Merger: An Early Innovation

Five years later Hoshiro Mitsunaga merged the two companies into one and called it "Nihon Dempo Tsushin-Sha," which translates to "Japan Telegraphic Communication Co., Ltd." The rather long title was abbreviated to "Dentsu" combining the "Dem" (but pronounced as "Den") and the "Tsu," in casual conversation, although the name of the emerging company didn't officially become Dentsu until 1955. The full name was actually "Dentsu Advertising Ltd." in 1955. The company changed its name to "Dentsu Incorporated" in April 1978, and then to "Dentsu Inc.," its current name, in September 1987.

The Playing Field Changes

The Japan Telegraphic Communication Co., Ltd, or Dentsu, enjoyed a prosperous existence for almost 20 years. Then, in 1932, the Japanese government called on all the news services to merge into a single national government-operated news agency called "Domei Tsushinsha." In 1936, Dentsu was ordered to transition its wire service to this new mandated organization. This led the company to reinvent itself as a specialized advertising agency.

Becoming a Media Powerhouse: 1946–1960

World War II was disruptive, to say the least, to Japanese business, and was not a time of prosperity for Dentsu. Hoshiro Mitsunaga, the founder, passed away in 1945. After two presidents, the fourth, and perhaps the most famous of all Dentsu company presidents, Hideo Yoshida, shown in Figure 1.2, took control in 1947.

To say the least, Yoshida was an interesting and dynamic leader. He was known as—depending on how you translate it from Japanese—"the big demon," or "the devil of advertising" due

Figure 1.2 Fourth President Hideo Yoshida.

to his aggressive leadership style. For example, executives were required to report to work one hour before the rest of the staff, and department heads were required to submit daily written reports of their activities.

Expanding the Meaning of "Agency"

Yoshida not only ran a tight ship, but he also made many significant changes to the Dentsu business and is credited with setting the course of advertising in Japan into a modern, prosperous industry. He created new departments devoted to activities beyond advertising and creative activity itself, including market research, audience samplings and ratings, publications of advertising statistics, and public relations. Yoshida also brought new focus to what was then the new media of the day: radio and, especially, broadcast television.

The practice of market research and analysis was quite progressive for the day. Dentsu introduced random audience samplings, first by polling movie theater audiences as early as 1948, and then by conducting surveys, initially for the pharmaceutical industry. These activities not only increased understanding of customers to make advertising more effective, but they also helped establish solid relationships and credibility with both clients and media outlets.

Yoshida's vision was to consolidate the functions of advertising and marketing into a single agency, delivering a more complete service and making commission structures more favorable. Essentially this was a "win-win" for clients and the agency—better, more complete, and comprehensive services for clients and more revenue and margin generated for the agency. Yoshida extended this vision beyond the agency itself into the media, and he played a big role in the establishment of the first commercial radio stations and, later in the 1950s, television.

Yoshida believed that advertising was an "integration of science and arts" and worked hard to develop the quality of creative activity at Dentsu while at the same time incorporating the latest advertising and marketing theories and measurements. His work went beyond elevating the quality of advertising at Dentsu; he set out to improve the industry as a whole. In 1948, he started the annual "Dentsu Advertising Awards" for advertisements with outstanding creative quality. He created advertising trade organizations to measure audience size and behavior, and to measure advertising activity and quality itself. He contributed to the initiation of the Japan Audit Bureau of Circulation Association and the establishment of the Japanese Advertising Association in 1950, a predecessor of the Japan Advertising Agency Association.

Not surprisingly, Yoshida is credited with turning the traditional Mount Fuji climb, which had first started in 1925, into a venerable Dentsu institution. He set the trip, an overnight ascent of the 12,388-foot peak, not only as a yearly test of staff strength and commitment but also as a show of his leadership skills.

MOUNT FUJI: A SPECIAL SYMBOL

Completed in 2002, the new Dentsu Corporate Headquarters is an impressive skyscraper, located in the heart of Tokyo. On one of the upper floors, in the lobby among conference rooms, a visitor's eyes would turn instantly toward a painting in vivid colors of Mount Fuji done by a Japanese artist.

It isn't just another pretty picture. Mount Fuji has a special meaning for most Japanese, but for Dentsu, it has an even greater meaning, not just as a mountain to look at and marvel at, but as a mountain to climb. For Dentsu, the climbing of Mount Fuji signifies a journey toward a high goal, not easily attainable, and to instill a fighting spirit in the hearts of the company's employees.

And so each year, since 1925, over 500 Dentsu employees make the two-day adventure to climb the mountain. All participants try to reach the peak by the dawn of the next morning to watch the sunrise. At the summit of the mountain the employees pray at Sengen Shrine for business growth and their clients' prosperity, as well as mail postcards containing summer greetings; there is a post office at the summit of Mount Fuji. The postcards also serve as a reminder of the strengths and solidarity of Dentsu and the importance of taking a 360-degree view of our clients and client needs.

Accessing the Power of Radio and Television

Yoshida recognized that private-sector broadcasting was vital not only for Dentsu but for the advertising industry as a whole. Dentsu devoted a lot of energy to the rise of the broadcast media. From that effort, Japan's first commercial station was launched in 1951.

As a result, Dentsu became a big part of the history of Japanese broadcast media. See Figure 1.3.

Seeing the potential of television, Dentsu helped the fledgling television stations and networks find advertising sponsors. The company also created a special group within Dentsu to make the best use of the medium. Dentsu created the first television commercial ever shown in Japan; it was for Seiko Ltd.

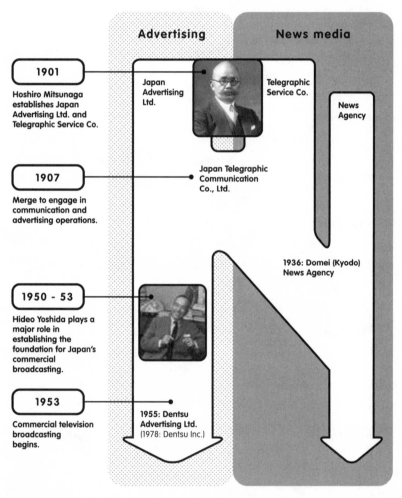

Figure 1.3 Dentsu's enduring relationship with the media.

In 1961, Hideo Yoshida became the "Man of the Year" of the International Advertising Association (IAA) for his outstanding contribution to the international development of advertising. See Figure 1.4. While still active with the company, he died in January 1963 at the age of 59. He was conferred Japan's "Order of the Sacred Treasure" posthumously, and there is a prominent bronze statue of Yoshida at the Dentsu headquarters building in Tokyo.

Yoshida not only achieved acclaim in Japan as a genius of advertising, but he also was famous for his stringent business ethics, which ultimately were compiled as President Yoshida's Ten Spartan Rules.

Figure 1.4 President Yoshida (on right) receiving the IAA "Man of the Year" award.

PRESIDENT YOSHIDA'S TEN SPARTAN RULES

Hideo Yoshida's quest for management excellence was no doubt driven by his visions for Japanese marketing and media, but also by an overall worry about Japan's economic prospects after World War II. As a result, he developed a set of business and work principles, or rules, which he called the "Ten Spartan Rules":

1. Initiate projects on your own instead of waiting for work to be assigned.
2. Take an active role in all your endeavors, not a passive one.
3. Search for large and complex challenges.
4. Welcome difficult assignments. Progress lies in accomplishing difficult work.
5. Once you begin a task, complete it. Never give up.
6. Lead and set an example for your fellow workers.
7. Set goals for yourself to ensure a constant sense of purpose.
8. Move with confidence. It gives your work force and substance.
9. At all times, challenge yourself to think creatively and find new solutions.
10. When confrontation is necessary, don't shy away from it. Confrontation is often necessary to achieve progress.

These traditional work rules still guide Dentsu's employees, and are carried around in their notebooks.

Multimedia and Multinational: Dentsu in the 1960–1990 Period

In 1959 Dentsu started an international expansion, first by establishing an office in New York, and then by establishing branch offices and subsidiaries in London, Paris, Moscow, Taipei, and Beijing. The goal was to help the by-then-booming Japanese companies deploy their business in these countries.

With the growth of the Japanese economy in the 1960s and 1970s, Dentsu expanded from a mere advertising agency into a major communications powerhouse. We continued to maintain strong relationships with the media as well as with sports and entertainment organizations. The 1964 Tokyo Olympic Games was a fusion of sports and media, and a great momentum builder for Dentsu to expand its business. See Figure 1.5.

At the same time, the Japanese economy was growing in double digits through the 1960s and 1970s, and Dentsu rode the tide. By 1968, Dentsu's billings were just behind the leading American firms. By then the company had 5,000 accounts, including not only many of the biggest Japanese firms but also the business of some large American companies marketing in Japan.

Figure 1.5 The 1964 Tokyo Olympic Games.

Becoming #1: 1973

In most global markets it is considered unethical for a firm to handle the accounts of two competitors. In the worldwide model the two accounts are often handled through separate subsidiaries. Dentsu, on the other hand, made it standard practice to accept competitor accounts, for example, multiple automobile companies. Where possible, these accounts were handled in separate buildings or on separate floors if necessary. We also had many strict security policies for information control. The arrangement worked well in Japan and helped Dentsu obtain greater dominance of the local industry. By 1973, Dentsu had become the largest advertising agency in the world.

Total Communications Services

Gohei Kogure became the new president of Dentsu in 1985. He reaffirmed the company's commitment to gain an international presence, but he also served up a new philosophy and slogan to communicate Dentsu's position as a total communications supplier: "Communications Excellence Dentsu." This slogan can also be translated as "Total Communications Services," which is what it became better known as later on.

The Total Communications Services idea followed some of the early philosophies of founder Mitsunaga and President Yoshida, and was created to convey the fact that Dentsu combined all the key elements of marketing communications services under a single roof. Those elements included strategic planning, branding, market research, traditional media advertising, media buying and planning, creative design, marketing analytics, sales promotion, public relations, and database marketing. The company also blended in a few nontraditional services, like sports marketing and event planning. The upshot was that a client could get any necessary mix of services created and delivered in a neutral manner (not favoring one service or platform over another) and uniquely tailored to the client's needs and the market. It was "total" in the sense that it covered the breadth of marketing services; it was "communications" because it transcended the limits of traditional mass advertising; the word "services" is self- explanatory.

Kogure reiterated the positioning difference between Dentsu and most worldwide agencies, which specialized in mass-media advertising only. This "breadth" strategy became a good foundation, especially with new forms of digital marketing to arrive later, for the "depth" strategy—deeper levels of involvement with consumers leading to greater action and interaction between them and the client. Here, the foundation was laid for the later "Integrated Communication Services" strategy and the "Cross Switch" application of "Cross Communication," a Core Idea of The Dentsu Way and the subject of this book from Chapter 3 onward.

The 1990s: Globalization and Digitization

The expansion of consumer economies in Asia shifted Dentsu's expansion plans toward Asia. Dentsu expanded its presence in Asia by expanding its own offices and by buying Asian advertising agencies.

Dentsu had always viewed China as a growth opportunity, even back in the days when few others did. In 1994 the company formed a joint venture with two Chinese advertising agencies and called it "Beijing Dentsu." In 1996, as part of Dentsu's 95th anniversary activities, the company launched a special "Japan-China Advertisement Education Exchange Project," which focused on the mutual development of advertising education in both countries.

Expanding Total Communications Services

In 1993 Yutaka Narita became the ninth president of Dentsu. Narita's primary contribution was to more firmly establish the positioning of Dentsu's services as "Total Communications

Services," while also undertaking to enrich the company's offering through the adoption of investment in new technologies, most particularly the Internet.

As Narita put it, "The progress of technology will make human communication of the utmost importance. If people communicate better they can reach a higher level of mutual understanding and get one step closer to happiness. In this sense, Dentsu is positioned on the right track."

Dentsu Enters the Technology and Digital Age

Besides looking to Asia for new growth, Dentsu turned to new technologies as a source of future income. In 1996, Dentsu launched a new Japanese venture called "Dentsu Tec Inc.," with the "Tec" standing for "Technology for Exciting Communication." Dentsu Tec's mission was to "perform integrated sales promotional services and product planning based on marketing ability, creativity, and technology." The focus was using new technologies of the time for sales promotions. Later, Dentsu Tec would use new digital, networking, and Internet technologies to expand marketing and develop new promotional opportunities.

At almost the same time, Dentsu also founded another Internet advertising joint venture with Tokyo's Softbank Corporation, called "Cyber Communications Inc.," or CCI. CCI was Japan's first firm to specialize exclusively in advertising on the Internet, not only developing and expanding the use of the technology but also buying and selling advertising space on the Internet in the style of the early Dentsu days.

2000s: Moving Outward and Upward

The technology boom of the late 1990s and the steady march of globalization were thought of as a revolution in Dentsu's collective mind. Dentsu continued to move forward to stay at the cutting edge of not only communications methods, but also communications strategies, to make the best use of them. Indeed the world had become much more complex and required a deeper understanding and deeper approach to communications management. With so many more ways to touch the consumer and so many more ways for the consumer to tune out your touch, it became imperative to take a more "holistic" and "technical" view of the customer communication process.

As President Narita put it at the turn of the millennium: "The years to come are expected to see revolutions of both technology and globalization. Dentsu will continue to be on the cutting edge of communication, providing innovative solutions around the globe," and, "Nowadays much effort is being made toward pursuing, fostering, obtaining, and investing in digital expertise in order to react and respond to the flood of new technology, including the Internet."

As early as 1998, the company declared its intention to "go public" (it was a closely held company at the time) and list its shares on the Tokyo Stock Exchange. On November 30, 2001, the shares were listed on the First Section, which is reserved for the largest Japanese companies.

Global Commitment: Bcom3 Group and Publicis Groupe

Dentsu didn't waste much time ringing in the new millennium with change. In March 2000, Dentsu made official its investment and participation in the Bcom3 Group, which had a total of 520 offices in 90 countries; this was Dentsu's biggest venture yet toward achieving global reach. Bcom3 was itself a combination of well-known and recently merged agencies—Leo Burnett, MacManus, and D'Arcy Masius Benton & Bowles—and it was the seventh-largest company in its space in the world at the time.

In 2002, the relationship with the Bcom3 Group was supplemented by another new relationship with France's Publicis Groupe. Dentsu gained another alliance with which it could grow internationally and especially in Europe. This alliance gave Dentsu vast opportunities to provide the best integrated communications services to its clients in global markets through strong global networks in Japan, the United States, and Europe, which were made possible by the partnerships with the Bcom3 Group and the Publicis Groupe.

Polishing the Corporate Image

In 2002, Tateo Mataki became the tenth president of Dentsu. He started with extending our corporate image by finishing our new world headquarters in the posh Shiodome district of downtown Tokyo, and he also created a new logo. See Figure 1.6.

The biggest success of the Mataki era was that Dentsu surpassed 2 billion yen in net sales for the first time in Dentsu's history.

Digitalization and Globalization Take Shape

In 2007, Tatsuyoshi Takashima, shown in Figure 1.7, became Dentsu's eleventh president.

Figure 1.6 Dentsu headquarters, a new corporate logo, and hundred-color business card.

Figure 1.7 Eleventh President Tatsuyoshi Takashima.

At the ceremony marking the 106th anniversary of the founding of the company, Takashima stressed the need to adapt to today's changing digital market and the needs of globalization. He announced the intent to integrate and unify management of digital businesses at Dentsu and the Dentsu Group, and to achieve even higher quality one-stop solutions. To this end, on January 1, 2010, we established an internal "Digital Business Division" and the business management company called "Dentsu Digital Holdings" to integrate digital-related businesses.

Under Takashima, our globalization strategy evolved considerably, especially in the Americas. In 2009, Takashima also presented the "Good Innovation." philosophy, previously discussed in the Introduction. This was a big step forward in identifying Dentsu as a creative and entrepreneurial leader, as well as a force in innovative marketing processes and integrated solutions.

We expanded our international presence, especially in the Americas, with the hiring of Tim Andree and with several key acquisitions to expand our skills, client base, and overall presence in the region. Andree's mission was to help achieve the vision held by Takashima, and many before him, to globalize the Dentsu model and to help clients take advantage of Dentsu's integrated approach.

Andree was instrumental in helping our management team in recasting and restructuring the existing Dentsu offices in the region, and in making three compelling acquisitions to bolster the Dentsu offerings outside Japan and particularly in the United States.

The ATTIK Acquisition

One of the first acquisitions targeted the creative and digital agency ATTIK, a San Francisco and UK-based agency, known for its edgy and youth-oriented campaigns. ATTIK and Dentsu had already worked together on the U.S. campaign for Toyota's Scion brand, paving the way for the relationship.

The acquisition was considered a win-win: Dentsu gained greater U.S. presence and access to digital and youth-oriented marketing talent, while ATTIK gained from being able to apply its talents to Dentsu's client base. ATTIK had been looking for a merger partner to expand its client base for some time, claiming that it was ". . . too small for big clients and too big for small clients." The ATTIK acquisition also brought important new clients, including Coca-Cola Co. and Lexus, as well as solidifying the Scion AOR to the Dentsu roster. Scion was the beneficiary of one of Dentsu's first Cross Switch campaigns in the United States, which is presented as an example in Chapter 6.

Old World, New World: McGarryBowen

In late 2008, Dentsu announced the acquisition of the relatively new advertising firm McGarryBowen.

McGarryBowen had been founded in 2002 by John McGarry, a former Young & Rubicam executive and the mastermind and CEO; Gordon Bowen, the chief creative officer; and Stewart Owen, the chief strategic officer. By 2008, the company had grown to become the largest *independent* agency in New York and the tenth-largest in the United States. The company was widely recognized in the industry for combining good old-fashioned Old World client-centric service and modern, digital New World creative and technical expertise, delivered with what one client called an "open and refreshing" transparency and collaboration. This combination naturally fit well into the Dentsu portfolio; both companies recognized this from the beginning.

The result of the acquisition must be considered one of the most successful in industry history. McGarryBowen not only brought a strong tradition to Dentsu, it was also very successful in winning new business during tough times. While most agencies were chasing shrinking slices of accounts to stay afloat in the bad economy, McGarryBowen was grabbing large chunks of blue-chip business in 2009. While best known for sentimental television commercials for Disney, Marriott, and others, McGarryBowen also took on leading-edge technology products like Verizon's Droid. McGarryBowen's clients also included Chevron, JP Morgan Chase, Crayola, Kraft, and Pfizer.

McGarryBowen helped Dentsu gain access to key U.S. accounts. More visibly, the company won *Advertising Age*'s prestigious "Agency of the Year" award in 2009 for the following reasons:

1. McGarryBowen's unwavering focus on clients and relationships

2. The agency's record year in 2009, with 10 new business wins and a 25-percent increase in revenue

3. The dramatic results the agency delivered for its clients' businesses in 2009, despite the challenging economic climate

It marked Dentsu's position on the U.S. and worldwide marketing map much more clearly.

Acquiring a Digital Powerhouse: Innovation Interactive

While the previous two acquisitions bolstered Dentsu's digital capability and brought other new assets both in the form of creative skills and client lists, Innovation Interactive was a large, award-winning, and wholly digital shop strong in search marketing, social media, and audience targeting. Like McGarryBowen, the agency was relatively new, founded in 2002, and had 300 people in nine offices in four countries. Innovation Interactive had three operating units:

- 360i, an award-winning digital marketing agency
- SearchIgnite, a leading paid search management technology
- Netmining, an audience optimization platform

Like the other acquisitions; this combination gave Dentsu access to leading technologies to build into its integrated marketing solutions, while giving Innovation Interactive access to a wide base of global clients, including Kraft and Coca-Cola (once again) but also Adidas and H&R Block.

Among other things, the acquisition of Innovation Interactive was really a play on the rapid expansion of social networking and search engine marketing in the business space. According to a University of Massachusetts survey in January 2010, 80 percent of the "Inc. 500" companies make use of social media platforms for marketing and general business, and some 87 percent of those report success with those platforms. Innovation Interactive put Dentsu squarely in line with and even out in front of this important trend.

Takashima explained it this way: "This acquisition is continuing evidence of our determined pursuit of innovation in the digital and global arenas." Indeed, the acquisitions of ATTIK, McGarryBowen, and Innovation Interactive really moved Dentsu forward toward building a competitive global operation and applying Dentsu methods and the "Good Innovation." policy for clients anywhere—all in the interest of winning global business.

From TCS to ICD: 2009 and Beyond

In 2009, we repositioned the long-standing "Total Communications Services" (TCS) moniker to "Integrated Communication Design" (ICD), in the policy of "Good Innovation."

In an excerpt from the corporate philosophy shared in this book's Introduction, our President and CEO Tatsuyoshi Takashima summed it up this way:

> Up until now, we have defined our business domain as "Total Communications Services." However, we must now have keener insight into the essence of changes in consumer behavior and branding challenges so that we can offer high-quality services which are integrated and concrete. We believe that the phrase "Integrated Communication Design" best expresses the current business domain and the strength of the Dentsu Group. We aim to evolve into a Group that as a whole is capable of designing, proposing, and implementing communications that provide true solutions in an integrated way.

We believe that the Internet is now fully integrated into the Dentsu offering. While other global agencies operated with separate units for digital and Internet marketing, Dentsu bundled it together with other media. This approach offers not only a better and easier experience for clients, but it also creates accountability: "If the Internet and mass media are handled separately, you cannot measure the effectiveness . . . this approach makes AISAS possible, as well as integrated planning and Plan-Do-Check-Act, or PDCA."

This is how The Dentsu Way has evolved into the year 2010. With this background in mind, it makes sense now to move to Chapter 2 to further explain our current capabilities and reach. From there, Parts 2 and 3 examine the Cross Switch implementation of Cross Communication, the cornerstone product of The Dentsu Way.

CHAPTER 2

BREADTH AND DEPTH: AN OVERVIEW OF DENTSU'S SCOPE AND SERVICES

C hapter 1 tells the story of how Dentsu started and how it evolved to become *the* top advertising and communications agency in Japan and *one of the* top agencies in the world. No doubt the company achieved its success through a combination of flexibility, innovation, and total client focus. Moreover, we at Dentsu, more than any other agency, brought to the table a "360-degree" view of marketing and what the company could deliver for a client, a "one-stop-shop" agency in a complex world of highly fragmented marketing agencies.

All along, we approached the agency practice with the business domain of Integrated Communication Design; although Dentsu assigned this name in 2009, it has been practiced since the 1980s. As ninth president Yutaka Narita described it a few years back: "Many advertising companies assign their communication activities to expert companies. Dentsu approaches each of the clients with comprehensive integrated solutions to serve the clients' brands."

With this background in mind, and the upcoming chapters describing the Cross Switch application of the Cross Communication platform also in mind, it makes sense to describe today's Dentsu: our skills and expertise, our products and offerings, and how—and where and to whom—those offerings are delivered. This chapter is not meant to be a sales pitch; rather it is intended as a high-level overview of the Dentsu business and how it is delivered to clients. By necessity, this chapter doesn't cover the details of how we deliver campaigns or any individual element of those campaigns. For that, readers should contact us directly or refer to the Dentsu English language Web site at *www.dentsu.com.*

Together, these ideas describe today's Dentsu. This chapter starts with an appraisal of our strengths and opportunities today; then it gives a description of the business in three views:

- Expertise and Capability

- Business Domains

- Delivery Model for those Deliverables

These "views" will be described in more detail shortly.

A Dentsu Self-Appraisal

As the second decade of the twenty-first century unfolds, we at Dentsu continue to be extremely proud of our heritage, our innovations, our ideas, our technologies, and our entrepreneurial spirit. Today, Dentsu is one of the top desired companies to work for in Japan. But, not surprisingly if you read the Chapter 1 story, we at Dentsu won't "rest on our laurels" in blind acceptance of that status. We continue to strive to be one of the favored choices in international domains, not just the best Japanese agency, but one of the top choices overall.

A company like Dentsu constantly appraises its own achievements and opportunities, sort of a Plan-Do-Check-Act, or PDCA, cycle of corporate success. We like to look at ourselves in the mirror, as well as view ourselves in our clients' eyes. As the decade unfolds, here is an inventory of our strengths and opportunities, presented here to give you our appraisal of who we are and where we are going.

Here is what we see as our biggest strengths:

- *Strength and durability of client relationships.* Our clients are partners; in the Japanese way, for the long term, and continue to be the center of our existence.

- *Total integrated services.* Our position of providing the "360-degree" set of marketing services continues to be hard to match. Other advertising and marketing companies have strived to do this for years. Dentsu already does it.

- *Resources.* We have the resources to create the ideas, apply the technology, implement, execute, and measure.

- *Creativity.* We have some of the best creative people in the world, and the advertising world has recognized this through numerous awards. See the section "Creative Strokes, The Dentsu Trophy Case," later in this chapter.

- *Commitment to Plan-Do-Check-Act, or PDCA.* Not only do we execute on "creative" but we can measure the results—the successes and return on investment (ROI)—of our marketing campaigns. We apply a true Japanese precision-engineered design and measurement to every campaign.

- *Innovation leadership.* As a result of all of the above, we are in a good position to lead the way in the creation and deployment of new, broader, deeper marketing technologies and platforms. The Cross Switch Cross Communication platform is an excellent example.

While leading the way in many areas, we also recognize some opportunities:

- *Establish strong presence and reference cases outside of Japan.* We still know there is a lot of work to do in bringing our models into the global market.

- *Continue to build digital capabilities.* While our acquisitions, especially Innovation Interactive, bring us closer to leadership in digital marketing, we know there is still much to learn and to do in this area.

- *Build components for Cross Switch overseas.* There are many system tools and databases used to gain consumer insight and provide structure and measurement for Cross Communication.

- *Improve international understanding and recognition of Dentsu.* Admittedly, Dentsu is a mystery to many potential international clients. It's a different culture, and a different, more holistic approach to doing things.

With this self-appraisal in mind, we can proceed to describe today's Dentsu and The Dentsu Way.

Describing the Dentsu Business

It is hard to comprehend the depth and breadth of a company like Dentsu—to understand all of its resources, expertise, products and deliverables, and the organizational structures behind it all that make it all work. Marketing, especially the integrated form of marketing practiced by Dentsu, tends to be extremely broad, deep, and multidimensional—working across multiple market targets, multiple products, multiple media, multiple channels, and multiple consumer Contact Points. Furthermore, these "dimensions" are becoming even broader, deeper, and more complicated with the new technologies and media available today. Consumer "touch" is being done in ways—for example, through mobile phones, never dreamed possible 20 years ago.

As a result, Dentsu recognized long ago that there is no "single" solution that fits every situation; every client is different and is given a highly customized and tailored marketing solution to fit its needs. The Dentsu Way goes well beyond typical advertising agency work, that is, beyond developing and delivering a creative message through traditional mass marketing venues. Dentsu does perform that service, and with its excellent relations with the media, does it well. But where Dentsu really excels is in delivering integrated, holistic communications that transcend the typical mass advertising models; Cross Communication is a leading-edge example.

So with that in mind, to describe Dentsu, it makes sense to look at the company from three viewpoints and describe each:

1. *Expertise and capability.* The core skills and capabilities Dentsu can deliver to its clients

2. *Business domains.* How Dentsu applies its capabilities to deliver elements of the marketing mix

3. *Delivery model.* How Dentsu organizes to deliver marketing solutions to its clients

Dentsu's Capabilities, Awards, and Global Rankings

Over time, Dentsu has invested in and built a very broad and deep set of marketing skills and resources to apply to marketing solutions for clients. The breadth is notable; further, what separates Dentsu from other agency companies and groups is that almost all of these skills and resources, and the specialists who apply them, are in-house within Dentsu. There are 6,000-plus individuals working for Dentsu; most are centralized in the Tokyo headquarters office.

This allows Dentsu not only to deliver *media- and technology-neutral* solutions—there is no bias toward a particular method because it happens to be available in house—but it also allows Dentsu to combine the specialized skills needed to meet a client's exact requirements. Beyond that, since the solutions are developed in house, Dentsu has the ability to implement and execute them as a complete package, which would be more difficult if they came from elsewhere. This concept will become clearer when you take in the examples of Cross Communication in Chapter 3 and especially Chapter 6.

Creative Strokes: "The Dentsu Trophy Case"

To maximize marketing impact, Dentsu provides its clients with unique media strategies that involve media planning built around highly creative concepts. Dentsu, over the years, has brought some well-recognized creative ideas to the advertising and communications world. Recently, international advertising awards have created a new category for this type of media solution, and Dentsu's work has been recognized internationally. We received the "Media Agency of the Year" award at the Cannes Lions International Advertising Festival 2009 and the "Interactive Agency of the Year" award at ADFEST 2009, the Asia Pacific Advertising Festival. These trophies are displayed in Figure 2.1.

Every individual, and every firm, for that matter, likes to display tangible signs of recognition and excellence as they come along. Over the years Dentsu has reaped a considerable number of awards in the advertising industry for creative excellence and innovation. Figure 2.2 graphically shows our presence in two key award venues: the Cannes Lions International Advertising Festival,

Figure 2.1 Two Dentsu award trophies: (Right) "Media Agency of the Year" award from the 2009 Cannes Lions International Advertising Festival. (Left) "Interactive Agency of the Year" award from ADFEST 2009.

and the Asia Pacific Advertising Festival (ADFEST). A more detailed listing of the awards won by the Dentsu Group at the Cannes Lions International Advertising Festival and ADFEST appears in Appendix 2.

Dentsu in the Rankings

Industry trade magazine *Advertising Age* publishes worldwide rankings annually for both holding companies and aligned agency networks, among other rankings. Figure 2.3 shows rankings published in December 2009.

The Geography of Dentsu

While Dentsu's business and geographic investments continue to be centered in Japan, the company now has 139 subsidiaries and 19,169

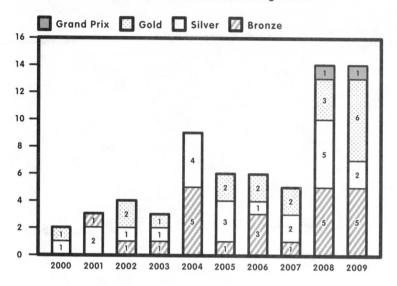

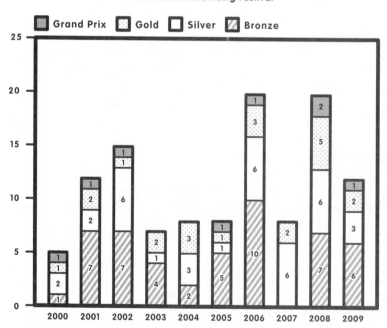

Figure 2.2 Grand prix, gold, silver, and bronze medals won by the Dentsu Group at the Cannes Lions International Advertising Festival and the Asia Pacific Advertising Festial (ADFEST) between 2000 and 2009.

Advertising Age Agency Rankings
Worldwide revenus, 2009

World's Top 10 Agency Companies	2009 revenues ($M)
1 WPP	$13,598
2 Omnicom Group	$11,721
3 Publicis Groupe*	$6,287
4 Interpublic Group of Cos.	$6,028
5 Dentsu*1	$3,113
6 Aegis Group*	$2,109
7 Havas	$2,010
8 Hakuhodo DY Holdings*	$1,522
9 Acxiom Corp.	$750
10 MDC Partners	$546

1. Reported worldwide revenue, excludes Innovation Interactive (360i), acquired in January 2010. Revenue supplied by companies via Ad Age questionnaire, obtained from public documents or estimated by Ad Age. Asterisk indicates estimate. Some U.S. figures reflect North American revenue 2009 and 2008 revenue data based on data collected and/or adjusted in 2010.

World's Top 10 Advertising Agencies	2009 revenues ($M)
1 Dentsu*	$2,335
2 McCann Erickson Worldwide* [Interpublic]	$1,419
3 BBDO Worldwide* [Omnicom]	$1,141
4 DDB Worldwide* [Omnicom]	$1,110
5 JWT* [WPP]	$1,066
6 TBWA Worldwide* [Omnicom]	$1,023
7 Hakuhodo* [Hakuhodo DY Holdings]	$956
9 Y&R* [WPP]	$932
8 Publicis* [Publicis]	$875
10 Leo Burnett Worldwide* [Publicis]	$777

Asterisk indicates estimate. Bracket shows affiliation with top agency firm

Figure 2.3 *Advertising Age* agency rankings based on worldwide revenue for 2009. *Source:* Advertising Age *Agency Report, April 2010.*

employees worldwide (as of March 31, 2010). The following maps show Dentsu's presence in Japan and worldwide, including subsidiaries like ATTIK and Beijing Dentsu. See Figures 2.4 and 2.5.

Overview of Dentsu Services—Business Domains

"Business Domains" is how we at Dentsu categorize the actual solutions and services Dentsu provides for clients, recognizing that depending on the client and the situation, Dentsu may mix, match, and/or alter any of these to get the right "fit" for that client. What follows is essentially a menu of solutions crossing a menu of media and a menu of technologies—a highly integrated, team-oriented, media-agnostic approach covering all kinds of media, and special spaces like sports, events, and even content generation. These services all fit under the umbrella of Integrated Communication Design.

Our Business Domains include Integrated Branding Services, the Creative Sphere, Integrated Media Services, Sales Promotion, the Content Business, Digital Solutions, Social Planning, and Cross Communication Planning Service.

Integrated Branding Services

Dentsu views strategic and tactical brand management as one of the most important activities a client can undertake. Good branding is not only essential to defining and positioning a product in the marketplace, but it is also fundamental to designing the proper communications and interactions with consumers.

Dentsu views branding as a "holistic and long-term" proposition; it is not something that happens overnight. A brand is *built*, not just created—built gradually by consumer contact with all the Contact Points with which they are surrounded. The use of Contact Points is essential to communicate a brand's core value. Like most Dentsu deliverables, branding is a process; we have pioneered original branding methods to ensure that each phase of a brand's life is dealt with effectively.

Dentsu also views branding as part of a larger one-stop service, that is, our services not only cover brand consultations and strategies but also their implementation through communications initiatives. We provide a broad range of branding services, including brand identity strategy, positioning, portfolio strategies, transition strategies including new brand development, extensions and brand consolidation, global brand management, and the measurement and evaluation of brand success. See Figure 2.6.

The Creative Sphere

"Creative" (short for "creative work" in industry parlance) could be counted either as a "skill" or as a "service"; it is so pervasive at Dentsu that we think it merits coverage in both places. Essentially, the goal of creative design is to best "capture the imagination" of consumers to first create attention, and then drive home a marketing message with sufficient impact to create search, action, and sharing results.

When Dentsu develops creative content, first ideas are gleaned from clients through many meetings and consulting sessions, and consumers' real feelings are deduced from marketing research. From these interactions, we gain insight in and understanding of developing communication ideas and messages that "touch the hearts" of consumers.

Dentsu has a dedicated creative staff of 800. Some specialize in specific media. Some creative directors are responsible for coordinating creative work to television commercial planners, copywriters, art directors, and other creative individuals. The members of this creative staff work with other departments on creative development for a wide range of media, including the Internet and mass media.

Dentsu provides creative services both in Japan and in many locations internationally. Dentsu collaborates with leading Asian

107 offices of 78 companies in 45 cities, 27 countries (as of October 2010)

● Subsidiaries and affiliated companies
● Holding companies and branch offices

San Francisco
Attik
Prophet Brand Strategy

Los Angeles
Dentsu America (Los Angeles)
Dentsu Entertainment USA

Chicago
mcgarrybowen

Toronto
Dentsu Canada

New York
Dentsu America (New York)
mcgarrybowen
Innovation Interactive
Dentsu Sports America
Dentsu Network West
Dentsu Holdings USA

Buenos Aires
Dentsu Argentina

Sao Paulo
Dentsu Latin America
Dentsu Network West (Latin America)

London
Dentsu UK
Sharp Image
Dentsu Sports Europe
Dentsu Network West(Europe)
Dentsu Inc., London Office

Brussels
Dentsu Brussels Group

Porto
Caetsu

Paris
Head quarters
for Europe,
Dentsu Inc.

Milan
cayenne

Johannesburg
Match Event Hospitality

Jeddah
Drivecommunication

Dubai
Dentsu Marcom Middle East

Figure 2.4 Dentsu's worldwide network.

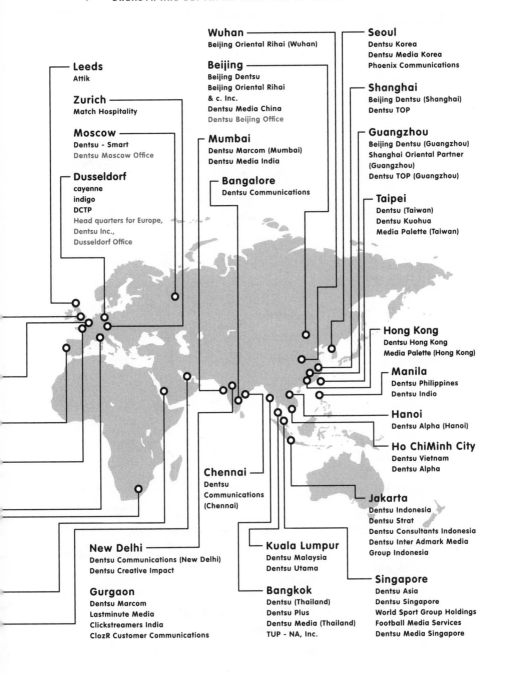

Wuhan
Beijing Oriental Rihai (Wuhan)

Seoul
Dentsu Korea
Dentsu Media Korea
Phoenix Communications

Leeds
Attik

Beijing
Beijing Dentsu
Beijing Oriental Rihai
& c. Inc.
Dentsu Media China
Dentsu Beijing Office

Shanghai
Beijing Dentsu (Shanghai)
Dentsu TOP

Zurich
Match Hospitality

Guangzhou
Beijing Dentsu (Guangzhou)
Shanghai Oriental Partner
(Guangzhou)
Dentsu TOP (Guangzhou)

Moscow
Dentsu - Smart
Dentsu Moscow Office

Mumbai
Dentsu Marcom (Mumbai)
Dentsu Media India

Dusseldorf
cayenne
indigo
DCTP
Head quarters for Europe,
Dentsu Inc.,
Dusseldorf Office

Bangalore
Dentsu Communications

Taipei
Dentsu (Taiwan)
Dentsu Kuohua
Media Palette (Taiwan)

Hong Kong
Dentsu Hong Kong
Media Palette (Hong Kong)

Manila
Dentsu Philippines
Dentsu Indio

Hanoi
Dentsu Alpha (Hanoi)

Ho ChiMinh City
Dentsu Vietnam
Dentsu Alpha

Chennai
Dentsu
Communications
(Chennai)

Jakarta
Dentsu Indonesia
Dentsu Strat
Dentsu Consultants Indonesia
Dentsu Inter Admark Media
Group Indonesia

New Delhi
Dentsu Communications (New Delhi)
Dentsu Creative Impact

Kuala Lumpur
Dentsu Malaysia
Dentsu Utama

Singapore
Dentsu Asia
Dentsu Singapore
World Sport Group Holdings
Football Media Services
Dentsu Media Singapore

Gurgaon
Dentsu Marcom
Lastminute Media
Clickstreamers India
ClozR Customer Communications

Bangkok
Dentsu (Thailand)
Dentsu Plus
Dentsu Media (Thailand)
TUP - NA, Inc.

Subsidiaries and affiliated companies
Holding companies and branch offices

As of October, 2010

Chicago
mcgarrybowen
360i

Detroit
360i

Toronto
Dentsu Canada

San Francisco
Attik
360i
Prophet Brand Strategy

Los Angeles
Dentsu America (Los Angeles)
Dentsu Entertainment USA

Atlanta
360i
Search Ignite

New York
Dentsu America (New York)
mcgarrybowen
Innovation Interactive
Dentsu Sports America
360i
Netmining
Dentsu Network West
Dentsu Holdings USA

Brazil (Sao Paulo)
Dentsu Latin America
Dentsu Network West (Latin America)
Argentina (Buenos Aires)
Dentsu Argentina

Figure 2.5 Dentsu's network: The Americas.

creators to provide creative services that are in tune with the national character of people in different countries and regions in Asia. In 2003, Dentsu began building an independent network of creators based in Hong Kong with the creative planning boutique, "Clipper Mother Asia."

As we mentioned earlier, Dentsu is a regular winner of advertising awards both in Japan and internationally, leading all Japanese companies in such competitions including the CLIO Awards, the Cannes Lions International Advertising Festival, and the Asia Pacific Advertising Festival (ADFEST). Figure 2.7 summarizes Dentsu's 2009 creative success both in traditional and digital media.

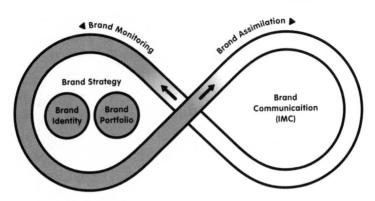

Figure 2.6 Dentsu's one-stop branding services.

Integrated Media Services

Dentsu has long been a big player in media services, and takes a highly integrated and holistic view of designing media strategies; implementing them through effective content design, media planning, and media buying; and finally, measuring the results. We make this possible through an assortment of proprietary systems and databases, and a staff of 1,000 professionals in the field with a wealth of experience and expertise in the various media. The range of Dentsu's media knowledge and practice is broad and deep, including not only conventional mass media like television, radio, print, and outdoor advertising, but also newer technologies like the Internet, mobile media, satellite, and social networking.

For media buying, over the years, Dentsu has built extensive and productive relationships with the media in Japan and elsewhere, and has learned to leverage those relationships to achieve scale, pricing advantages, and placement advantages. As the data from 2009, shown in Figure 2.8, indicate, the company has large shares of the media-buying pie in Japan for television (36.7 percent) and newspapers (18.2 percent) in what is usually a

Performance in Major Advertising Awards

Traditional media category

1. DDB London
2. Almap BBDO
3. Dentsu
4. Goodby, Silverstein & Partners
5. Del Campo Nazka Saatchi & Saatchi

Digital media category

1. Goodby, Silverstein & Partners
2. Crispin Porter + Bogusky
3. Bascule
4. Farfar
5. Dentsu

Figure 2.7 Creative expertise of Dentsu. *Source: The Gunn Report 2009.*

highly fragmented industry, and has even larger shares of "prime" space and time in many markets.

Sales Promotion

Sales Promotion activities occur where brands and consumers meet, that is, in stores or on the Internet. The promotional activity

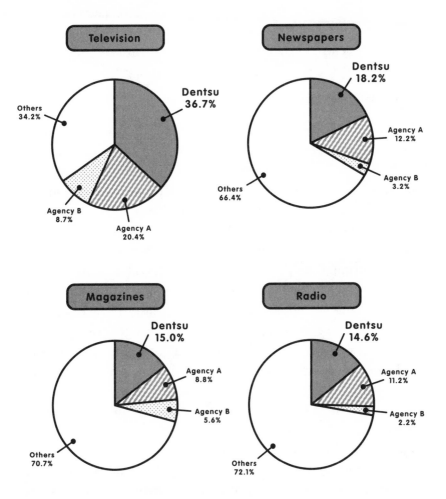

Figure 2.8 Dentsu's share of the advertising markets in Japan (2009). *Source:* Advertising and Economy, *April 1, 2010.*

is designed to complement—and produce results from—other mass media and Cross Communication promotional activities. The goal is to provide dynamic vehicles for clients to deliver their messages via on-the-spot interactive communications.

Dentsu uses traditional and proprietary methods to make the most of information technology. Campaigns can include in-store video and electronic displays, for example, touting a brand or offering more information about a product. The idea is that traditional mass promotion methods, on their own, no longer exact *enough* influence on the traditional consumer.

The Content Business

Part of The Dentsu Way is also finding and capitalizing on unique and powerful opportunities to create and/or leverage content to get consumer attention. The Content Business is engaged in things like sports event marketing, movies, stage production, and music.

Dentsu provides marketing opportunities via sports events like the Olympic Games and the FIFA World Cup™, and has established content and promotional tie-ins with a number of movie and performing arts productions. Dentsu has also created movies, television shows, and movie shorts with specially created characters and themes and tied these themes to advertising campaigns. In all of these sports and media venues, we generate revenues from diversified sources by securing and distributing broadcasting and marketing rights for these blockbuster events and content releases.

Dentsu has been actively participating in the financing and distributing of filmed entertainment. Recent films that Dentsu financed include *Departures* (Academy Award winner for best foreign language film) and *Spirited Away* (Academy Award winner for best animated feature film). With its versatile functions, Dentsu supports the local distribution of the films in terms of advertising, cross promotion, and financing.

Digital Solutions

Digital Solutions are a fast-growing and increasingly important component of integrated media services, as the Internet has penetrated every aspect of our lives. Not only does the Internet make new kinds of interaction *possible*, but, at the end of the day, it has actually changed consumer *behavior*. On the plus side, interactive media give us many new Contact Points and, really for the first time, they allow us to get information *back from* the consumer. They also allow consumers to readily share information with each other and with the masses. On the downside, the consumer, who was already "stretched" by so much interaction, has expanded "Information Barriers" (see Chapter 3) to filter out what has become a severe excess of communication.

To effectively deliver communications on the Internet, Dentsu has been researching, building, acquiring, and otherwise developing a full capability to advertise and promote on the Internet. As of today, the company provides five specific interactive services:

- *Internet media services.* To create communications and marketing campaigns covering the assortment of Internet, mobile, and other "new" media

- *e-Marketing services.* To develop longer range e-marketing strategies, including complete Customer Relationship Management (CRM) solutions

- *Platform development services.* To create actual communications infrastructures, like Web sites and other delivery venues, to help clients take advantage of interactive media

- *e-Branding services* (like e-Marketing services). To step back to the strategic level to help position and brand a client's product or service effectively on the Internet

- *Interactive campaign production services,* To deliver the interactive portion of Cross Communication campaigns

Social Planning

With the globalization of economic systems and today's environmental concerns as a backdrop, a company's products and services are no longer unaffected by or unrelated to the social issues of the day. We at Dentsu recognize this and have established a new mission to provide social perspectives in the framework of conventional marketing communications. At the same time, we provide communications planning toward increasing corporate image and perceived value, as well as overall consumer perception of a company.

We handle themes that are essential to maintaining environmental sustainability, for example, in terms of biodiversity, energy, and food, and also solution development required to resolve not only corporate issues like Corporate Social Responsibility (CSR) and consensus forming, but to address a variety of social issues as well. We created the unit called the "Social Design Engine" to develop optimum solution methods in collaboration of these two themes.

Cross Communication Planning Service

Cross Communication is really the apex of integration and achievement across all of the skills and services described so far. The goal is to create a broad and deep multimedia, multicontact scenario that moves target consumers who might otherwise tune out the message with Information Barriers. The trick is to create campaigns that create active brand experience where the consumer has special interest or wants to become involved.

Not surprisingly, the Cross Communication team within Dentsu has its own knowledge base but also works to assemble the necessary expertise and fact base to develop structured campaigns combining all Dentsu resources according to the designed scenarios. Dentsu has created its own brand for its Cross Communication solutions: Cross Switch–using "Cross" Communication to flip a "Switch" in the consumer's mind.

The Cross Switch application of Cross Communication solutions is the specific subject of Parts 2 and 3 of this book, and is one of the crown jewels of The Dentsu Way.

The Dentsu Delivery Model

Finally, to understand the Dentsu business, it helps to understand how all the skills and services are assembled and delivered to clients. The company is quite complex with numerous internal departments and organizations set up to develop and execute across all skill sets and services. But for any client to work separately with these groups and individuals would be impossible; therefore Dentsu deploys an active account management model to meet client needs. Figure 2.9 illustrates this account management model.

Here's how it works in practice: In a major advertising campaign, we typically assemble a team consisting of core members, as shown in Figure 2.10. The members cooperate closely all the way from planning and execution to follow-up evaluation of the campaign. An account executive assumes the role of leader, assisted by a strategist and a creative director. They are joined by promotion and interactive media directors, and also by other specialists, if necessary. We believe our distinctive strengths lie in this account management model, which effectively delivers high levels of expertise, improves our ability to integrate input from experts in diverse fields, and takes advantage of our proven ability to cooperate and work together as a team.

Summary

Dentsu is a large, integrated company dedicated to the proposition of delivering Integrated Communication Design as part of the corporate philosophy of "Good Innovation." The company is set up to deliver on all parts of this promise rather than to rely on outside sources. Through its expertise, experience, and vast amounts of data and research, Dentsu is well positioned to deliver complete, integrated customer solutions. The company has a history of strong client relationships and substantial creative and

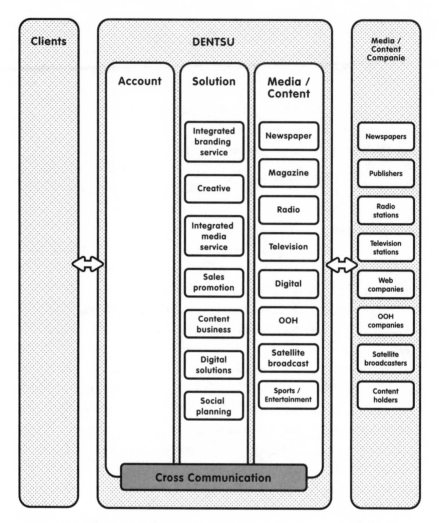

Figure 2.9 Dentsu's business structure*
*Figure shown here differs from actual Dentsu organizational chart.

innovative successes especially in Japan, and is strategically and tactically committed to expanding those services into the Americas, Europe, and elsewhere.

Understanding Dentsu's history and current business is obviously the key to understanding The Dentsu Way. From here,

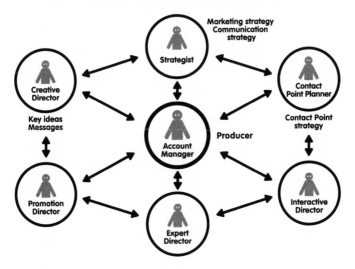

Figure 2.10 Dentsu's account management team.

we narrow the focus to cover Cross Switch, Dentsu's innovative and leading-edge implementation of Cross Communication—and a Core Idea of The Dentsu Way.

PART 2

THE CROSS COMMUNICATION IMPERATIVE

CHAPTER 3

FROM AIDMA TO AISAS: THE GROWING IMPORTANCE OF CROSS COMMUNICATION

In this day and age, businesses are struggling to get customers to pay attention to their brands and to their products and services. At Dentsu we hear this all the time: "It seems more difficult than ever to get our message across to consumers."

Why? Are people less interested in buying things? Are they less interested in learning more about what they buy? Obviously not. The central issue is this: in an era that is overflowing with information, many people put up what we like to call "Information Barriers." What does that mean? It means that people pay attention only to the information that they are specifically seeking, or the information that they are interested in. As a result, to remove these Information Barriers and to communicate effectively in the future, it will become increasingly important to adopt approaches that build consumer interest from the very beginning of a marketing campaign and maintain it all the way through. These new approaches are designed to draw consumers out from within the Information Barriers they naturally—and subconsciously—set up.

It turns out that "Cross Communication"—the smart application of multiple forms of media in a manner calculated to deliver a marketing message—is gaining popularity as a way to make marketing messages more compelling. Cross Communication as an application is more interesting to consumers and gets them more involved, both of which serve to remove Information Barriers.

In this chapter, we will look at consumer behavior and in particular how changes in consumer behavior have demanded a new look at traditional consumer response models, specifically, the traditional "AIDMA," or Attention, Interest, Desire, Memory, Action response model. The resulting evolution of consumer response forms the basis of and background for Cross Communication and what is required of effective Cross Communication marketing today. Along the way we will show some results of consumer survey data collected in Japan to support the Cross Communication approach. Finally, we will share an example of a Cross Communication advertising campaign used to draw consumers out from behind their Information Barriers. The sample campaign is for a Japanese manga, or comic, publication called *Jump Square*, which was carried out in the Tokyo area.

What Causes "Information Barriers"?

Professional marketers have been hearing the same questions repeatedly from their clients lately:

- "Is it okay to keep communicating in the same way as we did in the past?"

- "Can we achieve better results just by advertising more than our competitors?"

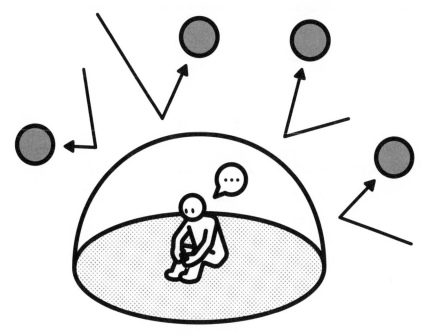

Figure 3.1 Consumer who has put up an Information Barrier.

There is no doubt that the information environment that surrounds us has changed dramatically in recent years. The growth of the Internet, the proliferation of mobile phones, and the increase in the number of television channels have brought about an enormous diversification and fragmentation of media. In this environment, consumers take one look at information, and despite the fact that that the information might have been considered valuable in the past, today it doesn't fly. Consumers simply feel: "This has nothing to do with me," and unconsciously isolate themselves from it. The Information Barrier, as we refer to it at Dentsu, is set in place. See Figure 3.1.

In examining the causes of Information Barriers, we come up with three main factors:

1. Information volumes are increasing rapidly.

2. Consumers have begun to seek information actively.

3. It is becoming more difficult to differentiate products.

Let's look at these one at a time.

Rapid Increase in Information Volume

The volume of information circulating in our modern world is increasing at an explosive rate. With the proliferation of the Internet and mobile devices, an increasing number of consumers are using both of these media to transmit their own information through, for example, blogs and other "Word-of-Mouth" Web sites. There are also more television channels available today than ever before.

Even as information volumes increase, however, our ability to process that information has not increased proportionately; essentially it has not kept up. If we tried to process it all, we would be unable to manage the business of our daily lives. This situation has made it necessary for consumers to pass up a lot of the information that they come into contact with. As a result, they put up Information Barriers.

Statistical data from the Japanese Ministry of Internal Affairs and Communications (MIC) suggest that the volume of "accessible information" continues to increase, but that the volume of "consumable information"—that is, the amount consumers can process—has not increased as much. The result, according to the MIC, is that about two-thirds of the information in circulation remains unused. In this sense, the "information age" has given way to the "era of excessive information." See Figure 3.2 for a tabulation of information volume and "information overload" in Japan.

Information volumes
[Unit: 10^{15} bits]

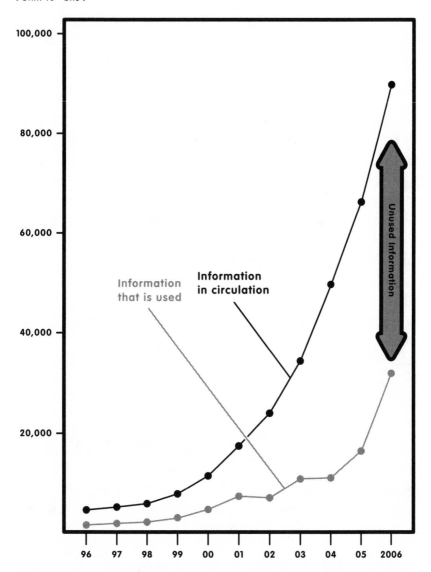

Figure 3.2 The rapid increase in information volumes: Japan. *Source: Information Distribution Census Survey, Japanese Ministry of Internal Affairs and Communications (MIC).*

Today's Consumers Actively Seek Information

Internet technologies and environments have evolved to the point where it is possible to instantly seek virtually any information, anytime, from anywhere, using a personal computer (PC) or mobile phone, or a similar device. Even for very specialized, detailed information there are sources due to the large number of individuals, corporations, and independent Web sites collecting and distributing that information. You can get information and answers about almost anything in today's environment from these Web sites or from other individuals. "If I want some information, I'll seek it out for myself" is an approach and behavior that has become commonplace. One new resulting trend is that consumers are no longer willing to accept at face value the information transmitted unilaterally by corporations.

The fragmentation of consumer interests and preferences has added further momentum to this trend. Consumers are less dependent on corporate Web sites. Now, as a result, when consumers decide that the mass information provided by corporations does not meet their needs, their natural reaction is to create an Information Barrier.

It Is Becoming More Difficult to Differentiate Products

Companies develop and sell products and services with the goal of pleasing large numbers of consumers. Not all products, however, can be "hit" products, as we know. Few products these days are truly differentiated or resistant to being imitated by competitor companies.

Beyond that, the "product supply cycle" is growing shorter and shorter, as technology evolves and as consumer preference changes become faster and faster. As a result, the points of differentiation between a new product and an existing or competing product are becoming increasingly minute. Furthermore, because technical capabilities for most products have reached an equilibrium at a very high level among various companies, even when a truly innovative product is released, in many cases similar products are quickly developed and marketed by competitors.

As a result of all of these factors, when new products are released, even if elaborate campaigns are rolled out, consumers soon begin to believe and feel that, "All the products are basically the same." If all products are really the same, why should I pay attention? Their Information Barriers go up.

Drawing Consumers Out

So what can we do, then, to ensure that our message reaches consumers within their Information Barriers? Naturally, that's the key question asked by most marketing professionals today.

In the field of advertising communications, fortunately, breaking the Information Barrier through the power of creativity is still an effective method. But creativity works best with products that by nature have a clear differentiation point, or where one can be created by advertising. In our business we look for the "unique selling proposition," or USP, a sales or value proposition that cannot be easily matched by competitors. A particularly strong campaign ensues when a product with a strong USP is meshed with a powerful creative marketing force.

A strong creative force, or campaign, however, still may not reach consumers with the increase in the Information Barriers we see today. In recent years a new option has gained attention; namely, campaigns based on the concept of encouraging consumers to come out from within their Information Barriers *on their own accord*. In other words, this approach serves to "draw out" consumers from within their Information Barriers by presenting information that is particularly engaging or intriguing, or better yet, information with which the consumers *want* to become involved.

FROM DARKNESS TO LIGHT
IN JAPANESE MYTHOLOGY

There is an episode in the Japanese myth of "Amano-Iwato," or the "Heavenly Cave," that symbolizes the approach of drawing consumers out. The Sun Goddess Amaterasu, no longer able to bear the atrocious behavior of her brother, Susano'o, shuts herself away in a cave, throwing the world into utter darkness. In order to draw Amaterasu out, eight million gods gather and have Ame-no-Uzume, the goddess of merriment, sing and dance in front of the cave door while the other gods raise a huge ruckus, yelling and laughing. Wondering what all of the fuss is about, Amaterasu comes out of the cave, and the world is once again bathed in light.

In today's marketing, we recommend slightly more subtle approaches, but you get the idea.

In summary, the traditional "breaking in" approach to getting consumers to pay attention to marketing messages is getting harder and harder to execute successfully. That's why we think the "drawing out" approach will be very important to marketing strategies going forward. It is a way to provide added value and create engagement with consumers. See Figure 3.3. That's a big part of where Cross Communication fits into today's and tomorrow's environment: Cross Communication gives marketers powerful new ways to draw consumers out and to get them more involved.

"We Told Them to 'Stay Away'; They Came in Droves"

Since ancient times, people have talked about the importance of moving others not by force, but by sparking their interest and

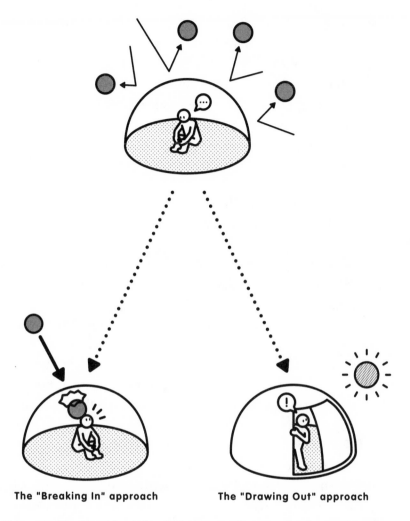

The "Breaking In" approach   The "Drawing Out" approach

Figure 3.3 The "breaking in" and "drawing out" approaches for reaching the consumer who has put up an "Information Barrier."

encouraging them to move of their own volition. The lesson has been learned time after time in everything from politics to raising children. Interestingly, we hear this message as a lesson over and over because we fall back into old "forceful" habits—it is probably human nature—and we tend to forget how important it is to get people to move by choice.

So with that "choice, not force" idea in mind, we'll illustrate the concept with a powerful example. We developed a very successful and innovative campaign for a Japanese publisher, Shueisha Inc., which sells manga, or comic fiction. Shueisha Inc. sought a campaign to market a new manga anthology called *Jump Square*; the campaign was based on the "sparking interest" and "drawing out" approaches to the readers.

"Don't Search!"—Shueisha Inc.'s *Jump Square* Inaugural Issue Campaign

Manga are a very popular blend of art and entertainment in Japan in which stories are published and sold as large comic-style magazines, usually in an anthology with serial issues released over time. The characters and artwork are drawn with strong visual images and a lot of action, and the stories and themes can range from children's themes to some that are quite adult-oriented. Teens and young adults are the sweet spot for manga, but they appeal to almost all ages in Japan. Figure 3.4 shows the *Jump Square* manga magazine.

Although this case is about the comic-style magazines, it can be applied to other new magazine launch campaigns. This is a case of a campaign that succeeded in gaining extremely high sales in an age in which magazines don't sell as much as they used to. This case is a good reference for creating a campaign in this magazine category.

The first issue of Shueisha Inc.'s monthly manga anthology *Jump Square* was published in November 2007 as the successor to *Monthly Shonen Jump*, the publication of which had already been suspended. As you'll see, the announcement campaign effectively used the Internet, television commercials, and advertisements on public transportation routes, drawing out readers who were not originally interested in such manga anthologies; that is, readers who had put up Information Barriers. As a result of the campaign, the inaugural issue sold out at an unprecedented rate and was so successful that an additional printing was required to meet the demand.

A Challenging Environment

In recent years, the sales of manga magazines have faded somewhat, probably in part due to the growth of the Internet, electronic gaming, and mobile phones.

Despite these unfavorable conditions, Shueisha Inc. set the first printing of *Jump Square*'s inaugural issue at 500,000 copies. This was far in excess of the final printing for *Monthly Shonen Jump* before that publication's termination (in June 2007), at 350,000 copies, and even more so when compared to the actual sales for that final issue, at 250,000 copies. This meant that in addition to the core manga fans who had been reading *Monthly Shonen Jump* up to that time, Shueisha Inc. had to secure some 250,000 *new* regular readers. This was a formidable challenge, to say the least.

Core manga fans would not be satisfied with typical, run-of-the-mill advertisements announcing the new monthly anthology. It was important to appeal to these readers and make them more loyal to *Jump Square* and—more importantly—to get them to help acquire a group of new regular readers. No matter how many such advertisements were published, Shueisha Inc. would be unlikely to secure the new readers it needed who were never really interested in manga to begin with. It was clear that advertisements focused on describing the content of the new magazine, by themselves, would be ineffective. Shueisha Inc. needed a campaign that would successfully attract the interest of both groups, and it would need its core readers to take action to help acquire this group of new readers.

The "Stay Away" Message

About three weeks before the release of the first issue, a rather dramatic and startling television commercial was broadcast, mainly during late-night time slots. The words "Jump Square" appeared in an Internet search window, crossed out by an "X." The accompanying voice-over was as follows: "This is a request from Shueisha. The inaugural issue of *Jump Square* will be released shortly, but please do not search for 'Jump Square' on the Internet." The official Web site had been open since August, introducing authors and stories a few at a time. Now, Shueisha Inc. was sending the message, "Don't search for 'Jump Square'."

It is human nature to want to do what you are told not to do. Right? That instinct probably originates from childhood, but no matter. There's no need to analyze it. Anyway, the commercial caught the interest of many people, who, of course, began entering the words "Jump Square" in their search engines all at once. When they tried to access the official Web site, they found that it was closed. All they saw was a text-only page with the heading "Request from the Editorial Division." This page contained only a simple, polite message apologizing for not being able to provide information about *Jump Square*.

Not surprisingly, the group of noncore readers was disappointed by this plain, unaffected message, and simply left the site. The reaction of core readers, however, was quite the opposite. "The official site was up until yesterday, and now it's suddenly closed. They are definitely up to something."

The Web site viewer needed to wait and do nothing for about 20 seconds, and then . . . action! Manga characters scheduled to appear in the inaugural issue suddenly began moving about in flash animations. They ran around the cramped spaces in the Editorial Division's "apology," tearing a hole through the middle of the page, climbing up the text, and generally causing damage and mayhem. Around ten different types of characters took turns appearing every 20 seconds.

Figure 3.4 Cover of the inaugural issue of the *Jump Square* manga anthology.

Core readers who saw this message became even more convinced. When they were told, at the end of this message, to "Please search for something else," they immediately entered the words "Jump Square" in the search window (again, defying what they were told to do, or not to do). Not once, but three times in a row. Finally, these readers were led to a "hidden site" that began with the message, "We give up. We are just no match for your enthusiasm and determination." This site offered detailed information on the stories to be published in *Jump Square*, along with videos introducing the authors' writing styles and a variety of other premium content.

Figure 3.5 shows the "Please don't search" kickoff television commercial and the connected "apology" site.

Building the Buzz

Core readers quickly posted comments on blogs and other sites describing how they had discovered this "hidden information." In

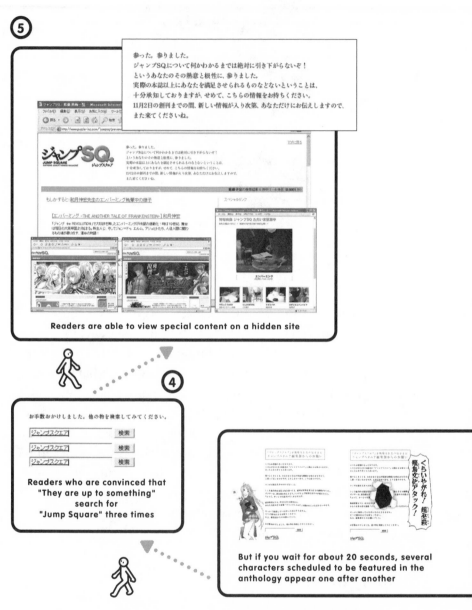

Figure 3.5 *Jump Square*'s "Don't search" television commercial and Internet campaign.

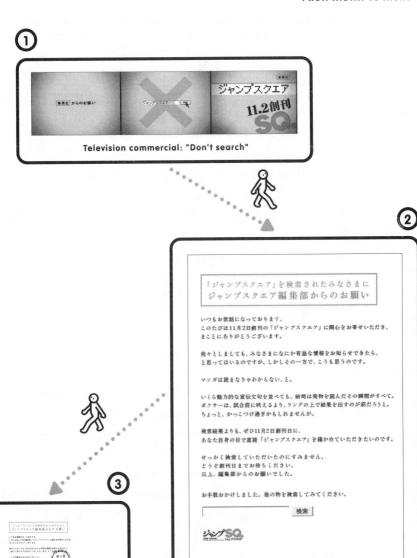

① Television commercial: "Don't search"

②

「ジャンプスクエア」を検索されたみなさまに
ジャンプスクエア編集部からのお願い

いつもお世話になっております。
このたびは11月2日創刊の「ジャンプスクエア」に関心をお寄せいただき、
まことにありがとうございます。

我々としましても、みなさまになにか有益な情報をお知らせできたら、
と思ってはいるのですが、しかしその一方で、こうも思うのです。

マンガは読まなきゃわからない、と。

いくら魅力的な宣伝文句を並べても、結局は実物を読んだその瞬間がすべて。
ボクサーは、試合前に映えるより、リングの上で結果を出すのが筋だろうと。
ちょっと、かっこつけ過ぎかもしれませんが。

検索結果よりも、ぜひ11月2日創刊日に、
あなた自身の目で直接「ジャンプスクエア」を確かめていただきたいのです。

せっかく検索していただいたのにすみません。
どうぞ創刊日までお待ちください。
以上、編集部からのお願いでした。

お手数おかけしました。他の物を検索してみてください。

検索

Apology site: "We can't disclose any information"

③

no time at all, discussions of the hidden site spread like wildfire by Word-of-Mouth on the Internet! What happened next? Both the readers who were discouraged by the original message and left and readers who were hearing the story for the first time flocked in unison to the *Jump Square* Web site.

Further Word-of-Mouth tie-ins were created using mobile phone sites and advertisements in Tokyo train stations. The Word-of-Mouth tie-ins didn't stop there. The hidden site provided open access to a mobile site that allowed users to preview a full manga story scheduled to be included in the inaugural issue before the publication date. First, the core readers accessed the mobile site, and then those readers boasted to their friends about it, as though competing to see who could get there first. The address for the mobile site was sent from friends to friends of friends. The mobile phone—the tool most familiar to modern youth—had been instantly transformed into a tool for Word-of-Mouth promotion.

The public transportation venue—that is, railway stations, railway cars, and areas adjacent to stations—is a very important advertising venue in Japan and especially urban Japan. We created an unusual device using the Yamanote Line, the central loop railway line that encircles metropolitan Tokyo. Readers could participate in a "manga relay," which used a story written by one of the writers featured in the inaugural issue. The only way to read every segment of the manga serial was to get off the train at each station. We realize this approach wouldn't work in every market around the globe, but in a place where rail transportation is a way of life, it worked well.

Figure 3.6 shows examples of how the campaign used train station advertisements and the mobile phone site. In the illustration, the mobile phone site tells the audience to "Read one story from the inaugural issue for free (on your mobile phone screen), and pass it on to your friends!" At the train stations, posters touted the Yamanote Line Limited Edition Manga as "Manga Journey around the Yamanote Loop: The SQ. Rescue Team is On the Way!"

As a result of the train station campaign, the buzz was irresistible:

- "I read it on Platform 4 at Shibuya Station."

- "I saw one at Komagome Station."

- "I read them all!"

Once the campaign was under way, information about the new *Jump Square* traveled by Word-of-Mouth from core readers to prospective readers, and further to their friends and acquaintances. Suddenly, everyone was talking about how much fun it was to "Go on a manga hunt." In fact, before the first issue was published, descriptions of the Yamanote Line Limited Edition Manga had appeared in as many as 30,000 blogs. See Figure 3.7 for statistics on *Jump Square* blog postings.

Sold Out!

The inaugural issue of *Jump Square* was released on November 2, 2007. The original printing was set at 500,000 copies, but the anthology sold out at bookstores all over the country in just a few days. For the first time in 32 years, Shueisha Inc. decided to release a second printing of 100,000 copies for one of its magazines. A total of 600,000 copies was printed, and almost none were left unsold. Many of the buyers were male office workers and adult women, an indication that *Jump Square* had successfully transcended its traditional reader base and captured the interest of new readers who had drifted away from reading manga. The core strategy to capture the hearts of core manga fans as a means of securing a large number of new readers had worked.

We felt that noncore readers would not show any interest in advertisements that simply introduced the content of a new manga anthology. It seemed that the best way to draw these readers out from within their Information Barriers was to make special tips

Mobile phone site: "Read one story from the inaugural issue for free (on your mobile phone screen), and pass it on to your friends!"

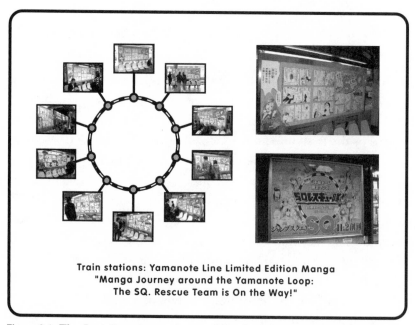

Train stations: Yamanote Line Limited Edition Manga
"Manga Journey around the Yamanote Loop:
The SQ. Rescue Team is On the Way!"

Figure 3.6 The *Jump Square* campaign: mobile phone site and train station advertisements.

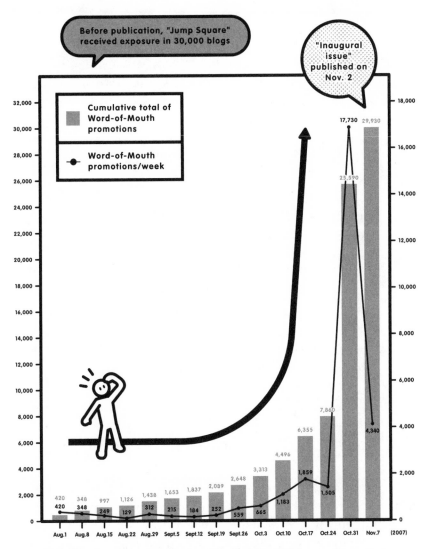

Figure 3.7 The *Jump Square* campaign: Word-of-Mouth blog postings. *Source: Dentsu Buzz Research.*

and "insider information" available person-to-person from core manga fans. To accomplish this, we first concealed the information and then rigged up a demanding "treasure hunt" to ensure that priority would be placed on transmitting the new information to the core readers. They would, in turn, pass it on.

We confirmed our belief that core readers—the most loyal and valuable consumers—like nothing better than searching for hidden information, except perhaps telling others what they have found. We also confirmed our idea that the "information gap" between core readers and noncore readers would lead to rapid ripple effects, spreading from core readers to less frequent readers, and from less frequent readers to still other readers.

The *Jump Square* inaugural issue campaign won numerous awards in 2008:

- "Bronze Lion" at the 55th Cannes Lions International Advertising Festival

- "Bronze Award" in the "Direct Lotus" category at the 11th ADFEST

- "Bronze Award" at the 49th CLIO Awards

- "Gold Award" in the "Integrated Campaign" division of the 6th Tokyo Interactive Ad Awards (TIAA)

The Internet Isn't Just for Young People

Some of you might think: "*Jump Square* targets younger readers, so it stands to reason that they want to gather information on their own. But will this approach really work for other products and services?" This has become a misconception. Today's reality is that it is no longer just young people who actively seek out the information they want. Consumers of all ages get information today by selecting from among various media, and combining or linking these media as the situation demands. All types of media can be connected: both traditional mass media like television and newspapers, and interactive media including mobile phones and the Internet.

As Figure 3.8 shows, people of all ages have searched keywords found in traditional advertisements in the past month. It shows us that people from all generations—even those in their forties and fifties—search for information on the Internet. More specifically, it tells us that:

* Net searches triggered by advertisements are common in all age groups, even for people in their forties and fifties.

* Of the people we surveyed, 67.7 percent said that within the past month, they had "used the Internet or a mobile phone to search for a keyword seen in an advertisement."

* Looking at the breakdown by gender and age, we can see that in every age group, the ratio of search behaviors is higher for men and that the group with the highest ratio is men in their thirties, at 76.7 percent. But even in the group with the lowest ratio—women in their fifties—the ratio is 44.6 percent, which means that nearly half of these women also use the Internet to seek out information.

As a result, it is safe to say that consumers actively and independently access information about advertisements that catch their interest. It is also interesting to note that the characteristics and trends observed in the United States are similar to those observed in Japan.

The "Cross" in Cross Communication

Cross Communication operates under the growing assumption that people connect different media types; that is, they use more than one medium to acquire information, and in some cases, to share information. In modern times it is probably true that people have never relied on one medium exclusively. Multiple media—television, radio, newspapers, magazines—have been

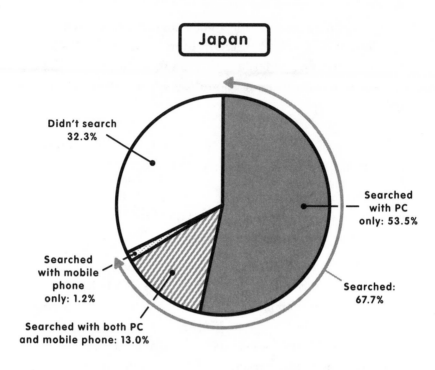

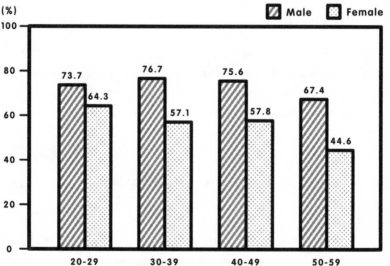

Figure 3.8 Percentage of age groups searching for keywords found in advertisements during the previous month. *Source: Dentsu Japan Cross Communication Behavior Survey, February 2008; Dentsu USA Cross Communication Behavior Survey, March 2010.*

around for a long time, and people responded to each of these media in their own way. Occasionally one might have heard a radio advertisement suggesting that the listener "check out our ad in this Sunday's newspaper," but such campaigns were far more the exception than the rule.

Today people are clearly relying on multiple media for their information, particularly with the advent of the Internet and the ubiquity of Internet access through mobile phones and other "on the go" devices. Mass media messages can spawn new media responses, including searches for more information or to see what the rest of the "community" has experienced with a product. These new media actions can occur on the Internet through company Web sites and social media such as shopping comparison sites, like cNET, or through social networking services (SNS) to name a few.

To learn more about such Cross Communication responses, Dentsu researched the tendency to engage with multiple media. A survey conducted in Japan in early 2008 found that 38.3 percent of respondents said that they "sometimes do Internet searches on the spot to find out more about something they saw on television." Importantly, we found that the responses do not differ significantly between genders and age groups. Incidentally, the survey was our "Cross Communication Behavior Survey," an Internet survey conducted to gain an overall grasp of real information trends and purchasing behaviors among consumers. For the outline of this survey and a similar survey done in the United States, see the "Cross Communication Behavior Survey" in Appendix 1 at the back of the book.

Other findings included the following:

- Despite the notion that the "older generation" tends to rely less on online tools, respondents in their forties and fifties had high scores, at 44.6 percent for men in their forties and 39.6 percent for women in their fifties.

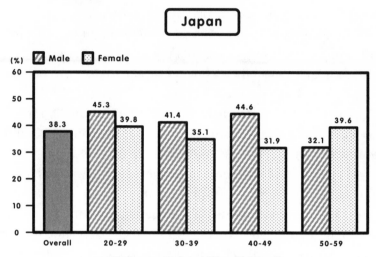

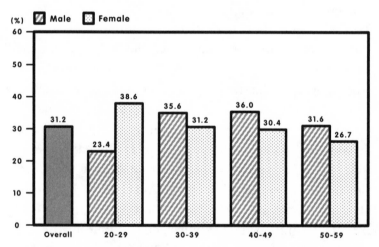

Figure 3.9 Internet access triggered by media type and age group, Japan and United States. *Source: Dentsu Cross Communication Behavior Survey, February 2008; Dentsu USA Cross Communication Behavior Survey March 2010.*

United States

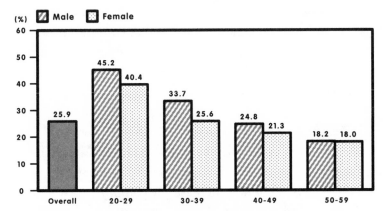

(%) Male Female

"I often search for additional information
about the program online while watching television"

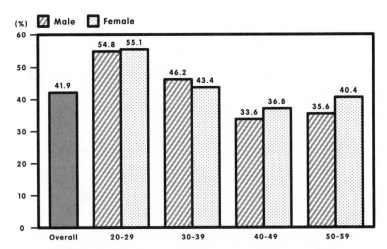

(%) Male Female

"I sometime visit an advertiser's Web site in response to a magazine ad."

- Out of all respondents, 31.2 percent said that they "sometimes access official sites for companies or products because of something they saw in a magazine advertisement." For women, this ratio peaked among those aged 20–29, at 38.6 percent, and decreased with each successively older group. For men, the peak appeared among those aged 30–49.

Our conclusion from the survey was that although ratios differed depending on the media in question, there is no question that accessing the Internet to seek out information on mass media content is becoming increasingly common even for people in their forties and fifties. And again, we find that the trends and characteristics in the United States are similar to those observed in Japan.

SUPER BOWL SUNDAY: BEER, CHIPS, SALSA

At one time, the Internet was considered to be a major threat to television. Television audiences would simply go away as people began to get their information and entertainment directly from the Internet. That fear seems to have subsided. In fact, according to a *New York Times* article in February 2010, media market researcher Nielsen found that during recent Super Bowl and Olympics broadcasts, some one in seven in the audience were on the Web at the same time—either searching for information or connecting with friends on social media.

In this environment, can you imagine how much yardage an effective Cross Communication campaign would have gained?

The Emergence of AISAS™

It's clear that the information environment that surrounds us today is changing dramatically, as are consumption behaviors. Because of these changes, we decided it was time to take another look at the traditional consumer behavior models that marketers and advertisers have been using for years. From our analysis, we believe that the traditional AIDMA behavior model—Attention, Interest, Desire, Memory, Action—is too linear for today's world. That is, the AIDMA model assumes that the information flow goes in only one direction and that consumers, rather than drawing information from companies or from each other, simply respond to information given by the company. Because of Information Barriers, and because of new abilities to interact provided by emerging technologies, we believe the old model has become obsolete for a substantial portion of today's marketing.

From AIDMA to AISAS

What is the process that takes place from the moment a consumer comes in contact with an advertisement, or a piece of information, to the moment a purchase is made? Numerous models have been developed to explain consumption behavior, but the AIDMA model is perhaps the most well known. The AIDMA model was first advocated by Roland Hall in the United States in around 1920, and is still used extensively to this day.

The AIDMA model describes the following steps from the point where a consumer notices a product, service, or advertisement up to the purchase:

Attention → Interest → Desire → Memory → Action

Advertising served to get the consumer's *attention,* and create some *interest* which would, hopefully, turn to *desire.* If the advertisement was effective, that desire would be committed to *memory* and hopefully remembered long enough so that the consumer would take *action*—buy that product or brand—upon his or her next visit to the store.

AIDMA is a simple but effective model for traditional advertising of relatively simple products where the real objective is to get the consumer to choose your brand from among many choices. It assumes that the information provided by the company through the advertisement is all that a consumer needs, and the objective is, as much as anything, to get the consumer to remember the brand and the brand promise at the point of purchase. The advertising models of many consumer products companies for years have been based on this model.

The AIDMA model may work for companies where consumers have little reason to learn more about products beyond the advertising message before their purchase. In the Internet era, however, where anyone can easily access information, we have seen a great proliferation of what we call "active contact with information," that is, after consumers notice a product, service, or advertisement, they voluntarily dig deeper, and share with others the intriguing information that they have obtained. In addition to the flow of information from companies (the senders) to the consumers (the receivers), two unique behaviors of consumers themselves—searching for (i.e., gathering) and sharing information—have become important factors in the purchase decision.

Based on these changes in the information environment, Dentsu now advocates a new consumption behavior model called AISAS (Attention, Interest, Search, Action, Share). If we were to compare this model to AIDMA, we would see that the psychological transformation process (A I D M) has been scaled back, and the final (A) for Action process has been expanded to encompass Search Action Share. So the model becomes:

Attention → Interest → Search → Action → Share

You can see these steps—and how they compare with the AIDMA model—in Figure 3.10. Dentsu created the AISAS model in 2004 and registered it in Japan as a trademark in 2005. Dentsu uses the AISAS model as the basis for many of the campaigns—and all of the Cross Communication campaigns—that we design today. Thus, the AISAS model serves as a framework for what you'll learn in the rest of the book.

The AISAS Process

Here is how the AISAS process works in more detail. A consumer who notices a product, service, or advertisement (attention) and takes an interest in it gathers information (searches) about the item in question. That search may be performed on the Internet on blogs written by others, product comparison sites, and official corporate Web pages, or by talking to family or friends who have actually used

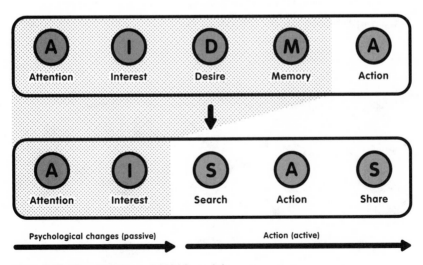

Figure 3.10 The AIDMA and AISAS models.

that product or service. The consumer then makes an overall judgment based on the information gathered and information presented by the company, taking into account the comments and opinions of those who have purchased and used the product or service. If successful, that then becomes a firm decision to make a purchase (action). After the purchase, the consumer becomes a transmitter of Word-of-Mouth information, by talking to others or by posting comments and impressions on the Internet (sharing).

AISAS as a Nonlinear Model

Fundamentally, the AIDMA model is linear; it represents a step-by-step process, starting with "attention" and finishing with "action." However—and it is extremely important to recognize—the AISAS model does not necessarily move through each of the five stages, as shown in Figure 3.11.

A step may be skipped, or it may be repeated. For instance, the consumer might see a television commercial for a similar product, and immediately go to the store to buy it (Attention → Interest → Action), or he or she might be so interested in the actress appearing in the television commercial that he or she sits

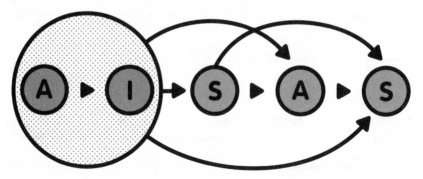

Figure 3.11 AISAS as a nonlinear model.

right down at his or her PC to write about the commercial in his or her blog (Attention → Interest → Share). And, perhaps in today's world, some consumer sits down right up front at his or her PC to search without being prodded by an advertisement in the first place.

The Importance of AISAS

The net result is that AISAS is a comprehensive model that anticipates the diverse behaviors of modern consumers, and at the same time functions as a model that operates in accordance with real-world activities. As we will see throughout the rest of *The Dentsu Way*, the AISAS model plays a critical role in the design of Cross Communication. As marketers we must strategically design mechanisms that will capture consumers' hearts in each of the AISAS processes.

Starting with A I, for example, we need to create mechanisms that will lead consumers to the corporate campaign site and motivate them to conduct searches. It is important to design the Web site to offer a variety of brand experiences so that the consumer will empathize with the brand and want to head for the store. Then, at the store, rather than simply encouraging the consumers to make the purchase, we must offer brand experiences unique to that store designed to ensure that the consumers are drawn to the brand in spite of themselves and that they enjoy themselves and want to return to make more purchases in the future. Examples of mechanisms to promote sharing might include Internet community sites where consumers can easily post comments, or mechanisms designed to increase the intensity of Word-of-Mouth communications.

With the AISAS model in mind, we can proceed to design the mechanisms that capture the consumers' hearts. By doing so, we can expect to:

- Establish a clear path to the purchase.

- Build "engagement"—a relationship—with the consumer.

The remainder of this book, and in particular Chapter 5, explains how the AISAS model is integrated into Cross Switch, the Dentsu approach to Cross Communication marketing.

Summary

As can be seen from the discussions up to this point, consumers often put up Information Barriers to marketing communications in general, while at the same time actively gather information on topics that interest them. In order to effectively approach these consumers, new and different forms of communication must be adopted.

As an example, in the world of manga publishing, the consensus for many years had been that sales of manga magazines were driven by the strength of the stories they contained. The example of *Jump Square*, however, demonstrated that even in the case of a magazine that always had particularly strong content, sales volumes could still be increased dramatically by creating an advertising device to attract the readers' attention and draw them out. This case is by no means unique; an increasing number of companies are experimenting with new forms of communication that cannot be defined within the framework of traditional advertising campaigns.

As a result, the questions we must ask when creating a modern campaign are:

- Can the campaign draw out consumers?

- Can it actively involve consumers and stimulate their behavior?

- Can it effectively use communication to build strong relationships, or engagement, between the consumer and the company or the brand?

The AISAS model has emerged from the new world of multimedia and online communication. Cross Communication is becoming more recognized as the new way to make marketing work in this evolved and more complex environment.

CHAPTER 4

CROSS COMMUNICATION: A LOOK AT WHAT MAKES IT WORK

In Chapter 3 we introduced the term "Cross Communication" and defined it tentatively as "the smart application of multiple forms of media in a calculated manner to deliver a marketing message." This definition is true, so far as it goes, but as we pointed out in the Introduction to this book, the term "Cross Communication" is used broadly. So now it's time to define Cross Communication the way we see it and the way we use it at Dentsu.

Defining Cross Communication

Often the best way to explain something is first to define it. . . .

We define Cross Communication as "the creation of a scenario or path for moving the target." The "scenario" is a path for the "target" (the consumer) to follow to get more information, take more action, or share information with a friend.

Sometimes it's best to define what something *is* by defining what it *is not*. Most marketers and advertisers are familiar with the term "media mix," and indeed, Cross Communication may sound like it refers to media mix. But there's a key difference: Cross Communication demands depth of penetration into the consumer's mind.

We'll soon see that, in the Dentsu version of Cross Communication, there is an important "depth" component to the involvement and response, whereas media mix to a greater degree addresses the "breadth"—the number of different channels or media—from which a message can arrive.

Cross Communication Is the Creation of Scenarios

The term "Cross Communication" has been subject to a wide range of interpretations, but essentially, it refers to a method of transmitting information, that is, using multiple media to express a given piece of information. In the context of corporate advertising and sales promotion activities, it is most often used, as the original meaning of the words suggests, to signify a "crossing over or combination of two or more media."

When viewed from the perspective of campaign planning aimed at resolving issues faced by companies, however, this interpretation is not only insufficient, but it could actually result in a negative outcome. The central question is *not* about whether there is use of multiple media. As we saw in Chapter 3, the objective of campaigns now and in the future should be *to actively involve consumers and stimulate behavior.*

A More Complete Definition of Cross Communication

The definition "creating a scenario for moving the target" is a good one-sentence definition, but to get a full understanding of our approach, here is a more elaborate version:

(1) Based on target insight and media insight, and (2) taking into consideration both "breadth" (reach and frequency) and "depth" (degree of involvement), (3) create a "scenario" for communication (4) that effectively combines multiple Contact Points.

The first component, item (1), of this more complete definition concerns *consumer psychology*. You cannot create an idea that will draw the target's attention without a deep insight into that target's characteristics, lifestyle, and approach to using media. Media insight, in particular, requires not only insight into trends related to media that the consumer comes in contact with, but also insight into new media and technologies that are emerging.

The question raised by item (2) concerns the addition of a depth dimension to the typical "mix" issue of breadth. Breadth can be measured and expressed "quantitatively" as a multiple of *reach* (the number of consumers who come in contact with the media or advertising) and *frequency* (the number of times the consumer sees the media or advertising). Depth adds a "qualitative perspective" regarding the degree to which the target has become involved; think of it as a measure of *quality*, in contrast to the *quantity* elements of a campaign.

We know that depth has been achieved if contact with the information creates a strong impression on the target. Depth has been achieved in cases where some other behavior results; for example, the consumer wants to learn more, so he or she begins to gather information, and eventually becomes a loyal user of the brand in the long term.

Based on the situation described in item (2), item (3) asks the critical question, "Has a scenario been designed to move the target?" If not, then a campaign may be doomed to failure before it begins.

There was a time when all we needed to do was position an advertisement in a conspicuous location above a well-traveled street and wait for consumers to notice it. Recently, however, it is important to create an engagement which moves the consumer and inspires that person to seek out information voluntarily.

The Scenario and Contact Points

It should be possible to create a path that is triggered by some form of contact with information, and which ties into the next action on the part of the consumer. Unlike the path of movement that makes up the consumer's day-to-day lifestyle activities, our goal is to achieve a creative path that starts from contact with information prepared by the company and that induces the next action. The campaign's "scenario" is complete when this path is properly designed. The result is that consumers have a truly active brand experience: they come in contact with the information and are intrigued by it; they follow the path, and before they know it they are a fan of that brand, making purchases, and telling their friends about it.

Finally, we come to the question raised by item (4), "Has the campaign been designed with Contact Points in mind?" The Contact Points, which connect the consumer and the brand, can take a number of forms; for example, television commercials, point-of-sale advertising, or even Word-of-Mouth communication.

Figure 4.1 illustrates the scenario definition of Cross Communication.

It is important to design the scenario based on a flow of Contact Points that is suited to the consumer's behavior. In other words, we must create the scenario from a media-neutral perspective that is not confined to a specific medium. It's worth pointing out here that the Internet is not necessarily the key element to Cross Communication, although in most campaigns it plays a part.

When defined in detail, as we have here, it becomes clear that Cross Communication is, in fact, a planning method that focuses on a combination of Contact Points. This planning takes place in the broader context of "Integrated Marketing Communication,"

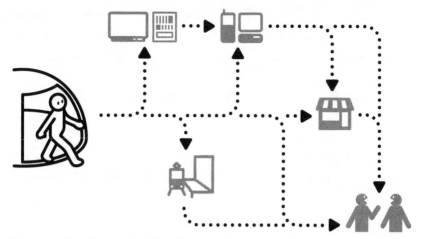

Figure 4.1 Creating a scenario, with paths, for moving the target.

which refers to continuous marketing activities that attempt to achieve synergy by integrating corporate communication activities that were traditionally undertaken by separate divisions, such as conventional advertising, sales promotions, public relations (PR), direct marketing, events, and interactive communications. The main goals of these activities are to strengthen long-term relationships between the brand and the consumer and to maximize the desired purchasing behavior.

Cross Communication and Brands with Little News

When should Cross Communication be put to use?

As we like to say: "Cross Communication works well on brands with little news." It's true that some campaigns capture the consumer's heart with a single, overwhelming creative element, which leads directly to purchasing behavior. This approach, which has been around since the dawn of advertising, is still extremely effective today.

In many cases, however, this approach demonstrates its greatest effects when the brand can be clearly differentiated from the competition. If a product or service that is clearly different from any before it can succeed in attracting attention, then popularity can spread like wildfire, and Word-of-Mouth communications naturally abound. This is why it is important to be the first to draw the consumer's interest.

Cross Communication, on the other hand, works well when there is little news or "buzz" about the brand. Examples include:

- Long-selling brands for which the novelty has worn off

- Brands that have undergone minor renovations

- Brands with characteristics difficult to communicate in simple terms

- Brands in categories where differentiation is difficult

- Brands in categories with low levels of consumer involvement

When it is difficult to attract the consumer's interest, it is important to lay out a clear path that draws consumers out from within their Information Barriers (see Chapter 3), increases their involvement, and ties into their purchasing behavior. Of course, Cross Communication is also extremely effective even when the brand has already secured a high level of involvement. In these cases, the "clear path" noted above is the path that brings the consumer to the point of purchase.

Differentiating "Media Mix" from "Cross Communication"

We are often asked, "What is the difference between 'media mix' and 'Cross Communication'?"

Media mix is a term that has been used for many years in advertising campaigns. In most cases, the term "media mix" refers to the distribution of advertising budget or the combination of media that achieves the campaign's objectives efficiently. In this context, "efficiency" means using a variety of media to communicate a message to as many consumers as possible (i.e., achieve maximum reach and frequency) at a minimum cost. The media mix approach can be a powerful tool when a company has an outstanding creative message that it wants to get across to as many consumers as possible, in order to maximize recognition of that message.

In this next section, we will examine the differences in planning approaches and perspectives for media mix and Cross Communication, making reference to the four definitions noted earlier.

Four Perspectives on Media Mix and Cross Communication

To solidify the contrast between traditional media mix and the Dentsu Cross Communication approach, it is helpful to compare them with respect to each of the four elements of the Cross Communication framework.

Target and Media Insight

First, we compare how we think about the target. In media mix, the "target" is often defined in terms of demographic characteristics like age or generation; for example, M1 is males aged 20–34, and M2 is males aged 35–49. This approach is effective when there are no significant individual differences in media environments, that is, in the degree to which information is able to penetrate among consumers. The Dentsu Cross Communication approach, on the other hand, emphasizes *combined* insight into both the targets *and* the media. We feel that the starting point for the creation of new ideas is to know what consumers are thinking and what they want, know the targets' lifestyle values and media behaviors, and know the details of how they view and react to information—in combination.

Breadth and Depth

Media mix places an emphasis on how *efficiently* the intended message can be carried across to consumers. The central concept is that if the message can be communicated to a larger number of consumers for the same cost, then the result will be greater recognition and a higher degree of purchase intent. Cross Communication, on the other hand, places an emphasis not only on reaching a broader audience, but also on *resonating more deeply* within consumers' minds, in order to motivate those consumers to take action of their own accord. In Cross Communication, the goal of communication is to strike a balance between the "breadth" and the "depth" that tie into purchasing behaviors.

The Scenario: A Path for Consumers to Follow

To maximize depth, or deeper penetration, of the marketing message toward getting action, there is a key additional dimension to the planning process. Media mix focuses on the volume and distribution of communication budgets that will maximize the efficiency of communicating the intended message. In contrast, for Cross Communication, the most important output is the "communication scenario"—the proposed action path or paths that will draw the target consumers outside of their Information Barriers, and motivate them to voluntarily launch themselves toward the product or the brand. This is a critically important concept in Cross Communication planning and will be covered extensively in the remaining chapters.

Contact Point Planning

There are also important differences between media mix and Cross Communication in the way that planning is implemented, particularly in terms of the media (or Contact Points) that are emphasized. Media mix most often starts out by looking for "efficient combinations" of advertising media, such as television commercials, magazine advertisements, and billboards or posters positioned outdoors or on major transportation routes. In Japan, this usually means on trains or in train stations. Sales promotions, PR activities, events, and interactive communications are then devised to run in parallel with this advertising.

For Cross Communication, the focus of planning is the Contact Points that link the consumer with the brand. The goal is to select from a wide range of Contact Points on many levels, but from a media-neutral standpoint. For example, planning might encompass a combination of mass media like television commercials and magazine articles, interactive media like Web sites, and in-store media like point of sale (POS) promotions. Together these media are used in a neutral and unbiased way at all levels of the consumer experience.

In Short . . .

Media mix emphasizes the distribution of media that will communicate the message to the target most efficiently. It is effective in achieving breadth of communication.

The key to Cross Communication is using a Core Idea to create a scenario for effectively moving the target to action. Cross Communication becomes necessary when the company needs to motivate consumers to voluntarily launch themselves toward the brand.

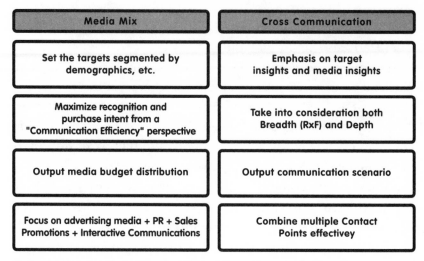

Figure 4.2 Perspectives of media mix and Cross Communication: summary comparison.

Figure 4.2 summarizes the comparison across the four elements of Cross Communication planning.

Figure 4.3 illustrates the increasing depth of communication via the generation of a scenario in addition to gaining the breadth through different Contact Points in the consumer experience.

Perspectives of Media Mix and Cross Communication: The Use of Data

The implementation of Cross Communication entails new and different ways of using existing and new media databases.

The data contained in traditional media databases include television viewer ratings as well as the circulation and readership rates for newspapers and magazines. Because the main perspective for media mix is "reach effect," if the target was, for example, "married men in their thirties," then the contact volumes for each media would be calculated by checking against the media database for this group. The media mix plan might show that a budget with

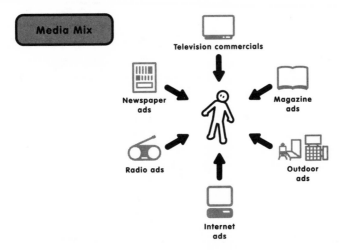

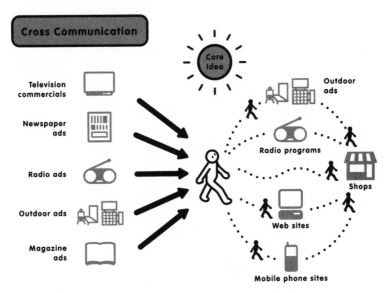

Figure 4.3 Difference between media mix and Cross Communication.

an emphasis on television commercials would reach 60 percent of married men in their thirties and that a higher budget would reach 70 percent.

How would the Cross Communication approach differ? Even for Cross Communication, it is very important to secure breadth by effectively using mass media such as television and Internet portal sites, so we continue to use data that indicate the spread and reach of data.

In addition to this, however, it is also important to actively incorporate data indicating the depth of media contact with consumers, as well as the *connections* between the various Contact Points. In Cross Communication, the cross-tabulation of response between different Contact Points, such as television *and* the Internet, becomes very important. In other words, Cross Communication identifies Contact Points from the consumer perspective and collects and uses data to provide an understanding of the depth of response and the depth of connections between media. We will discuss this approach in more detail in Chapter 5 in the section "Identifying Consumer Connections with Contact Point Management."

Core Ideas and Scenario Ideas

Now we come to one of the most critical aspects of Cross Communication and the Cross Switch application of Cross Communication: the generation of a "Core Idea" and a "Scenario Idea" to guide and frame the campaign. The "scenario," as we just discussed, is an operational plan—a script—for increasing the depth of interaction with the consumer and moving the consumer toward action.

Cross Communication entails the creation of a scenario for moving the target. However, the scenario doesn't exist in a vacuum. Rather, it originates from a Core Idea, or a central campaign theme, designed to "capture consumers' hearts."

At the Heart of the Cross Communication Campaign: The Core Idea

For an idea to attract the consumer's attention, it must, at the very minimum, be *interesting, innovative,* and *powerful.* "Innovative" is by far the most important of these three elements. No matter how faithfully you imitate a truly outstanding campaign, you will never be able to achieve the surprise and wonder that is generated when consumers come in contact with something they have never seen or even imagined before.

The idea that lies at the heart of the campaign, and which is emphasized during the planning process, is generally referred to as the "Core Idea." This is the concept that expresses the allure, novelty, and power of the campaign in simple terms. At the same time, it is the engine that moves the target. The ultimate success of the campaign will be determined by how attractive the Core Idea is to the consumer.

When developing the Core Idea, we must take into consideration a variety of factors, including target insights, industry trends, current activities in the market and particularly among competitors, and the true nature of the brand's value. Figure 4.4 illustrates these inputs.

The form of the campaign changes dramatically depending on which of these factors are incorporated into the Core Idea; for example, the strategic directions, the identification of the target, the use of media, and the development of creative communications. The Core Idea is usually fairly simple and can be expressed in a few words. The resulting Scenario Idea and scenario may be more complex.

As an example, the Core Idea for the *Jump Square* campaign described in Chapter 3 was: "information gap"—more specifically, "Intentionally create an information gap to induce Word-of-Mouth communications." In itself it was a fairly simple idea, or strategy, to move the audience toward a goal, which was to capture more noncore readers. The more tactical Scenario Idea and scenario add tactical detail to the basic Core Idea.

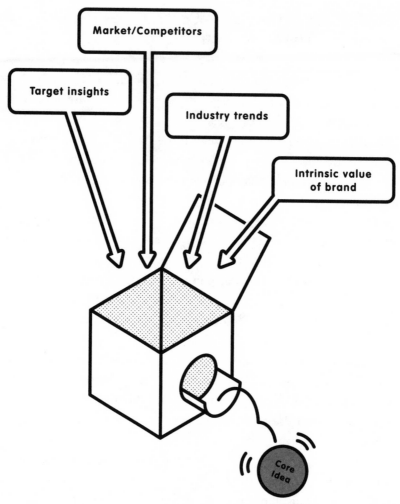

The Idea at the Heart of the Campaign

Figure 4.4 Factors in developing a Core Idea.

There will be many more examples of Core Ideas in the next few chapters and several tips for developing your own Core Ideas in Part 3.

Giving Form to the Core Idea: The Scenario Idea

Next, in order to give form and life to the Core Idea, we must create a conceptual framework for what drives the campaign; that is, we must create a specific scenario for moving the target. As discussed earlier, by preparing a variety of paths, we create the engagement with the consumer. At Dentsu, we refer to this framework as the "Scenario Idea." We believe that the creation of Scenario Ideas represents a new approach to Cross Communication.

The Scenario Idea touches on three major elements or considerations:

- Contact Points

- The Message

- Psychological Approach

As Figure 4.5 shows, the Scenario Idea is a conceptual path for the consumer to follow in response to various messages, at defined Contact Points, delivered in a planned sequence.

At this point it makes sense to take a closer look at each of the three elements, or considerations, in developing a Scenario Idea.

Contact Points

The Contact Points, which connect the consumer and the brand, can take a number of forms. They transmit a message that is appropriate to the consumer's circumstances and lifestyle activities, in keeping with the time, place, situation, and how the consumer feels at that particular moment.

The important thing here is to position an appropriate message in the appropriate circumstances to give proper form to the Core Idea. In some cases, the message changes depending on the

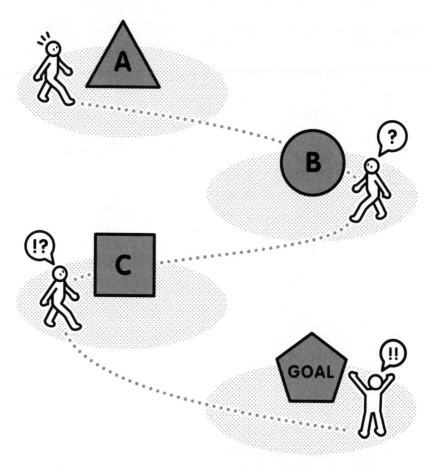

Figure 4.5 The Scenario Idea is the framework that gives form to the Core Idea.

circumstances; in others, a single message can be used effectively to reach the consumer.

The Message

When creating The Message, the most important thing is to ensure that it will catch the consumer's attention. To do this, we must develop The Message from the consumer's point of view, in order to establish a connection between the consumer and the brand.

Specifically, we talk about the brand in the context of the target's preferences and day-to-day interests. "Message" not only includes the actual message itself but also the context or environment in which it is delivered.

For example, suppose that we chose the theme of a journey surrounded by relaxing classical music. We could then create a context in which a person with an interest in classical music hears this message and senses that the brand has functions that will bring feelings of relaxation.

Psychological Approach

The "Psychological Approach" is a stimulation that puts consumers in a frame of mind that will lead them to the next behavior. The "puzzle" in a suspense novel is an example of this approach. The reader's motivation to continue reading the book is rooted in the desire to find out who the culprit is, or how the crime is perpetrated. If the book is really well written, the reader becomes completely absorbed in the story and can't stop turning the pages until the very end.

If we think of this in terms of an advertising campaign, we could design a path that begins, for example, by hiding some intriguing information to stimulate the consumer's curiosity, and then gradually expand on that theme. Cross Communication is most often designed to incorporate psychological motivations that lie deep within the human psyche. Because these psychological triggers differ from one target to the next, the search for the most appropriate message must take into consideration the unique characteristics of the target in question.

Keeping Scenario Ideas "On Task"

Creating Scenario Ideas for campaigns tempts the creative mind—it is easy to visualize intricate and exciting paths lined on both sides by continual stimulus and response. But we must remember that consumers can absorb only so much; we don't want to waste people's time. We must also remember that, in many cases, less is more.

The scenario can take on a variety of forms depending on the Core Idea, but in any case, it is important to remember that Core Ideas and Scenario Ideas should be conceived as a method required to resolve a brand issue. The scenario should never be designed to lead the consumer unnecessarily. If a campaign is put together with a design that simply leads to one dead end after another, the consumer will generally tire of it quickly and will consider it futile just as quickly.

Our definition of a scenario is "a path designed to link the consumer and the brand." In its design, you should ensure that the experience derived from the path, or experience path, *reduces* the distance between the consumer and the brand.

The Jump Square *Example*

It will help to examine Core Ideas and Scenario Ideas using the example of Shueisha Inc.'s *Jump Square* inaugural issue campaign from Chapter 3.

The Core Idea of the *Jump Square* inaugural issue campaign was to choose the target in such a way as to generate a "buzz." In order to capture many regular readers of manga magazines in general, we deliberately focused on the core readers—that is, the faithful readers of *Monthly Shonen Jump.* By creating an "information gap," in which core readers were always first to receive key information and noncore readers could only obtain fragmented information, we were able to generate a ripple effect in Word-of-Mouth communications, whereby information flowed from core readers to regular readers, and then on to others. Stated simply, as shared earlier, the Core Idea was: "To intentionally create an information gap to induce Word-of-Mouth communications."

Next is the Scenario Idea that gave form to this Core Idea: "Send the core readers on a complex information hunt, and motivate them to pass on this insider information that only they know. Use this Word-of-Mouth communication to draw in new readers who were not originally *Monthly Shonen Jump* fans."

From this "base" Scenario Idea we can examine the Contact Points, the Message, and the Psychological Approach. First, the following Contact Points were selected as the most common means of reaching the core readers:

- Late-night television commercial spots

- Internet sites accessed by PCs and mobile phones

- Advertising media in train stations

The message communicated by the television commercials— "don't search!"—stimulated the curiosity of the core readers, who thought, "They are up to something." This formed the starting point of a path for drawing readers to the Web site.

We set up a special site that could only be accessed by the tenacious readers who entered the words "Jump Square" in the search field three times. Only those tenacious readers were able to obtain detailed information on *Jump Square*, including videos introducing the authors' writing styles. By offering a reward only to those readers who were able to decipher the trick, we aroused a sense of superiority and induced these readers to pass the information on to other readers, for example, through comments posted on blogs and other sites, saying, "Actually, this is how it works . . ."

We created a mobile phone site that allowed users to read a full story scheduled to be published in the inaugural issue of *Jump Square* before the publication date, and motivated the core readers to access this site. After accessing the mobile phone site, the core readers told their friends about the site, boasting about how they had found it. The intent was to have the mobile phone site address passed from friends to friends of friends.

For advertising in railway stations, we created a series of manga posters that formed a complete story going around the Yamanote Loop train line, but the readers had to get off at each station in order to read the full story. The result was that core readers who found the advertising first posted comments on the Internet saying, "I read one at such-and-such station," or, "I read them all!" This motivated other readers to go on an adventure to find the manga themselves.

Such was the form given to the completed Scenario Idea. The core readers voluntarily went to the trouble to seek out the hidden information, which was, to them, a pleasing experience. Then, through the Internet or face-to-face conversations, they showed off their hard-earned insider information to others. The interest of regular readers was piqued by coming in contact with special information that they were unable to obtain on their own, and this motivated them to imitate the actions of the core readers, or to pass on the information to other regular readers. The final outcome was that many of these readers were interested enough to go out and buy the first issue of *Jump Square*.

Three Scenario Idea Approaches

The possibilities for creating Scenario Ideas seem almost endless. At Dentsu we find it helpful to design Scenario Ideas around one of three common approaches. We created these approaches based on an analysis of specific case studies and real Cross Communication implemented in Japan and other countries over the past few years. All three take into consideration Contact Points, the Messages, and Psychological Approaches, and all three are structured around experiences that motivate the consumer to voluntarily come into contact with multiple types of information and advertising, and eventually make the consumer a fan of the brand.

Note that the three types of ideas can be merged in any combination. Also note that all three are designed to get the audience curious about, "What's next?"

The three approaches are:

1. *Power variation scenario.* Presents variations to a message using a similar format

2. *Timeline scenario.* Creates a message that changes over time

3. *Media split scenario.* Attracts interest using only a key fragment of the message and presents the rest of the message using a separate medium

Power Variation Scenario

This type of scenario (illustrated by Figure 4.6) involves using information or advertising configured with roughly the same format, and presenting several variations via Contact Points with the target as a means of drawing interest.

The key here is to use a large number of variations, in order to stimulate a specific psychological reaction when the target comes in contact with several variations of the information or advertising; namely, the desire to seek out even more variations: "I've seen this, and this, and that . . . I wonder what else there is."

The number of variations will differ depending on the campaign, ranging from just a few to several hundred variations rolled out simultaneously. As a rule, the more variations there are, the greater the effect will be. This is because the rollout of new variations is extremely well suited to expanding the scope of location and space. Localized campaigns can be implemented very easily, for example, with simultaneous rollout in multiple cities, or by incorporating the unique characteristics of a given region or specialized themes related to specified locations. In Japan, scenario has a particularly high affinity with outdoor media,

Figure 4.6 The power variation Scenario.

such as posters or advertisements in train stations. Of course, multiple media can be used as well.

Following are the four main effects achieved by the power variation scenario:

1. *It may arouse a taste for the hunt.* Consumers who see one variation naturally want to find the next. This is the first step in motivating consumers to come out from within their Information Barriers.

2. *It may promote empathy.* When consumers see multiple variations of a given advertising message, they tend to compare the variations and choose the one that they empathize with the most; for example, "This one is the most interesting," or, "This is the one I like the best."

3. *It allows multiple messages to be communicated.* When the brand has numerous features that are difficult to communicate, this method makes it possible to show the brand from a variety of angles. If a particular feature is difficult to communicate, then several complementary variations can be used to convey the intended meaning. Some car advertising campaigns use this idea—you might see one ad touting appearance and another touting safety.

4. *It gives rise to Word-of-Mouth communications.* Consumers tell one another about how much fun they have had hunting for and finding the information:

   "Did you see the one with . . . ?"

   "I found one at . . ."

   "What do you think the other ones are like?"

   This also serves to increase the number of new participants in the Word-of-Mouth exchanges. Again, beer commercials and others with a degree of humor, suspense, or surprise fit into this category

Timeline Scenario

This type of scenario attracts attention by changing the message over time, and creating a chain of links for the consumer to follow. See Figure 4.7. There are two patterns for drawing the consumer's attention to the process that changes over time:

- A continuous story based on the premise of the changes

- A surprise story using unpredictable changes

The key to the continuous story pattern is the psychology of expectation, as consumers await the next message containing the next change. This pattern has two main effects:

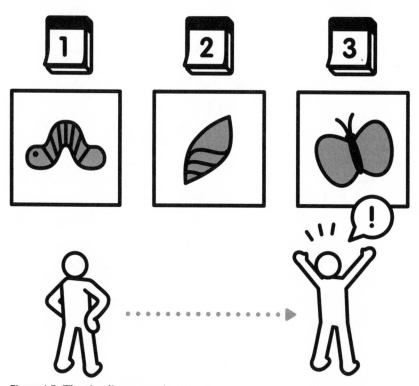

Figure 4.7 The timeline scenario.

1. Curiosity about what's next may induce the consumer to seek out information, perhaps by searches on the Internet or in the real world.

2. The pattern promotes a long-term focus on the brand.

As consumers become involved in the story line, they maintain a high level of interest until the entire story is complete. When the various segments are presented in a real-time format, it is particularly easy to encourage participation and promote interest, because the consumers feel as though they are part of the story.

When the campaign involves unexpected changes, the emphasis is placed on designing the surprises themselves. Unexpected changes aim to shock the consumer, in a Kafkaesque sort of way: "One morning, as Gregor Samsa was waking up, he found himself transformed into a monstrous bug." This method often uses media that consumers see on a daily basis and which is subject to long-term exposure. The consumer expects to see the same information or advertisement today that he or she sees every day, but what is found is in fact quite bewildering. This gap effectively attracts the consumer's interest.

The two main effects are the impact of the unexpected, and the resulting Word-of-Mouth communication, as absurdity always makes for an interesting topic of discussion.

Media Split Scenario

After drawing the consumer's attention with a key fragment of the message, this scenario leads the consumer to another medium where the remainder of the message is presented. By intentionally offering only a fragment of information, the consumer may take direct action in a desire to know the rest. See Figure 4.8.

One example of this campaign structure, which has gained popularity in recent years, can be seen in television commercials that present part of a story, and then say, "continued . . . on the

Figure 4.8 The media split scenario.

Internet," or, "For more information, please visit us at www.abc
.com." That said, such information can be broken up in many different ways, and the consumer does not always need to be led to a
homepage. A wide range of media can be incorporated, including
the four main forms of mass media (television, radio, newspapers,
and magazines), as well as outdoor media and live events. This
pattern is particularly well suited to the use of "teasers," when a
company wants the consumer to have some advance notice but
does not want to give away the entire package. For example, the
consumer might be told that if he or she goes to a specified place
on the specified date, all will be revealed.

The three main effects achieved by the media split scenario are:

1. *Increased involvement with the brand.* Motivated by a desire to learn more, angst arises from the awareness that, "If I don't go to the next step, I'll never find out what happens." As a result, even consumers who are not normally invested in the brand find themselves increasingly involved.

2. *Immediate focus on the brand.* In contrast to the timeline scenario, which promotes a long-term focus on the changes over time, this scenario generates a strong craving to resolve the frustration of not knowing, and so can fuel intense interest in a short period of time.

3. *Word-of-Mouth communication driven by action.* Because only those who take action can obtain the full story, consumers who have succeeded want to tell others, so they can show that they are ahead of the crowd.

CHAPTER 5

CREATING SCENARIOS FOR CROSS COMMUNICATION

In Chapter 3 we introduced the AISAS model for consumer response to marketing efforts. As a review, the five steps in AISAS are Attention, Interest, Search, Action, and Share. Consumers don't always follow the five steps in this order. The AISAS model has evolved as the digital age has made it possible—even likely—that customers will search for information during their buying process and that they will share information about their purchases and product experiences afterward. Refer back to Figure 3.10 on page 79 for a review of the AISAS model and the AIDMA model from which it has evolved.

So the next logical question is one that blends ideas together from Chapters 3 and 4: When examining today's buying behavior based on this model, what is required in the creation of scenarios for Cross Communication?

Capturing the Consumer's Heart:
Search and Share

We must strategically design mechanisms that will capture the consumer's heart in each of the AISAS stages. Starting with A I, for example, we need to create mechanisms that will lead the consumer to the corporate campaign site, and motivate him or her to conduct searches. It is important to design the Web site to offer a variety of brand experiences, so that the consumer will empathize with the brand and will want to head for the store (or buy it online). Then, at the store, whether brick-and-mortar or online, rather than simply encouraging the consumer to make the purchase, we must offer brand experiences unique to that store designed to ensure that the consumer is drawn to the brand willingly, enjoys the experience, and wants to return to purchase in the future. Examples of mechanisms to promote sharing might include Internet community sites where consumers can easily post comments, or mechanisms designed to increase the intensity of Word-of-Mouth communications.

By designing mechanisms that capture the consumer's heart, we can expect to achieve the following equally important results:

- Establish a clear path to the purchase.

- Build engagement—a relationship with the consumer.

Tying Search to Purchase by Product Category

One of the first important steps to consider in Cross Communication design is the likelihood of "search and share activities" in the consumer buying process. Clearly this varies according to the product category involved. For example, one will engage more in the purchase of an automobile than in the purchase of toothpaste. It turns out that regardless of the product category, search and share behaviors can easily be tied into purchases and the decision to make a purchase.

The results of a "Cross Communication Behavior Survey," conducted by Dentsu in Japan (see Appendix 1), showed that among consumers who had already made purchases, the ratios of persons who gathered information about the products in question were as follows: automobiles, 72.0 percent; mobile phone terminals, 70.6 percent; flat screen televisions, 57.6 percent; movies (at theaters), 66.0 percent; cosmetics, 53.5 percent; and snacks, 33.9 percent. Not surprisingly, the ratios differ from one category to the next, but in general, we can see that a large percentage of consumers gather information *before* making their purchase. Figure 5.1 shows the breakdown:

Figure 5.1 gives an idea of the relative importance of search in the consumer buying process for each of the six categories shown. Note that reported search rates in Japan are consistently higher than those in the United States; this is because many Japanese

Category	*Search rate(among purchasers)		Period
	Japan	United States	
Automobiles	72.0%	50.0%	Past year
Mobile phone terminals	70.6%	44.9%	Past year
Flat screen televisions	57.6%	52.0%	Past year
Movies (at theaters)	66.0%	35.0%	Past six months
Cosmetics	53.5%	29.8%	Past six months
Snacks	33.9%	9.2%	Past six months

Figure 5.1 Search rates by product category: the ratio of persons who shared or searched for information via the Internet, magazines, flyers, or at a store during the period indicated. *Source: Dentsu Cross Communication Behavior Survey, Japan (2008)/United States (2010).*

television commercials make a direct plea to have the consumer go to the Web for further information.

The next step is to tie search and share behavior to purchase behavior. Does the fact that consumers searched during the buying process suggest that they are more likely to buy? And does the tendency for buyers to also be searchers vary across product categories?

Indeed both of these are true—to a considerable extent. As Figure 5.2 shows, consumers who searched in the automobile category were far more likely to buy than those who didn't; in the snacks category, not surprisingly, search wasn't such an important element in the consumer buying process or a predictor of buying behavior.

Figure 5.2 shows the purchase rates for consumers who searched and the purchase rates for consumers who did not search, and calculates a "product purchase ratio"—the ratio of the two—for each category. Specifically, the product purchase ratio is:

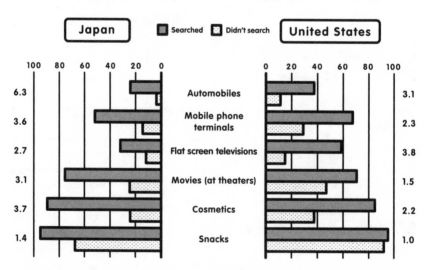

Figure 5.2 Relationship between search rates and purchase rates by product category, showing the rate of purchases by consumers who either searched for or did not search for information. *Source: Dentsu "Cross Communication Behavior Survey," Japan (2008), United States (2010).*

the ratio of persons who made purchases after gathering information in each category during the period indicated divided by the ratio of persons who made purchases without gathering information in each category during the period indicated.

These ratios are shown to the left of the Japan graph and to the right of the United States graph.

Looking at product purchase ratios, we might assume that purchasers have a high level of involvement, but in all categories, there is a higher purchase ratio for persons who gathered information than for those who did not, ranging from 6.3/1 for automobiles to 1.4/1 for snacks. Interestingly, the absolute percentage of respondents who search and purchase bigger ticket items is higher in the United States than in Japan, The product purchase ratios are also different, that is, the ratio of those who search and purchase to those who purchase without a search. U.S. consumers are more likely to purchase without a search, especially for less expensive items.

Tying Share to Purchase by Product Category

While "search activity" on the part of a consumer may be a simple quest for more, better, and deeper information, "share activity" is a stronger indicator of involvement and loyalty with the product and the experience of the product and the brand. Now, we will look at the relationship between information-sharing behaviors and product purchases.

Looking at a similar comparison of product purchase rates between persons who shared information and those who did not, we can see that although there is some variation among categories, the purchase ratio for information sharers is higher in all categories, ranging from 3.0/1 for automobiles to 1.6/1 for snacks. Of course, not all product categories are equally conducive to searching and sharing, but by closely examining the unique characteristics required of each category, it is fully possible to induce some degree of searching and sharing.

For example, in the automotive and digital camera categories, searching and sharing often focus on information related to the product's functions and specifications. In the case of food and beverages, however, instead of specific product information, we can expect that searching and sharing will focus mainly on topics related to television commercials and campaigns, or reading and posting comments on blogs about reactions and reviews after having actually used the product.

Figure 5.3 shows the linkage between share activity and purchase rates.

"Sharing" was defined in the survey as "talking to others" or "posting comments on the Internet." Although not as strong as the connections between search and purchase, the survey showed a greater propensity to buy for sharers than nonsharers. The comparison between the United States and Japan is similar to that for search: U.S. consumers are less likely to share information and purchase lower-cost products and more likely to share and

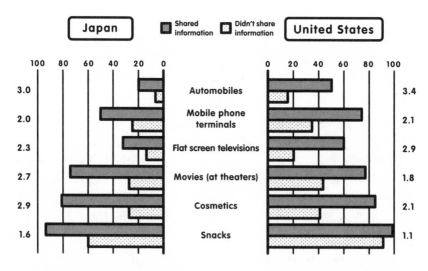

Figure 5.3 Share activity and product purchase rates in each product category, comparing the rate of purchases by consumers who shared or did not share information. *Source: Dentsu "Cross Communication Behavior Survey," Japan (2008), United States (2010).*

purchase higher-cost products. However, the product purchase ratios are more similar.

Search and Share in Scenario Design

When creating scenarios, it is important to design communications that will tie into purchases by promoting search and share, based on the types of category characteristics described above. In order to do this most effectively, it is important to consider both obvious and nonobvious forms of search and share; that is, what happens in the "real world."

The "Real World" as a Factor

The AISAS model was originally created to accommodate the emergence of interactive media such as the Internet and mobile phones, and it is easy to imagine that activities involving information searching and sharing might take place through these media. But we must also take into account real-world search and share activities that might take the form of obtaining product information from friends and family, or talking to others about one's reactions after actually using the product, or dozens of other possible communication channels.

The results of the Dentsu "Cross Communication Behavior Survey," discussed in Chapter 3, showed that in most categories, information gathering in the real world—for example, through magazines and flyers or at the store—accounted for the largest percentage of search activities. This trend was even more conspicuous in the case of sharing; in every category, the percentage of people who "talked to others" was greater than the ratio for those who "posted comments on the Internet."

When creating scenarios, we can promote search behaviors among consumers by using corporate Web sites, campaign Web sites, and social media. What we mean by social media includes the rapidly evolving assortment of blogs, SNS (social network services) like Facebook and Twitter, product comparison sites, and video-sharing Web sites. At the same time we can use more offline experiences to get the word out by actively using venues such as showrooms and trade shows, along with flyers and other promotional materials. With regard to share activity, it is worth investigating triggers for promoting Word-of-Mouth communications and frameworks for generating discussions in homes, at schools, in workplaces, and in local communities.

In any case, the important thing is to avoid drawing lines between the real and virtual worlds. Instead, we should seek out the Contact Points that are most likely to generate search and share activity in relation to the brand or the category in question and select the optimum combination of such Contact Points.

Creating Word-of-Mouth, or WOM

By now, you may have observed that information shared by one person, for example through Internet postings, is information searched for by another person. In the AISAS process, "Word-of-Mouth communications" are generated through a cycle that arises between the two "S" elements—search and share.

There are two types of Word-of-Mouth communications: those that arise spontaneously and those that are triggered deliberately. The latter type is referred to as Word-of-Mouth marketing, or WOMM.

In recent years, Word-of-Mouth communications have demonstrated an increasingly powerful influence. Videos posted on video-sharing sites have become extremely popular. Comments posted on blogs are picked up by mass media. Advertising on the street becomes hot topics in schools. Children appearing in television commercials quickly become the focus of attention. Figure 5.4 illustrates the search/share or "WOM" cycle as part of the AISAS process.

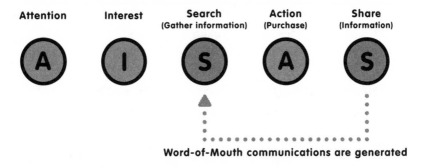

Figure 5.4   Word-of-Mouth communications as part of the AISAS process.

There are many brands that have achieved substantial sales through the spread of Word-of-Mouth communications. Because shared information is transmitted at a rate that was unheard of in the past, information is passed on from one consumer to the next in the blink of an eye.

The Importance of "Influencers"

With this backdrop, in order to deliberately generate Word-of-Mouth communications, it is important to strategically target those who have a high level of involvement with the products and who are adept at transmitting information to others. In Word-of-Mouth marketing, these people are referred to as "Influencers." We saw the importance of "core" *Jump Square* readers as Influencers in Chapter 3.

In Scenario design, it is important to ask:

* Which consumers are the most likely Influencers for the brand in question?

* What information will the Influencers help to distribute, and how will they distribute it?

The answers to these questions involve careful selection of targets, as well as strategic design of sharing behaviors.

Identifying Consumer Connections with Contact Point Management™

Contact Points that connect consumers to the brand are becoming increasingly diverse as a result of changes in the media environment and purchase behaviors based on the AISAS model.

The concept of "Contact Point Management" is important when creating Cross Communication scenarios; that is, identifying the Contact Points that are truly effective for consumers and effectively utilizing and managing those Contact Points. The Contact Point Management concept was registered as a trademark in Japan in 2004 in the advertising category.

What Is a Contact Point?

Consumers obtain information about products and services through a variety of routes, including some that we would not normally refer to as "media": family and friends, events, PCs and mobile phones, shops, and even the products themselves. At Dentsu, we call these connections between consumers and the brand "Contact Points." See Figure 5.5 for a sampling of common Contact Points.

Following are some of the most common types of Contact Points:

- The product itself

- Advertising, including television and radio commercials, advertisements in newspapers and magazines, and advertisements along transportation routes or in transportation vehicles

Figure 5.5 A sampling of common Contact Points.

- Programs and articles (programs on television and radio, and articles in newspapers and magazines)

- Shops (shop posters and displays, and sales promotions such as campaign goods)

- Service organizations, call centers

- Events (sports and music events hosted or supported by the manufacturer, outdoor events, etc.)

- PCs and mobile devices (corporate home pages, advertising on PCs or mobile phones, etc.)

- Word-of-Mouth (conversations or e-mail exchanges with friends, acquaintances, and family)

Recently, the following types of Contact Points have also gained attention:

- Social media such as blogs, social networking services like Facebook and Twitter, and product comparison sites

- Product placement (use and exposure of products in movies and television dramas)

Selecting Contact Points for Cross Communication

Consumers form a brand image or decide to purchase products based on an aggregation of experiences with a variety of Contact Points, including some that have been overlooked to a degree in the past. The identification and selection of effective Contact Points could thus be considered a fundamental step in Cross Communication.

When creating Cross Communication scenarios, it is important to identify and define, from a media-neutral perspective, the Contact Points that will act as the core of communications. Beyond that, it is important to consider developing new and innovative

Contact Points that will help to resolve brand issues, rather than simply using existing Contact Points.

Take, for example, the case of *Jump Square*, which was described in Chapter 3. In that campaign, late-night television commercials, train station advertising, and interactive media such as PCs and mobile phones were defined as the core Contact Points based on extensive analyses of the target consumers' lifestyle behaviors and frequency of media contact in specified time frames.

Our analysis also showed that the target consumers often read the Japanese comic-style manga anthologies on trains or buses on the way to or from school, so we thought that it might be possible to use the manga magazines themselves as a new Contact Point. This line of reasoning led to a unique approach: a *Jump Square* advertisement, drawn by a manga artist, was incorporated into a story published in the sister Shueisha periodical *Weekly Shonen Jump*.

Five Types of Contact Points

In this section, we will take a slightly more systematic look at these Contact Points. In the relationship between the target consumer and the brand, we have identified five main types of Contact Points:

1. *The product itself.* As long as the brand exists, there is always a Contact Point. When you think of the product as a Contact Point, however, you must think not only of the purchase, but of every experience that involves the use of that product.

2. *Outbound, or "push" contact.* Mass media advertising and promotional goods are Contact Points *created by* the company. These are used in communicating the needed message "outbound" directly to the consumer.

3. *Inbound, or "pull" contact.* The third type of Contact Point assumes that the target has some active involvement with

the brand. For example, through the corporate Web site or events sponsored by the manufacturer; the company does something to bring the customer in. In this type of Contact Point, it is important to have some trigger that motivates the consumer to become actively involved in the brand and to ensure that the consumer finds some measure of satisfaction from that involvement.

4. *Externally generated contact.* In the case of the fourth type of Contact Point, the consumer learns of the brand through the activities of a company other than the one that produces or sells the product. Examples include television programs, articles in print media, or displays in shops.

5. *Word-of-Mouth.* In the case of the fifth type of Contact Point, the consumer learns of the brand through conversations with family or friends, or through personal postings on the Internet.

The fourth and fifth types of Contact Points are unique in that the company is not directly involved when the message or information is transmitted to the consumer. It is thus important for the company to establish good relationships with the mass media, distribution routes, or the individuals who generate these Contact Points, so that more positive information is passed on to as many targets as possible.

Figure 5.6 illustrates the different types of Contact Points.

Contact Point Management: Designing Scenarios from a Contact Points Perspective

How can we identify effective Contact Points to create Cross Communication scenarios? Contact Point Management, a method that has been advocated by Dentsu, is an effective way of doing this.

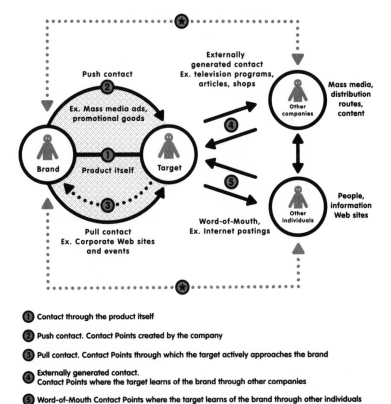

① Contact through the product itself

② Push contact. Contact Points created by the company

③ Pull contact. Contact Points through which the target actively approaches the brand

④ Externally generated contact.
Contact Points where the target learns of the brand through other companies

⑤ Word-of-Mouth Contact Points where the target learns of the brand through other individuals

★ Activities in which the company creates relationships with other companies and individuals

Figure 5.6 Types of Contact Points.

Simply stated, "Contact Point Management is a methodology for designing Cross Communication with a focus on a variety of Contact Points that link the consumer and the brand. Contact Point Management entails discovering and creating the best possible combination from among various Contact Points to design highly effective Cross Communication."

Designing Scenarios with Contact Point Management

The three main steps to designing scenarios with Contact Point Management are (1) identify all potential Contact Points, (2)

select effective Contact Points in keeping with the communication goals, (3) define the best timing for contact based on time, place, circumstances, and feelings. Here is a closer look at each of these steps:

1. *Identify all potential Contact Points.* The Contact Points that bring the consumer together with the brand carry more potential than we might imagine. The first step is to identify all Contact Points from the perspective of the consumer's day-to-day lifestyle, regardless of whether or not the company is directly involved in those Contact Points.

2. *Select effective Contact Points in keeping with the communication goals.* The next step is to select the most effective Contact Points from among those identified. Of course, the effects of each Contact Point differ depending on the target. Also keep in mind that effective Contact Points also differ depending on the objective, such as the brand image to be communicated or the action that the company wants the consumer to take.

   For example, let us assume that we first want the consumer to learn about a new beer, and to buy it once, just to try it. As with all Cross Communication campaigns, we want to assemble the most effective Cross Communication structure.

   In this case, television commercials are very effective in letting the consumer know about the new product, and premium goods are effective in motivating the first purchase. On the other hand, if the beer brand is a long-seller that has been around for more than 20 years, then the goal would be more to emphasize the "freshness" and "vitality" of the brand, and to encourage the consumers to continue buying it. In this case, in Japan, advertisements in train stations and on trains and buses, along with high-volume displays in retail stores, would be highly effective in communicating "freshness" and "vitality," while television commercials would help to promote continued purchases.

These are simplistic examples, but the aim here is to clarify the goals with regard to the intended image and the actions to be taken by the target, based on the issues and circumstances affecting the brand, and then to select the combination of Contact Points that will be most effective in achieving those goals. In this way, it will be possible to separate the effective Contact Points from the ineffective ones, so that communication resources can be utilized efficiently.

Figure 5.7 illustrates the idea of connecting Contact Points with specific campaign goals.

3. *Define the best timing for contact based on time, place, circumstances, and feelings.* When selecting effective Contact Points, it is important to define the most effective timing for the consumer to come in contact with the brand.

When communicating the message, greater depth of penetration can be achieved by ensuring that the consumer sees the brand information or advertisement when interest in the brand or category is at its peak. It becomes easier to define this crucial timing if you take into consideration not only "time," but also "the place," "surrounding circumstances," and "how the consumer feels."

For example, you can hear or see the same information or advertisement about a hamburger, but the effects and the way the message is received will be quite different at 11:00 a.m., when the consumer is hungry and looking forward to lunch, as compared to 1:00 p.m., when he or she has just finished lunch and is feeling full.

We can think of this in much the same way as the timing we choose when communicating with other people. For example, generally a person would not propose marriage in the middle of

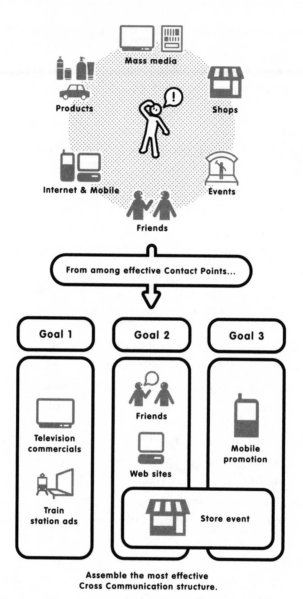

Figure 5.7 Selecting Contact Points to meet specific goals.

the day, on a crowded street with many people around, while the other person is feeling distracted or annoyed. No doubt, the message would be easier to communicate, and the other person would be much more receptive if the proposal took place on a weekend evening, on the beach, where the only other sound was the lapping of the waves on the shore.

When will the brand's message resonate most in the targets' minds? What are the time, place, circumstances, and feelings that will motivate them to voluntarily launch themselves toward the brand? If you can incorporate these questions into your planning perspective and properly utilize Contact Points, then you will be able to further increase the "speed" and "effectiveness" of your communications.

Figure 5.8 illustrates the idea of incorporating time, place, situation, and feelings into the Contact Point Management plan.

Evaluating Success in Contact Point Management

The final stage of Scenario design using Contact Point Management is the evaluation and management of results. Even if you've defined the most effective Contact Points and timing and have created a Cross Communication using a variety of Contact Points, the campaign will not always demonstrate effects in the way that you intended. When using these Contact Points, it is important to carefully examine the effects *after* the communications have taken place in conjunction with planning for the next phase of the campaign. Ask yourself: "What worked, and what didn't?"

Cross Communication methods can be refined and improved by evaluating the results in a variety of forms and accumulating knowledge of the effective Contact Points and combinations that should be given the highest priority. Contact Point Management is not only used in isolated applications of Cross Communication; it is a continuous process for achieving more effective, efficient communications.

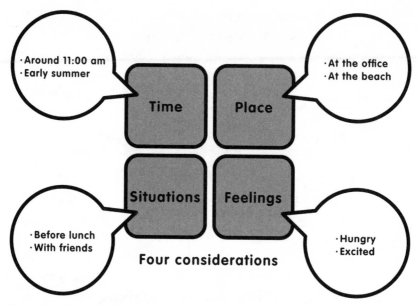

Figure 5.8 Four considerations in evaluating Contact Points.

The Intersection of AISAS and Contact Point Management

Up to this point, we have introduced two basic approaches to Cross Communication: AISAS and Contact Point Management. In fact, these two approaches are highly compatible—really, intertwined—in the rollout of a Cross Communication.

AISAS is a *consumption behavior model* created to capture the evolution of today's information environment. Contact Point Management is a *planning method* focusing on effective Contact Points linking the brand and the consumer. Model meets method, in effect. Contact Point Management produces a plan consistent with the AISAS model of the world. This is illustrated in Figure 5.9.

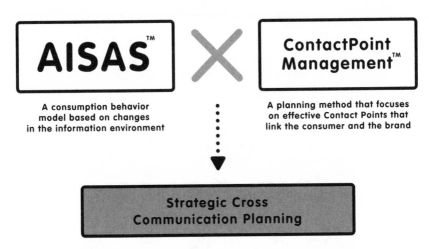

Figure 5.9 The intersection of AISAS and Contact Point Management.

Strategic Cross Communication Planning

The following statement explains the linkage between AISAS and Contact Point Management, as well as lays out the planning path for Cross Communication: "Analyze consumers' purchase behaviors through the AISAS model, and then use Contact Point Management to define and manage effective Contact Points that link those consumers with the brand." This approach makes it extremely easy to design the structure of Cross Communication.

Figure 5.10 illustrates the most common relationships between consumer Contact Points as they correspond to the various behaviors in the AISAS model. The structure of Cross Communication can be designed based on the optimum combination of Contact Points that is most effective for the brand by clarifying two key factors:

1. Which AISAS behaviors should be emphasized for the target in question?

2. Which Contact Points can be used most effectively to maximize those behaviors?

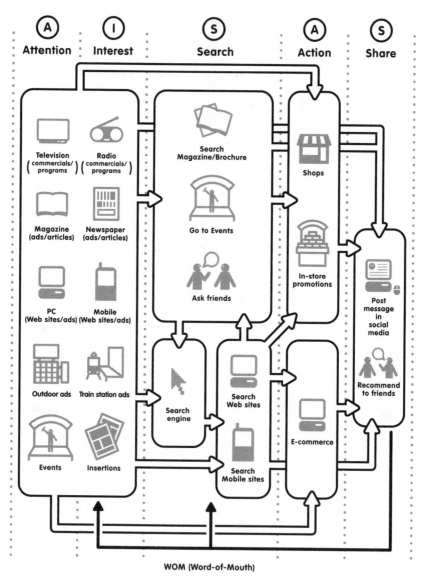

Figure 5.10 Designing campaigns using AISAS and Contact Point Management.

During the actual planning process, it is important to keep in mind that consumers' AISAS behaviors and highly effective Contact Points differ depending on the category, the target, and the communication goal being emphasized. It is wise to conduct consumer surveys to maintain a detailed grasp of these elements. Figure 5.10 not only shows the common relationships, but also shows how rich and intricate they can be.

Case Study: Japan Dairy Council's "Ask Milk!" Campaign

Here, we would like to introduce a specific example of Cross Communication that used AISAS and Contact Point Management: the Japan Dairy Council's "Ask Milk!" campaign, which was designed to increase flagging milk consumption and to reestablish milk's presence in Japanese society.

The key issue in this campaign was that junior high and high school students were drinking less milk than in the past. The campaign was designed to effectively and efficiently send a message to these students using Cross Communication: "To overcome the many trials of youth, drink milk!"

Specifically, attention and interest were promoted using television commercials as well as exposure through posters that were strategically placed in keeping with the lifestyle patterns of junior high and high school students. For example, posters were put up in karaoke rooms and cram schools where many students study in the evenings.

The students were then led to the campaign Web site by "Milk Manga," which appeared on mobile phone sites in conjunction with advertisements in manga magazines. The campaign site, designed around the concept of "a friendly advisor for junior high and high school students," was set up as a community where students could ask anything they wanted, and encouraged the students to post comments and visit the site often. At retail shops, in order to motivate students to pick up milk off of the shelf, the television commercial was shown on POPs, or point-of-purchase displays, using LCD monitors.

As a result, many students wrote about the "Ask Milk!" campaign on their blogs, and this in turn generated considerable Word-of-Mouth communication. This campaign won the "Promo Lion" (equivalent to the current "Gold Lion") at the 53rd Cannes Lions International Advertising Festival in 2006. Figure 5.11 shows details of the "Ask Milk!" campaign:

REAL-TIME MARKETING

The "Ask Milk!" campaign deployed POP ads displayed on LCD terminals at key locations in the store. The idea of displaying advertisements at the locations where consumers obtain the product is a relatively new concept in Cross Communication, but it is catching on with in-store displays and even using cell phones and other portable personal devices. As a consumer moves through a store, messages can be delivered at the right place with precise timing. Of course, this advertising can take a variety of more traditional forms, including standing or hanging displays, or posters on walls or in showcases.

The advent of real-time mobile phone driven advertising and purchase is just around the corner in the United States and in other countries. According to a February 2010 story in the *New York Times*, major retailers Walmart, Crate & Barrel, and Disney Stores are testing mobile real-time marketing applications, including a new application from IBM called "Presence" and one from Cisco Systems called "Mobile Concierge." Such tools help consumers find the products they're looking for and are expected to go a lot further to communicate product details to consumers and convince them to buy. What really remains to

be seen is how consumers respond; once they get the information, will they simply order the product online at a lower price
or continue with the shopping motion? That isn't clear, but either way it's pretty obvious that this new technology will spawn
a revolution in retail Contact Point marketing.

Motivation and Psychology Fundamentals for Scenario Creation

In this section, we will look at the psychological, motivational, and behavioral aspects of creating powerful Scenario Ideas. The goal, once again is to "capture the target's heart." In a sense, "capturing a person's heart" means stimulating that person's hidden needs. Offering a resolution or a path toward fulfillment of those needs will enable us to design the "path," discussed earlier.

To support the creation of scenario needs, Dentsu developed Communication Motivator™, a methodology that involves a categorization of human psychological motivations that can lead to capturing a "heart." Dentsu has classified them into a unique and original methodology. The Communication Motivator is based on the theoretical concepts of human desire derived from Henry Murray, Abraham Maslow, and other noted authorities on consumer psychology.

According to our methodology, human beings have 20 basic needs. Our lifestyles and communication patterns are formed according to the relative dominance of these needs. Our Communication Motivator is drawn from this set of deep-seated consumer motivations, which are shown in Figure 5.12 on page 140.

When creating Scenario Ideas, it is helpful to identify the psychological factors that form the triggers for those ideas, as well as the psychological states that are gradually aroused in the consumer as the campaign progresses. We went a little further than simply to observe the 20 needs. We categorized them into three perspectives:

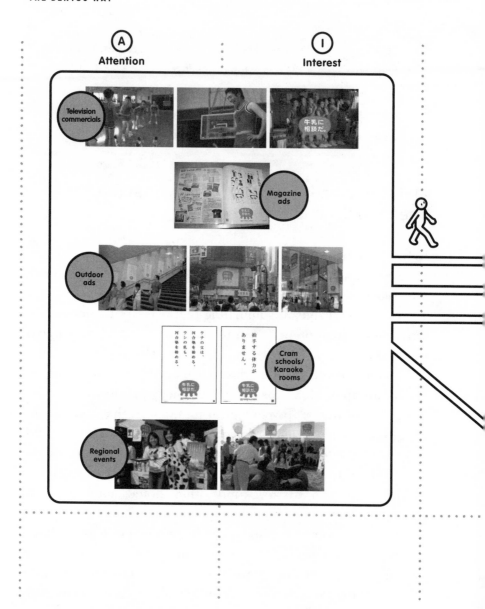

Figure 5.11 The Japan Dairy Council "Ask Milk!" campaign.

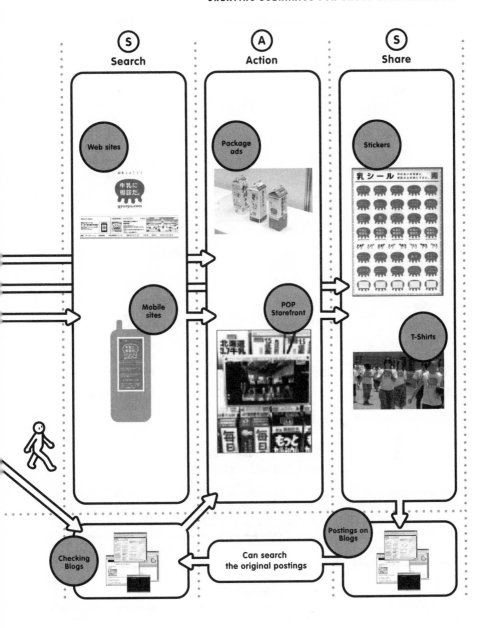

- Personal needs

- Interpersonal needs

- Social needs

These categories help us to apply this model to any type of campaign.

The best way to illustrate is by looking at these three examples: the "Magic Tower Project" for the movie *Harry Potter and the Order of the Phoenix*, the "Go with Roots!" campaign for Japan Tobacco's "Roots" brand of canned coffee, and the "Kanken DS" campaign for a game software application for the Nintendo DS. These examples follow.

Example 1: "The Magic Tower Project": Personal Needs to Satisfy Curiosity

The Warner Bros. "Harry Potter" films are extremely popular in Japan, but in fact this popularity peaked with the first installment,

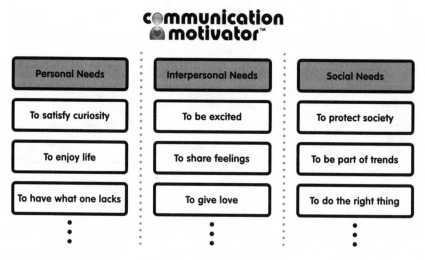

Figure 5.12 Communication Motivator (partial excerpt).

Harry Potter and the Sorcerer's Stone. Subsequent to this release, both box office revenues and attendances fell with each successive sequel up to the fourth in the series. A new campaign was thus rolled out in 2007 to increase ticket sales for the opening of the fifth installment, *Harry Potter and the Order of the Phoenix.* Rather than focusing on public relations (PR) for the new movie, the strategy decided upon was to revitalize interest in Harry Potter in general.

Specifically, the campaign was designed to have as many people as possible experience the excitement of "casting a spell," a central theme of the Harry Potter stories. People would learn firsthand how much fun they could have casting spells of their own. The venue for this magical experience was an event held on the day of the Japanese premiere (the preview screening), featuring a "Magic Tower" of light measuring 14 meters (about 45 feet) in diameter and shining some 600 meters into the sky. People were invited to gather at Roppongi Hills (an upscale commercial and leisure complex located in central Tokyo) to "cast a magic spell together" at the base of the light tower.

Mysterious notices were published in various media to attract people to the event and to promote "buzz" about the story. Samples of the notices included:

- "Magic is coming, June 28, 7:30 p.m., Roppongi Hills."

- "On the evening of June 28, leave your mobile phone behind, and bring your magic wand."

The advertisements never said a word about what was actually going to happen; they just said that on June 28, at Roppongi Hills, if they cast a magic spell, then something would happen. These advertisements appeared mainly on trains and in train stations in Tokyo, and word of the event spread rapidly.

On the morning of the event, a full-page advertisement appeared in morning newspapers, generating even greater expectations: "Today, go out on the town and cast a magic spell." That day, some 1,500 people gathered at the event venue to cast a spell along with Daniel Radcliffe, who plays the title role of Harry Potter in the film. At that moment, 29 searchlights lit up at once, projecting a huge tower of light into the night sky. The next day, the event was covered extensively in newspaper articles and television programs. Figure 5.13 illustrates the campaign.

The key point of this campaign was to stimulate curiosity with a teaser advertisement that presented people with a mystery—"Something magical will happen"—and then to entice people to gather at the venue to find out what would actually occur. Those who could not attend were encouraged to seek out information as well. The driving force behind the campaign was the needs to know the unknown—to solve the mystery and to find out what was behind it all. By emphasizing the simple fun of magic rather than trying to describe the complex plotline, the campaign was able to catch the attention of those who had stopped following the Harry Potter film series, and even those who had not seen the earlier films.

Harry Potter and the Order of the Phoenix succeeded in slowing the drop in box office revenues, becoming a major hit with revenues of 9.4 billion yen (about $100 million in U.S. dollars), which was the second highest for any film in 2007. Further, "The Magic Tower" campaign won the "Most Outstanding Advertising" award in the Film Division of the 64th Yomiuri Film and Theater Advertising Awards.

Example #2: "Go with Roots!": Interpersonal Needs to Share Feelings

In contrast to personal needs, which arise within individuals, needs regarding others are focused on the external environment. The "Go with Roots!" campaign of Japan Tobacco Inc. (JT) was a large-scale sales promotion campaign rolled out in 2007 to increase sales of the "Roots" brand of canned coffee. The campaign was an

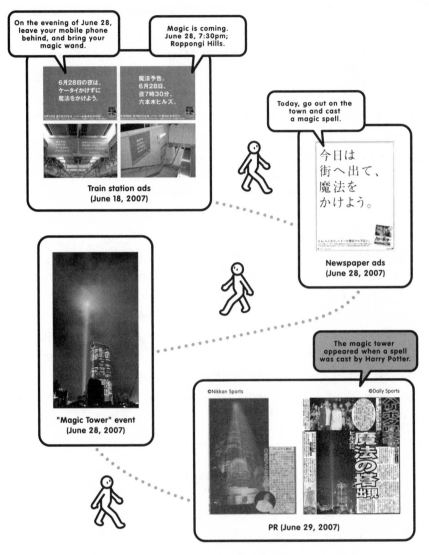

Figure 5.13 *Harry Potter and the Order of the Phoenix,* "The Magic Tower Project."

example of the "Interpersonal needs" group of motivators, specifically, the "needs to share feelings."

This was a case of a beverage product that succeeded in increasing its sales by capturing the target's sympathy. This case is a good reference for creating a campaign in product categories with low involvement such as groceries, cleaners, and other low-cost products used routinely.

The central issue for the "Roots" brand was that it did not have a familiar enough presence to adult users who represented the product's main market because the "personality" of the "Roots" brand was not sufficiently clear. In order to position the "Roots" brand as an intellectually stimulating, pleasing, and familiar experience, and to minimize the psychological distance between the consumers and the brand, we created a campaign based on the theme of "What businessmen are really thinking," sending the message: "The Roots" brand of coffee relieves the day-to-day stress experienced by the target consumers."

As Figure 5.14 shows, we displayed more than 600 types of posters at Contact Points focusing mainly on commuter routes for office workers in three of Japan's largest cities, Tokyo, Osaka, and Nagoya, offering thoughts on what these target consumers were feeling every day. The posters offered a wide variety of topics, including local themes related to the cities where they appeared, as well as themes focusing on specific settings such as train stations and staircases, and posters that expressed how working people often feel.

Sample feelings included:

- My manager is typing his PC password saying it out loud.

- After the kiss, she wiped her mouth.

- "Can you do me one favor?" he said, while ending up asking for many favors.

The target consumers—the office workers—would look at the posters and think, "That's happened to me too," or, "That's just how I feel. I'm glad someone said it!" Furthermore, they could be amused by this experience time and again on their way to and from work. In addition to the posters, the consumers were able to watch similar humorous themes in television commercials after they

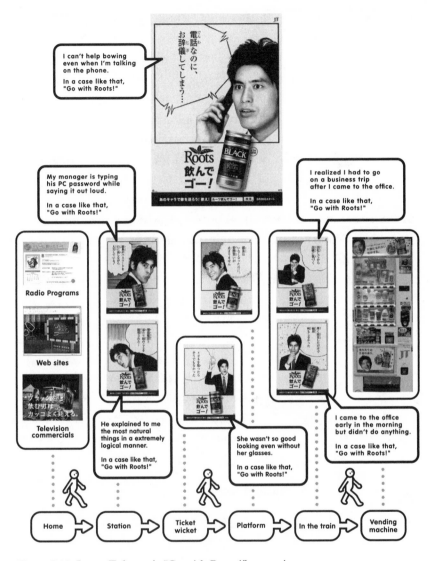

Figure 5.14 Japan Tobacco's "Go with Roots!" campaign.

came home from work. Because there were so many variations, consumers found themselves enthusiastically looking for new versions and telling others about the ones that they had found.

The underlying basis for the "Go with Roots!" campaign was to skillfully stimulate consumers' hidden psychological motivation to share their feelings with others. It focused on the sense of security that each of us derives from seeing simple, unadorned depictions of the real world that we live in and from knowing that we are not alone in feeling the things that we feel.

By using media on lifestyle routes that consumers come in contact with virtually every day over a long period of time and by offering "little truths" experienced by everyone in a variety of situations, we were able to inspire in consumers a natural feeling of security and peace of mind in reference to the "Roots" brand. The "Go with Roots!" campaign was expanded further to incorporate an Internet-based songwriting contest, in which consumers could actively participate by putting their feelings of stress into words—or, more specifically, into lyrics. The campaign was successful in securing new fans of the "Roots" brand of coffee and substantially increasing sales. The campaign won the "Bronze Award" in the "Direct Lotus" division of the 11th ADFEST, in 2008.

No Matter the Era, Concept Is the Key

The following interview was conducted with So Yamada, Planner, Strategic Planning Office, Dentsu Inc., and Planning Director of "Roots" project team, and Cannes Lions International Advertising Festival award winner. A more complete biography for Mr. Yamada can be found in Appendix 3.

We thought of jokes that you would tell friends at school.

In the Japan Tobacco (JT) "Go with Roots!" campaign, our goal was to establish Roots' position as a major canned coffee brand. We decided to increase Roots' popularity by taking the image held by existing Roots fans—that of "a canned coffee that makes you feel positive"—and carrying this image over to a broader range of canned coffee drinkers.

A key factor in the creation of the central idea for the campaign was a comment that we received from the client: "Put more thought into the brand's personality." The personality we decided on was the "class clown"—that intelligent but rather goofy friend that you remember from your school days. Once we settled on this, the direction for the campaign came together quite naturally.

When his friends are feeling down, the class clown never tries to encourage them by pushing them to work harder. Instead, he tells jokes or plays tricks on people to turn their mood around, for example, by sending funny e-mail messages or acting up at social gatherings. This is the exact concept used in the campaign.

Because canned coffee is a low-involvement product, in the past, the most common means of creating a strong impression had been through television commercials. The problem was, however, that the top brands were doing the same thing, and they had a larger budget, so it was difficult to compete. So, instead of just trying to reach as many people as possible, we placed priority on ensuring that our message struck a chord deep within each individual user.

My strongest impression during this campaign was that we were working closely with the client. I'm really glad we spent so much time in meetings and discussions with the client right up to the point where the final output was confirmed.

The concept is "New point of view to resolve issues."

A certain creative director once told me, "There are only three types of ideas in advertising: Brand strategies, creative ideas, and media plans." Of these three, I think, the most fundamental and most important is the idea related to the brand strategy; that is, the campaign concept. When you have a clear concept, any campaign can be effective regardless of the era. The concept here is the words which give us "New point of view to resolve issues"; not just flowery expressions and spur-of-the-moment inspirations.

I see four essential steps to develop and implement a campaign based on the concept:

1. Clarify the issue.
2. Identify the words that will lead to a resolution.
3. Develop concrete output.
4. Execute the campaign.

Let me explain them one at a time:

1. *Clarify the issue.* There are two things that we focus on here. The first is not to fall into the trap of "analysis for the sake of analysis." Of course, data is important, but you'll never get anywhere if you are constantly chasing after data and can never see the whole picture. I think it's important to "DON'T THINK, FEEL!" as much data as possible (quoting from Bruce Lee), and identify the key issues using both intuition and logic. You must also communicate fully with the client. The orientation sheet will indicate a number of issues, but it's impossible to place the same priority on resolving all of these issues. It's important to maintain a clear understanding of what the client really needs.

2. *Identify the words (concept) that will lead to a resolution.* Next, we find the direction that is most likely to resolve that issue, and put this into words as the concept to share with the team. After the "words" that form the basis for the concept have been presented to the team, we carefully discuss and refine the concept using the following three checkpoints as our guideline:

   - Is the concept firmly linked to the product?
   - Is the concept firmly linked to the consumer?
   - Is the concept firmly linked to the output?

   You could say that the concept evolves through this process. The way I see it, there is no point in hanging on stubbornly to the words or concept presented at the outset. The "metaphor" is an important device in the creation of the campaign concept, because it functions as a means of sharing the concept intuitively. In the case of Roots, by settling on the metaphor of a "prankster," we were able to develop the output with little difficulty.

3. *Develop concrete output.* Steps (1) through (3) are not necessarily successive stages; you go back and forth, gradually increasing the accuracy of the output. The accuracy of the concept also improves in the final stage of campaign

development, so by keeping that concept in sight, it becomes possible to create truly exceptional output. The "output" that I am talking about here is not simply the expressions appearing in the posters and commercials; it is also necessary to discuss the respective media at the same time, based on the limitations of the budget.

4. *Execute the campaign.* At this stage you put yourself in the target consumers' place and experience firsthand the campaign that you have developed. You combine your own intuitive reactions with data obtained through effect surveys and other sources, and return to step (1), where you once again clarify the issue to be resolved. The development and implementation of the campaign is a never-ending cycle.

In summary, I believe that regardless of the era, the concept is the key. Already, we have come to a point where clients are no longer satisfied with "funny and interesting ads" or "new media." Concepts will continue to be important, because it is the concepts that have the power to resolve issues for the client.

Example 3: Kanken DS: Social Needs to Protect Society

Social needs focus on various aspects of the society in which we live, such as the community or the environment. In this example, we examine "The needs to protect society." This case involves "Kanken DS," a game software designed to reinforce adult knowledge of "kanji" characters, one of the main character sets of the Japanese language. In Japan, society values an elevated knowledge of the thousands of kanji characters in a manner similar to—and really exceeding—the way English language speakers prize their knowledge of vocabulary. In Japan, it is a national goal to expand kanji knowledge not only for language fluency but also for cultural preservation. There is concern that the growth of the PC will cause a permanent decline in the use of handwritten kanji characters.

This was a case of game software that succeeded in gaining attention and increased understanding of the product category by public relations (PR) and Word-of-Mouth (WOM). This case is a good reference when you create a campaign for a complex product that is hard to explain such as software, new media devices, and so on.

Rocket Co., Ltd., which specializes in the development of game software, released "Kanken DS" in September 2006 for the Nintendo DS handheld video game system to enable users to have fun while improving their ability to read and write Japanese kanji characters. At its original release, the software was a hit among video game users, selling some 300,000 units. The campaign was rolled out to expand these sales further.

The first stage of the campaign involved strategic PR activities designed to attract the attention not only of video game users, but of regular consumers as well. Three months after the original release, on December 12, which had been designated in Japan as "Kanji Day," we announced the results of an independent survey, which found that "recently, 85 percent of adults feel that their kanji skills have deteriorated." The mass media all picked up on this theme at once, cultivating in the population at large a sense of impending crisis regarding poor kanji reading and writing skills—something it seemed that everyone was aware of intuitively but had not seen in figures.

The second stage was to design a trigger that would motivate consumers to reach for "Kanken DS" as a means of resolving this problem. This was achieved through a Word-of-Mouth campaign involving a dedicated Web site and the distribution of blog parts. "Blog parts" are tools that can be incorporated into blog pages to display information or content from another site in a small window.

When users clicked on the blog parts embedded in individual blog pages, they were able to enjoy a trial version of the "Kanken DS" game that was identical to the original. The results of these trial games were reflected on the official Web site. Here's the engaging part: users were able to check how their own kanji skills compared to the population at large and get a nationwide ranking. Users were also asked to input their home prefectures, so after the test, an overall ranking of prefectures (political divisions not unlike states or counties in the United States or other countries) could appear on the home page. Thus, users who scored well were able to get satisfaction from helping their prefecture score improve overall. See Figure 5.15 for an illustration of the "Kanken DS" Scenario design.

Interestingly, the blog parts did not simply offer a trial version of the game; they incorporated a mechanism that set the prefectures in competition with one another. This stimulated a form of patriotism among the participants toward their own prefectures and generated Word-of-Mouth communications at an explosive pace. Users contacted friends and acquaintances over the Internet in a rapid chain reaction, with messages like, "We're not going to let that prefecture beat us, are we?" Or, "I'd hate to see our home prefecture come in last." "Kanken DS" proved to be such a high-quality game that users became hooked, just by trying the Internet trial version, and this led to frequent postings on social networking services (SNS) and bulletin board sites (BBS). People were writing rave reviews about how much fun "Kanken DS" was, even before they had purchased the game.

Exposure for these highly popular blog parts was measured at around 8 million impressions, or times that a Web page was viewed by a visitor. More than 150,000 people played the trial version via blog parts, and the game became a major hit with sales of 650,000 units.

The key point to this campaign was to lay the groundwork by bringing to light concerns about deteriorating kanji skills, and to use this topic to trigger the psychological motivation of feelings of affection for the place where one was born or currently lives, the feeling of belonging to that community, and the need to protect this. By adopting the format of a competition between prefectures, we were able to make use of the feelings of solidarity formed over

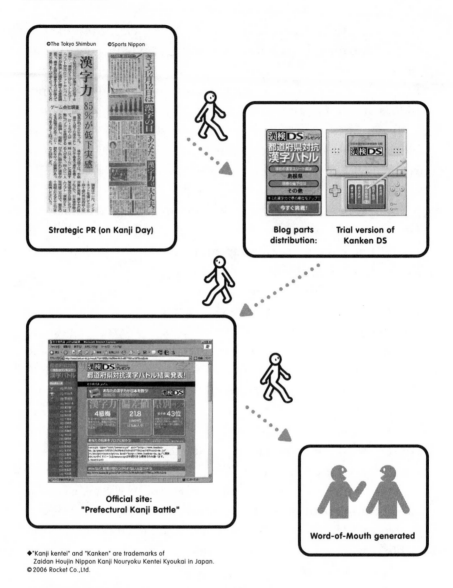

Figure 5.15   Rocket Co., Ltd.'s "Kanken DS" campaign.

the Internet to promote a rapid increase in Word-of-Mouth communication. This campaign won an award in the "Other Interactive Advertising" division at the 5th Tokyo Interactive Ad Awards (TIAA) in 2007.

Don't Design the Mechanism— Design Consumers' Feelings Instead

The following interview was conducted with Yuki Kishi, Communication Designer, Communication Design Center, Dentsu Inc., and Cannes Lions International Advertising Festival award winner. A more complete biography for Mr. Kishi can be found in Appendix 3.

"Kanken DS" uncovered a potential market through strategic PR.

Even before I started working on the project, Kanken DS was already a hit with sales of 300,000 units. The client wanted to add even more momentum to these sales. The game had already reached most of the main target users (video game fans). So in order to increase sales, I had to find new users outside of this target group. Rather than selling a product that wasn't selling, our job was to sell a product that *was* already selling. In a sense, this was a real and different challenge for us.

I began by using strategic PR to stir up awareness of deteriorating kanji skills, as a means of uncovering the potential market. I then used strategic PR to uncover new users in the general population because I knew that regular advertisements would have little effect on people who didn't usually play video games. Compared to an advertisement that says "kanji skills are deteriorating," a news report—in the "real" media—saying the same thing is far more effective. When something is reported in the news, it can draw the attention of people who were not originally interested in that topic. Somehow, being in the news makes it more personal, less biased, and more urgent.

The important thing was that even if the message got across, our job still wasn't finished. The campaign was only successful if consumers went out and bought the product. I could increase consumers' interest and awareness, but it would all be for naught if they ended up buying one of the competitor's games—or not buying anything at all.

I created an Internet-based trial version of the game, and then created an environment where consumers could actually play it. Specifically, I used blog parts to encourage a natural proliferation of the trial game. I also incorporated an element of "Prefectural competition," to make the game more interesting and promote more intense Word-of-Mouth communications at the same time. At the stores, I created point-of-purchase (POP) displays using the news article.

Picture the scene: "How will the consumer react?"

I had been designing the communications from the perspective of "The moment when the advertising reaches the consumer." To do this, I conducted detailed studies of what the targets see, and what type of psychology operates at the moment they see it. I began with the premises of "Thinking from a media-neutral perspective" and "Seeing potential in all media." Rather than starting with the media, I thought first about "What is the best way of ensuring that consumers get the message?" Then I thought about the media best suited to accomplishing that.

The most important perspective for planning in the era of Cross Communication is not designing the "mechanism," but designing consumers' feelings. The goal is not simply to use Cross Communication, or even to get the consumer to search for your brand.

It's important to picture the scene right at the point of contact—imagine the situation and the circumstances that the target is facing, and the feeling, or the psychology, at that very moment. It takes imagination, almost to the point of fantasy. You have to create a very strong image in your mind. The next important step is to design the communications based on that moment, when the message gets across. In the case of Kanken DS, one of these scenes included people talking about the "Prefectural ranking."

I think the important thing here is not to think of things after the expression has been defined. If the expression of the concept comes first, then your focus becomes narrow, and you have a tendency not to think of other possibilities. When that happens, it's easy to lose sight of the consumer, which is where our focus really should be. Whenever I give presentations to the client, I don't start with the expression or the media; I begin by asking the client to picture the scene where contact takes place: How will the consumer react?

It's important to explain in a way that gives the client a real, firsthand understanding, without getting caught up in the data. Of course, you also have to come up with a concept that everyone can share on an intuitive level.

Demand for overall communication design.

Recently, an increasing number of clients are looking for a "grand design"—that is, a communication design with a firm grounding. More and more clients have come to realize that significant effects of communication can only be achieved with an overall design, and I think that's why I have received so many requests in this area.

In that sense, in the planning process, I think it's important to take a stance of seeing the big picture, from start to finish, rather than just focusing on one segment of the campaign. The best way to do this is to avoid limiting the roles of the people involved in planning; instead, you have to adopt a flexible approach, in which anyone can take on any task—if you can do it, then you do it.

These days, there is too much information available, and a greater number of consumers have taken a very defensive attitude toward advertising. Simple messages won't get across. In communication design, it has become increasingly important to identify the moment that moves those consumers' hearts.

Summary: Using the "Psychological Approach"

The Psychological Approach increases consumer involvement, and motivates the consumer to take the next action. The approach differs depending on the unique characteristics of the target and the brand, so it needs to be modified for each unique situation. In today's Cross Communication, the process that stimulates that "pressure point" becomes even more important.

By using Dentsu's Communication Motivator concept, it will be possible to identify effective psychological needs and develop suitable ideas. We will provide an overview of planning practices in Chapter 8, in the section titled "Creating the Scenario Idea Through Team Discussions."

The "Horizontal T Model"

Finally, we get to one of the most important ideas—or visualizations of an idea—in The Dentsu Way. When creating Cross Communication Scenario Ideas from the perspective of AISAS, Contact Point Management, and Psychological Approach, having a basic framework will help to eliminate unwanted variations in the idea and will make it easier to share the idea within the team. By actively using the "Horizontal T model," you can transform the Scenario Idea into a concrete and visible image and confirm its effectiveness before implementation.

Visualizing a Scenario Idea Using the Horizontal T Model

Dentsu developed the Horizontal T model as a basic framework for the creation of Scenario Ideas.

The underlying concept when creating Cross Communication scenarios is to pleasantly draw out consumers who have put up Information Barriers, and to have them actively come in contact with product information and advertising and develop deep relationships with the product so that they will be positively motivated to buy that product. Based on the AISAS approach, we must first establish Attention and Interest in the product information or advertising and then design a path that will motivate consumers to actively Search, take Action, and Share information.

In order to maximize the effects of Cross Communication, we must see that the process described above occurs not just in a few individuals, but in a large group of target consumers. In other words, we must create an idea that actively involves a "broad" target group, and at the same time promotes "deep" involvement with the target consumers. This is the "breadth" and "depth" dimensioning described in Chapters 3 and 4.

The purpose of the Horizontal T model is to visualize, in a single integrated structure, the consumer's transition from "passive to active" and from "AI to SAS," as well as the perspectives of breadth and depth in the creation of scenarios. The name, as you will see in Figure 5.16, is derived from the image of a T rotated 90 degrees.

Using the Horizontal T Model to Check Scenario Ideas

The Horizontal T model can be used to check the validity of the Scenario Idea you've created. The two questions to ask are:

* Have you formed a relationship between the offer and the campaign host?

* Does the scope of the scenario demonstrate depth as well as breadth?

Let's consider these two questions, one at a time.

1. *Have you formed a relationship between the offer and the campaign host?* The transition from passive to active and from AI to SAS can be viewed from the following perspectives. When the information or message that draws out the passive consumers becomes the offer or "invitation," what is the "treat" that welcomes the now active consumers and meets their expectations? We must carefully calculate the relationship between the offer and the host. If the Scenario Ideas created freely by the team are plotted on the Horizontal T model, then the situation becomes very clear. Perhaps the consumers have been successfully drawn out, but the subsequent connec-

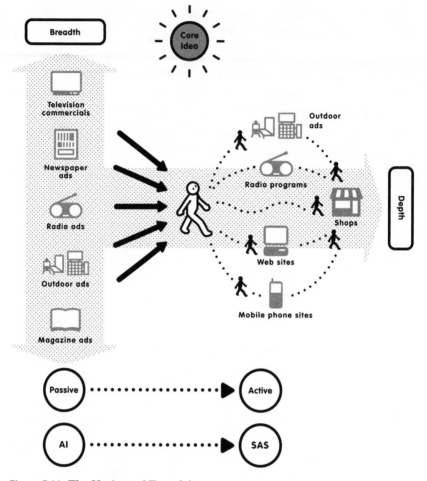

Figure 5.16 The Horizontal T model.

tions are still unclear. Has an appropriate Psychological Approach been selected to act as a host that will not to betray consumer expectations? Which Contact Points have been selected to act as the next host on the consumer's path? This model will no doubt be useful in confirming and strengthening the connections for each individual path as the scenario gradually takes shape.

2. *Does the scope of the scenario demonstrate depth as well as breadth?* Normally, because "reach" is included in the concept of "breadth," it is easy to assess roughly how many target consumers will see the information, and how many will show an interest in it.

Depth, however, has a more qualitative focus—how to increase the consumer's involvement and how to motivate the consumer to take action—so there is a tendency to overlook the issue of numbers.

The scenario for moving the target was unique, but the trigger was so complex that few people could follow it. The content offered an experience that was sure to make fans of the consumers, but the Contact Points were limited, so in fact, few people could enjoy that experience. These are situations that can and do arise in the real world. A strong awareness of both breadth and depth is essential to the success of Cross Communication.

When creating the Scenario Idea, we need to take the elements that tend to fill up most of our field of vision in the foreground and draw them back to a more neutral perspective. This is the effect that can be achieved through the check process that utilizes the Horizontal T model. For a more detailed description of how to design scenarios with both breadth and depth, please refer to Chapters 7 through 9.

PART 3

PUTTING
CROSS SWITCH
INTO PLAY

CHAPTER 6

CASE STUDIES OF THE CROSS SWITCH WAY

Part 2 gave an overview of the building blocks of Dentsu's Cross Communication platform, or Cross Switch. The three chapters in Part 2 each had moderately sized case examples of the Cross Switch concepts presented in those chapters. Chapter 6 presents five more case studies, each of which includes all the core elements of Cross Switch as illustrations of an integrated model. The central focus is on illustrating creative and successful Core Ideas and Scenario Ideas and how they address the issues faced by the companies. As we describe the cases, we'll cover the other supporting elements of Cross Switch and how they are put into practice as well.

Nissin Food Products Co., Ltd.: "Cup Noodles" "FREEDOM-PROJECT"

In order to resolve brand issues, problems, or challenges through Cross Communication, we feel that it is important to create ideas that break away from existing frameworks. As a first case example, we'll present the "FREEDOM-PROJECT" used to promote Nissin Food Products Co., Ltd.'s Cup Noodles product. While this campaign was conducted in Japan, the product has a strong presence in the United States and other countries and is generally sold under the "Cup Noodles" brand. Conducted as a continuous campaign for two years from April 2006 to March 2008, this campaign used a variety of Contact Points to capture the hearts of young people and to create a new business model. We'll start with the brand issue.

Brand Issue: Revitalize the Brand by Improving the Brand's Impression among Younger People

Cup Noodles, first released in 1971, is a global brand that has sold a total of more than 25 billion units in some 80 countries around the world. At the same time, however, it faced a problem common to such long-selling brands: some 35 years after its initial release, the market had undergone a change in generations, and the company was concerned that young Japanese people in their teens and twenties did not have as strong an image of Cup Noodles as in preceding generations. The communication target for Cup Noodles was basically *all* generations, but the company decided that it was important to strategically increase awareness among young people, who represented the consumers of the future, that Cup Noodles was a brand they could empathize with in their daily lives.

So the central question became: "How could we create an active new image and secure new users, while at the same time maintaining the worldview of a long-selling brand that had been built up over 35 years?" We examined the possible approaches that would be effective in resolving this issue. We created a Core Idea.

Core Idea: Have Consumers Experience the Culture of Cup Noodles through Creating Original Japanimation

In the case of a long-selling brand like Cup Noodles, our strategy was not so much to *sell the product* as it was to have consumers *experience the culture of the brand* in order to win over new fans while also winning back old ones.

The starting point was to establish that Cup Noodles was not just a product; it was a culture. Since its release in 1971, it had become quite common to see people walking down the street eating Cup Noodles with a fork. This had come to be accepted by the Japanese as a new food culture. Cup Noodles won overwhelming support because it offered the value of "Freedom," the freedom of being able to eat whenever and wherever you wanted to.

Thus we decided that "Freedom" expressed the essential value of the brand in a single word, and so it was chosen as the main theme for the campaign. The next idea was to create "Original Japanimation" as a means of expressing this essential value in a modern format. Japanimation is, as the name implies, Japanese animation and usually takes the form of highly artistic short pieces designed to entertain or to convey a message. Like Cup Noodles, Japanimation is a globally recognized cultural phenomenon with origins in Japan.

As illustrated in Figure 6.1, we gave the campaign the name "FREEDOM-PROJECT."

Japanimation appeals to many audiences, but in particular it is a form of entertainment that modern youth is interested in. We felt that by incorporating the brand message into this medium without losing its sense of fun, it would be possible to establish a close, natural connection between young people and Cup Noodles. From this starting point, we created the Scenario Idea.

Figure 6.1 The Cup Noodles "FREEDOM-PROJECT."

Scenario Idea: Roll Out a Continuing Story in Real Time— through Television Commercials, and DVD Sales—to Foster Expectations

The animation was set up to tell an impressive story to be completed over the course of two years. The story was set in the twenty-third century. Human beings have moved to the moon and are living in a strictly regimented society where "freedom" is prohibited. In this story, which hinges on a hidden mystery, young people go out in search of "True Freedom." The noted manga artist Katsuhiro Otomo was chosen to create the original characters and the mechanical designs.

The Scenario Idea took the form of a *timeline scenario*—that is, the target comes into contact with multiple media through a continuing story that unfolds a little at a time. See the section titled "Three Scenario Idea Approaches" in Chapter 4. This continuing contact increases the target's sense of expectation in real time. The process is composed of two main elements:

1. Rollout of the brand campaign through advertisements and sales promotions in multiple media

2. Rollout of DVD sales and video distribution based on the same content

The brand campaign offered multiple Contact Points, mainly through television commercials but also including magazines and the Internet. The role of the campaign was to form the brand image by offering fragmented glimpses of a worldview as seen through animation and by tying this into product exposure for Cup Noodles.

The role of the DVD content was to form a full-scale worldview by creating a single work that allowed the target consumers to feel the "depth" of the project overall, and at the same time to engender a feeling of "empathy" with the high-quality content. The sale of DVDs was an independent venture, though it was still tied into the advertisements; it promoted active purchases by the targets and created a new Contact Point that had not been considered as part of the original advertising campaign.

In the execution of the campaign, "FREEDOM" was seen as a "project." Even while maintaining a central focus on advertisements, the DVDs were produced and sold as an original video *anime* series that showcased the characters in the story. Part of this concept was to sell related products, including novels and licensed goods, based on the worldview of "FREEDOM." This transcended the framework of a typical advertising campaign, becoming a Scenario Idea involving the creation of an entirely new business model.

The two main elements of this campaign demonstrated the two perspectives discussed earlier: "breadth," for drawing the targets' interest, and "depth," for increasing involvement. These elements worked in concert with one another, forming a structure that encouraged young people to reexamine the concept of "freedom"—the main theme for the brand overall. Next is a more detailed examination of each element.

Brand Campaign Rollout in Multiple Media

The first step was to secure "breadth of attention." To do that, we started with advertisements on trains and in train stations, television commercials, and magazine advertisements, among other media.

The Advertising Campaign

The train and train station advertisements were designed to stimulate discussion surrounding the concurrent television commercial broadcasts. We put up posters with *black-and-white* line drawings in three high-traffic train stations—Shibuya, Shinjuku, and Umeda—and then changed these posters to *color* posters a few days later, when the television commercials first went on the air. This innovative approach attracted the attention of passersby, and increased awareness of the new activities of Cup Noodles.

In April 2006, the "declaration" version of the television commercial was aired, and the campaign got fully underway. The story underwent continuous changes every three months, increasing expectations of what turns the story would take next. A total of 10 types of commercials aired until the final broadcasts in March 2008.

At the same time, advertisements were published in two popular manga magazines for young readers: *Young* and *Comic*. These advertisements included versions arranged in the style of American comic books and were designed to allow readers to experience the drama of the continuous story through synergistic effects with the television commercials. To secure "breadth of contact," we actively used the back covers of these magazines for maximum visibility. Figure 6.2 summarizes the mass media advertising campaign.

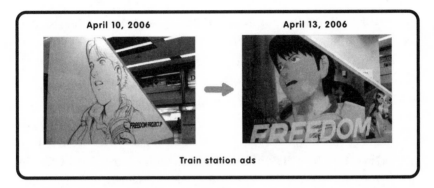

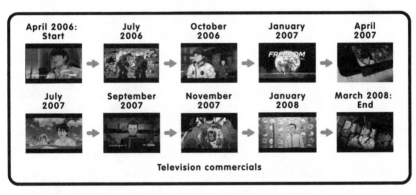

Figure 6.2 "FREEDOM-PROJECT"; advertising campaign.

After consumers saw the advertisements and developed an interest, to secure the depth to increase involvement, we also set up an Internet site, a mobile phone site, and various events.

The "FREEDOM-PROJECT.JP" Web Site

The FREEDOM-PROJECT.JP Web site was set up to act as the host for consumers to interact with it as their feelings of expectation increased. This Web site was established independent of the Cup Noodles product brand site as an official site dedicated to the worldview of the "FREEDOM" animation. It played a central role in linking the advertisements with the custom-created content. It also offered a comprehensive collection of all the information related to the "FREEDOM-PROJECT," including a list of advertisements, descriptions of the story and the worldview, and data regarding the DVDs and the campaign in general.

Mobile Phones and QR Codes

In Japan, and most likely the rest of the world eventually, mobile phones can be set up to read special "QR codes"—small two-dimensional bar-code-like labels that can be used to convey information or direct a mobile user to a certain Web site. We put QR codes on the reverse side of Cup Noodles lids as a path to bring consumers to a specially set up mobile site. In addition to having the consumers enjoy the site's content and increase their involvement, this system also recorded the time at which the site was accessed, making it possible to accumulate marketing data on when the targets were eating Cup Noodles.

Other Paths

Throughout the campaign, we set up other paths to increase consumer involvement. We established a path to draw the targets to a Cup Noodles 35th Anniversary Event (in the Odaiba commercial district of Tokyo), which offered free taste testings, screenings of the "FREEDOM" animations, and full-sized models of futuristic vehicles that appear in the story. The objective of this

Official Web site: "FREEDOM-PROJECT.JP"

QR Code on back of lid leads to mobile site

Cup Noodles 35th Anniversary Event (Tokyo, Odaiba area)

Figure 6.3 Campaign elements including Internet, sales promotions, and events.

event was to foster awareness of Cup Noodles as a familiar brand, from the perspectives of "eating" as well as "personal experience."

In the latter stages of the brand campaign, when the message "Seize Freedom" took a prominent position in the story, we rolled out a new type of approach to consumers: Through Cup Noodles, we posed the question, "What is freedom?" Through a tie-in with the *Yomiuri Shimbun,* one of Japan's most widely read newspapers, we published an advertisement asking: "Is it your desire to have FREEDOM?" Responses were gathered via the Internet. We also established a tie-in with the free magazine *R25,* a popular read among target consumers, with articles describing various writers' views on the concept of "FREEDOM."

The common element in all of these campaign elements was to encourage the target consumers to reexamine their own ideas about "freedom" from their own perspective. Figures 6.3 (on the previous page) and 6.4 summarize the campaign elements beyond the mass media advertising campaign.

Rollout of Content-Based DVD and Video Distribution

With the previously discussed campaign elements, we were already well along in increasing depth of consumer involvement with the FREEDOM-PROJECT.JP Web site, the QR code tie-in, and the "What is Freedom for you?" campaign. We carried the idea a big step further by turning the story into salable content and selling that content to the public.

DVDs of "FREEDOM" animations were released about every three months, in parallel with the broadcasts of new television commercials. Shops and outlets were also put to use through tie-ins with TSUTAYA and TSUTAYA RECORDS, Japan's largest DVD rental and sales company. We created a new and unprece-dented merchandising Contact Point between "Cup Noodles" and the consumers, and generated interest with outstanding breadth.

Newspaper advertisement: "Is it your desire to have Freedom?"

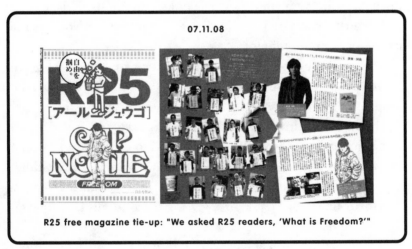

R25 free magazine tie-up: "We asked R25 readers, 'What is Freedom?'"

Figure 6.4 Newspaper advertisement and free magazine tie-up: "What Is Freedom?"

For a limited period, the Yahoo Video (Japan) site distributed "FREEDOM" series segments ahead of DVD sales, and the offer was boldly announced as top news right under the main "Yahoo!"

title. By offering limited streaming video for three days starting one week before each DVD went on sale, we succeeded in securing a breadth of interest—each of these videos was viewed an average of more than 700,000 times. This increased interest also tied into depth, in the form of actual DVD purchasing behavior. In TSUTAYA's weekly ranking of DVD sales, the "FREEDOM" series ranked No. 1 not only for animation, but in all DVD genres. Total cumulative sales for the series exceeded 450,000 units. Figure 6.5 shows DVD sales and activities at TSUTAYA shops.

The popularity of "FREEDOM" expanded even further as companies came with offers to arrange tie-ins with the project. A wide range of licensed goods was released, including blue jeans, T-shirts, skateboards, wristwatches, and sunglasses. A novel was also published, and numerous events were held throughout Japan.

Consumers expanded the scope of their shared experiences through a wide range of products, books, and events. This resulted in the construction of a new business model for Cup Noodles that had never been seen before.

Figure 6.6 shows an overview of the two key elements of this campaign as they apply to the Horizontal T Model introduced in Chapter 5; the dimensions are breadth (capturing interest) and depth (increasing involvement). The net effect of the campaign was to capture the hearts of young people and to elevate Cup Noodles into a brand that "always feels new" and "suits the individual." Figure 6.6 shows all elements of the Cup Noodles campaign along the Horizontal T model. Figure 6.7 further outlines key points of the campaign.

This two-year project gave rise to a major boom that came to be known as the "FREEDOM phenomenon." Every time a new commercial was aired or a new DVD was released, a huge buzz was generated, and countless comments were posted on blogs and other Internet sites throughout the year.

The main theme of the campaign was to change young people's impression of Cup Noodles, and the campaign was successful in bringing about a clear image change. The results of an inde-

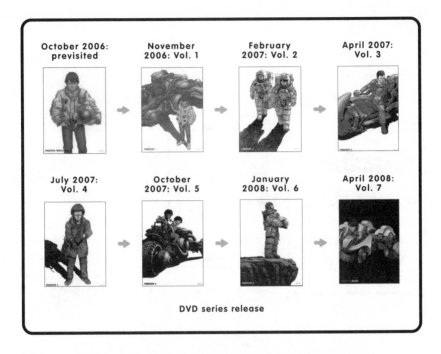

Figure 6.5 DVD sales and activities at TSUTAYA shops.

pendent survey showed that young people had a strong image of
the "FREEDOM" worldview as "leaving a strong impression,"
"interesting," and "high quality." Their image of the actual Cup
Noodles product was both active and empathetic, as indicated by
comments such as "it feels lively," "energetic," "always new," and

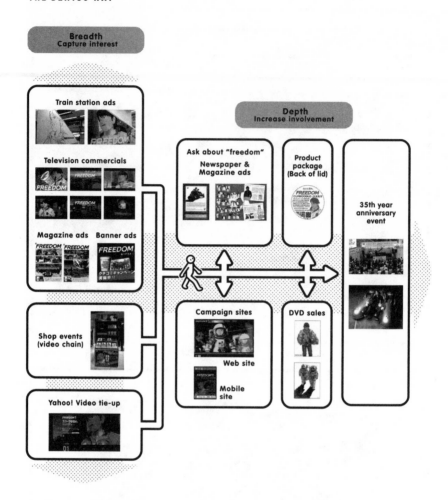

Figure 6.6 "FREEDOM-PROJECT"; the Horizontal T model.

"suited to my style." We believe that securing a brand reputation of "being suited to the individual's style" was extremely important in terms of establishing a future consumer base.

A key point of this campaign was to establish the "culture of freedom"—the fundamental value of Cup Noodles—as the Core Idea, and to communicate this through the media of Japanimation, with which the target consumers had a very strong affinity. We then created a Scenario Idea using a "Timeline scenario," in

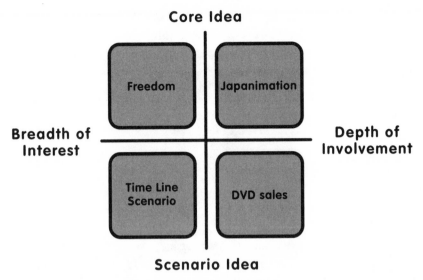

Figure 6.7 Key points of the "FREEDOM PROJECT."

which the targets' feelings of expectation were cultivated continuously and in real time, and added an entirely new approach with DVD sales tied into the campaign.

The "FREEDOM-PROJECT" received numerous awards, including:

- Two "Silver Awards" in the "Overall Campaign" division and the "Content and Contact" division at the 48th CLIO Awards, in 2007

- "Outstanding Work Award" in the "OVA" division at the Tokyo International Anime Fair, in 2007

- "Technical Incentive Award" in the "Anime/Video Package" division of the 7th Video Technology Awards, in 2007

- "Innova Lotus Grand Prix and Gold Award" and "360° Lotus/Gold Award" at the 11th ADFEST, in 2008

The Starting Point: "How to Create Ideas as Freely as Possible"

Figure 6.8 Satoshi Takamatsu

The following interview was conducted with Satoshi Takamatsu, Creative Director and representative of the Japanese creative agency "ground," and a Cannes Lions International Advertising Festival award winner. It shows some of the thought processes behind the campaign. A more complete biography for Mr. Takamatsu can be found in Appendix 3.

The real "mission" of the "FREEDOM-PROJECT" was to make junior high, high school, and university students feel that "Cup Noodles" was their own product.

I believe that campaign planning means creating a structure to achieve the client's mission. First, you have to start by thinking very carefully about what that mission is. Then you have to think about what is required to achieve that mission, in terms of strategy, design, and then expression.

In the case of "FREEDOM-PROJECT," through the briefing with the client, we realized that there were three missions:

1. To create a large-scale, universal campaign unique to "Cup Noodles"
2. To enable the use of sales promotions
3. To enable junior high, high school, and university students to share in an era with "Cup Noodles"

Of these three, we selected the third as the most important and our major objective: to form a new awareness among junior high, high school, and university students that "Cup Noodles" was their very own product. The next step was to create the strategy: What could we do to achieve this mission? The strategy had two parts.

Create commercials using full-scale, original animations; achieve this by producing and selling a DVD series.

In the previous "Cup Noodles" campaign, called "NO BORDER," we used outer space as our main setting. We started out by thinking of how we could create a new campaign that didn't feel like it had been scaled down. We decided that if we were going to use an animation, we could actually expand on this theme, by moving to the moon, or to Mars.

Anime characters are extremely easy to use in sales promotions. The commercials don't appear cheap or hastily made. Normally, it's very difficult to effectively create a commercial that is easy to use in sales promotions and is of large scale and high quality, but we were able to do this by using anime. When we mapped this onto the three missions mentioned earlier, we reached the conclusion that the medium of anime met all three conditions:

1. The scale wasn't reduced.
2. The commercials could be used in sales promotions.
3. The message would reach the targets; namely, junior high, high school, and university students.

You would think that anybody else could have come up with this idea, but in fact, there has never been a campaign that made use of a full-scale animation. When we looked into the reason for this, we found that it was next to impossible to gather truly outstanding anime staff, and get them to work on a major project for a full year just to create a single 30-second commercial.

We decided that if we couldn't put an anime staff together just for a commercial, we would attract them with the idea of producing and selling a DVD series. We took a reverse approach: We would create a studio for two years to produce a DVD series, and we would make television commercials at the same time.

Because the plan was based on the assumption that we would be selling DVDs, the production costs would be covered by the income from DVD sales. The client would not have to bear the financial burden. You could say that we reversed the commonly used approach of "product placement," in which a product receives exposure in a movie. With "FREEDOM-PROJECT," we were "placing" the DVD title and characters in a television commercial. This concept represented an equal "win-win" situation for both the client and the company financing the DVDs, and both parties agreed to the terms of the project at about the same time, so our basic strategy was ready to go.

Get the clients to buy into not only the commercial, but also the total campaign structure.

The next step was to create a specific "design." In our presentations, we explained the overall structure of the campaign. The goal was to have consumers buy into the campaign structure itself. For me, this is what set this campaign apart from the others.

Television commercials have the broadest reach; it's said in Japan that if you can achieve 3,000 GRP (Gross Rating Points), then you can reach 50 million people. Manga magazines reach 2 million readers. One million people watch Yahoo! Video. Each episode of the DVD was rented by 200,000 people, and purchased by 50,000. Those numbers appear to get smaller, but the smaller they get the stronger the engagement becomes. Think about it: those last 50,000 people are putting down 3,990 yen—about 40 dollars—to buy that video. When we designed this campaign, we proposed a structure that would bring together two consumer bases: "broad and shallow," and "narrow but deep." I think the main reason that we were able to put all these plans into action was that right from the first presentation, we offered a complete and convincing proposal to Nissin's top management showing the complete structure with all of its key elements.

Creating ideas as freely as possible, starting from "what will be most effective?"

The unique thing about "FREEDOM-PROJECT" was that we tore down the barrier separating advertising and content. With advertisements, the clients pay the costs, but with content, the consumers pay for at least some part of the campaign. In the "FREEDOM-PROJECT," we proposed commercials that the client would pay for, and content that the consumer would pay for, all using and sharing the same resources. I think this is one case where such duality was very clearly articulated.

Recently, I've had the opportunity to talk to various people in the advertising industry overseas, and I get the impression that everyone is trying to free themselves from the framework of "creating advertisements." In order to achieve the mission, you don't just have to use advertisements; you can create video games, or DVDs. I suppose you could even make clothes.

When you hear the words "Cross Communication," there is a tendency to limit the thinking to using a variety of media in an unrestricted combination, or applying the same content to other media. The goal, however, is not just to use Cross Communication, but to create a more effective campaign. The most important thing is to find an innovative idea that will achieve this goal. If that innovative idea comes from outside the traditional framework, the Cross Communication approach is a natural fit.

The baseline for Cross Communication is creating ideas as freely as possible, in conjunction with the strategy, to achieve the greatest effect.

Strategy and creativity working together.

In my approach, I write the marketing story from the first page of the plan. I worked in sales for many years, and even then, I used a marketing approach, so this might not be the typical way of doing things.

If we look at the differences in approach between Japan and other countries, we find that overseas, an emphasis is placed on "strategic planners." Planners have a substantial influence on what the campaign is supposed to say, and how to say it. Planners also have the trust of others. The strategic planner and the creative director work together to present the campaign message, and the staff put together the specific proposals and ideas. I think this is probably the standard approach. So if you don't have a really outstanding strategic planner, then even if you have a great message, it's hard to get it across to the client.

Japan may gradually move in this direction, but in order for this to happen, strategic planners will have to improve their skills, as well as their position. You have to train strategic planners with an understanding of creative elements, and you have to train creative staff who understand that without clear logic, the consumers won't accept it. I think this is the key issue.

Keep the budget in mind, while thinking on a grand scale, to come up with unusual ideas.

You might be curious about how budgetary considerations affect Cross Communication planning. I always keep the budget in mind. In fact, the smaller the budget, the more I think about it, and try to come up with ideas that normally would not be feasible within that budget. Along with the ideas, I am always thinking about how much it will cost, and how it will turn out if we apply that budget. Keeping a budget in mind motivates the creator to do the best communications for that amount of budget.

Of course, there is another approach, where you say, "Let's think freely without worrying about the cost, because we've hit a wall." But I really believe that starting with an awareness of the budget is what allows you to achieve important breakthroughs.

Giving form to new ideas is also an important function.

Negotiations leading up to the implementation of the plan are also important. For example, in the case of difficult contract negotiations,

such as with the Russian Federal Space Agency and FIFA, there was nobody else qualified, so I did the negotiations myself.

Some overseas advertising companies have dedicated teams to enable the execution of ideas. Their responsibility is to conduct a wide range of negotiations to find a way to give form to new ideas. Regardless of whether the advertising medium is television, newspapers, or outdoor billboards, or whether the client is the government or the police, this team does whatever is necessary to make the idea a reality.

I find that when you want to do something new, it would be much easier to work with Cross Communication if there was a person, a division, or a company devoted to the holistic challenge of making it happen.

The Toyota Motor Corporation "Harmony for Tomorrow" Campaign

Cross Communication is not just a sales promotion method used to build short-term sales. It can also be used as a form of brand communication to build medium and long-term relationships with the consumers, and to bolster a corporate brand.

Here, we will look at an example of a Scenario Idea that was successful in drawing the attention of a broad range of consumers, despite the fact that its main theme—Corporate Social Responsibility (CSR)—is generally considered at first glance to be difficult to follow and is often shunned by everyday consumers. Our case study is Toyota's "Harmony for Tomorrow" campaign, which began in June 2007.

Brand Issue: Communicate to Consumers the Intent of CSR Activities

In recent years, Corporate Social Responsibility (CSR) has gained importance in a wide range of situations, and companies are expected to play an increasingly important and autonomous role in the creation of a sustainable future. In this context, Toyota felt that it was important to communicate clearly the content of its CSR activities, which were being undertaken in response to meeting societal expectations. The key issue being studied when this campaign was being devised was not simply communicating the details of CSR activities, but finding a way to encourage consumers to work with Toyota in overcoming the problems being faced by the environment and society in general.

Core Idea: Establish a Connection between Toyota's Activities and the Consumers' Day-to-Day Lives from a Third-Party Perspective

When companies talk about their own CSR activities or try to describe these activities to consumers, there is a tendency to fall into a pattern of one-way communications. Toyota wanted consumers to think of Toyota as a partner in building a better future and felt that changing the way it communicated might just lead the way to a solution. With that in mind, what if a "third party" introduced Toyota's activities, and described them from the consumer's perspective? This approach would make it possible to establish communications that were not unilateral, but that allowed consumers to think of the environment and society alongside the company.

This concept opened the way for a new approach to communications: to assemble a third-party journalistic reporting entity with known media personalities called the "Editorial Division" to report on Corporate Social Responsibility issues.

Scenario Idea: An "Editorial Division" Draws Attention through Mass Media Advertising and Attracts Consumers to the Web Magazine

In June 2007, a virtual "Editorial Division" was created to think about the future along with consumers. Tamori, a well-known television personality, was selected as the editor-in-chief. Later on, various division members of all ages came forward to connect with consumers on all levels—Satomi Ishihara (actress), Kunikazu Katsumata (comedian), Yoshizumi Ishihara (television personality), Leiji Matsumoto (manga artist), and Yumiko Tomochika (comedienne).

These media members reported on Toyota's social contribution activities from a consumer perspective, mainly through television commercials. Magazine advertisements also introduced a wide range of environmental and social contributions that were not covered in the television commercials, thus further expanding the scope of the campaign. In both cases, when the targets came in contact with advertisements presented by editorial staff from the consumer perspective, they were naturally drawn into the story.

The "host" for this new interest was an Internet magazine called *Harmony for Tomorrow*. This Web site was designed to appear as an actual magazine; for example, consumers could flip through it easily as though they were turning the pages. Based on the concept of "things you can do today, on your own or with someone, to create a better future," the Web site offered light, enjoyable descriptions of ecology-minded projects and activities that simply made you feel good. Examples of titles included: "A Desktop Vegetable Farm," "Nationwide Tsunagari (connection) Spots," and "Strategies for Improving Stick-to-it-iveness."

Figure 6.9 shows the elements of the "Harmony for Tomorrow" campaign.

Visitors to the site were not just reading articles. They were viewing attractive videos driven by flash technology, a "tag"

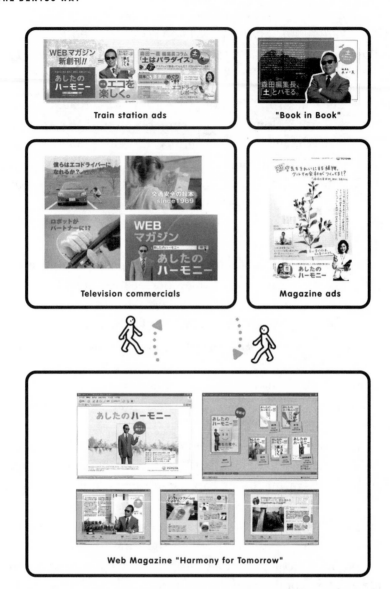

Figure 6.9 Elements of Toyota's "Harmony for Tomorrow" campaign.

function that allowed readers to leave comments on each page, and a page where readers could view other readers' comments. By providing an interactive format where people could participate freely, this Web site encouraged users to continue coming back and offered consumers an opportunity to think about what they could do based on these easy-to-read articles.

The desired result was to achieve greater proliferation of these activities. Consumers would also be able to empathize more closely with Toyota's activities. After the initial declaration of the words "Harmony for Tomorrow" in the path up to the first edition, this Web magazine sent one message after another focusing on a variety of themes: "Eco Should be Fun" in the first edition; "Growing the Future" in the second; "Strength in Doing Things a Little at a Time" in the third; "Connections Feel Good" in the fourth; and "Recharging the Future" in the fifth and final edition.

In addition to television commercials, the Web magazine, and magazine advertisements, train station and train advertisements were used to form paths, and a digest version of the Web magazine was distributed in a "book in book" format through various other magazines.

The campaign served its purpose to establish goodwill and empathy with a broad range of consumers. After the campaign, comments were received not only from fans of Toyota, but from a wide range of consumers in every age group. People said that they began wanting to start doing something good for society and for the environment and that environmental problems, which in the past seemed like "somebody else's problem," had become more personal for them. In a survey of impressions left by the advertisements, "goodwill" and "empathy" both scored high marks.

The key point of this campaign was the communication approach using the "Editorial Division" reports. These reports were able to promote communications between the company and consumers, from the same perspective—with a perspective toward society and the future. Another reason for the success of this campaign was that by placing the focus on a highly interactive Web magazine that enabled various modes of expression, it was possible to present Toyota Motor Corporation's Corporate Social Responsibility activities in detail, and at the same time in a format that felt familiar and interesting for consumers.

This is one example that demonstrates the effects of a "Media split" scenario (see Chapter 4), where television commercials were used as the trigger, and the targets were then led to the Web magazine. This "Harmony for Tomorrow" campaign was chosen as the "Judges' Recommended Work" in the "Entertainment" division of the 11th Japan Media Arts Festival, in 2007.

"Cross" Is Not Just About Media, But Also Creativity

The following interview was conducted with Koji Hirayama, Senior Creative Director, Communication Design Center, Dentsu Inc., and a New York Festival Gold Prize Winner. A more complete biography for Mr. Hirayama can be found in Appendix 3.

In "Harmony for Tomorrow," television commercials and the Web magazine played complementary roles.

We received a request from the client wanting to communicate its Corporate Social Responsibility (CSR) activities to the outside, and that it wanted to gain the attention even of people who were not fans of Toyota. In the past, at least in Japan, a company's social contribution activities were mostly undertaken tacitly and without fanfare, but now, they are conducted very much out in the open. There has been a change in awareness; rather than just doing good things for society, emphasizing those activities is now considered useful for consumers, shareholders, and the company.

The problem is, even if you transmit information about these activities, it is often very difficult to get people to take notice. We thus decided to avoid the traditional style of corporate advertising with Toyota talking about Toyota's activities. Instead, we positioned a third party to speak from as neutral a perspective as possible.

Specifically, we created a "virtual Editorial Division," with Tamori, the television personality, as the Editor-in-Chief, and published the contents in an Internet magazine. The television commercials focused mainly on Toyota's activities, but were also used as a trigger to lead consumers to the Web site, which touched on information like environmentally friendly actions that people were more likely to have a general interest in. The Web site also described the Toyota activities that appeared in the commercials, but almost all of the Web site content used an original reporting style, in order to downplay the image of a corporate PR activity.

As a result, I think the Web magazine and the television commercials played mutually complementary roles. The commercials were effective in terms of catching many people's attention; however, if that was all the campaign did, then it would just be another case of advertising using famous personalities. By adding the Web magazine, we were able to demonstrate a more apparent "third-party" stance. In fact, according to the results of a survey, people who came in contact with both the television commercials and the Web magazine reported dramatic changes in their attitudes.

Normally, it is difficult to incorporate an element of entertainment into an environmental theme, but we wanted to keep it light and interesting for everyone, and not too sophisticated. It was a good example of creating a win-win relationship between consumers and the advertiser.

In advertising and campaigns using tie-ins, creating a WIN-WIN relationship is important.

Recently, I worked on Asahi Kasei Corporation's corporate advertisement "Creating things that didn't exist until yesterday." As a spin-off from this campaign, we created a television commercial in collaboration with Fuji Television's drama series *Galileo*, which aired on Monday nights at 9 p.m. This project was a Cross Communication collaboration between a television program and a television commercial.

In the past, there have been many tie-ins between programs and products, mainly in the form of product placements, but *Galileo* was the first attempt at a collaboration between a corporate message and the worldview of a television drama.

Once again, I think that one of the main reasons we were able to pull this off was that we created a win-win relationship involving the client, the television station, and the performers. The clients were able to take advantage of the power of a television program; the program producers enjoyed advance public relations (PR) for their drama through exposure in the television commercials; and the performers saw the benefits of extra PR as well. So everybody was a winner. As a result, all the parties involved were happy to work together, and the project as a whole went very smoothly.

The "Cross" should also involve creative elements to ensure synergistic effects.

One more thing: I believe the "Cross" in Cross Communication is not just about crossing media types; it is about a strong and highly innovative synergy between media planning and raw creativity. In this era of Cross Communication I often see planning that relies heavily on well-known and existing content. The result is not so much a creative collaboration as it is a multifaceted sales promotion. In many cases, even though it's being presented as "Cross Communication," in fact it's really nothing more than a media mix incorporating multiple physical outlets or Internet Web sites.

When we talk about Cross Communication, we're not talking just about presenting the same creative elements through multiple media. It's important to "cross" not only the media types, but also the creative elements, in order to achieve the maximum synergistic effects. Even if the arrangement is well-thought-out, if the attempt at Cross Communication does not incorporate essential creative elements, then the desired effects aren't likely to be achieved. Today's creative directors need to generate new ideas taking this into account.

Another important thing, I suppose, is going back to thinking about "effectiveness." Not only is it important to try to do something new, but it is also important not to simply evaluate a campaign based only on "process." A "we did this on the Internet, and we did that on a

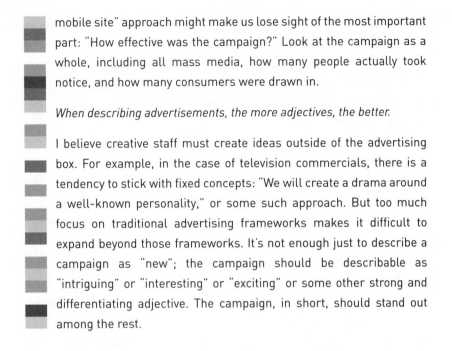

mobile site" approach might make us lose sight of the most important part: "How effective was the campaign?" Look at the campaign as a whole, including all mass media, how many people actually took notice, and how many consumers were drawn in.

When describing advertisements, the more adjectives, the better.

I believe creative staff must create ideas outside of the advertising box. For example, in the case of television commercials, there is a tendency to stick with fixed concepts: "We will create a drama around a well-known personality," or some such approach. But too much focus on traditional advertising frameworks makes it difficult to expand beyond those frameworks. It's not enough just to describe a campaign as "new"; the campaign should be describable as "intriguing" or "interesting" or "exciting" or some other strong and differentiating adjective. The campaign, in short, should stand out among the rest.

Cross Switch Comes to America: The Scion xD "Little Deviant" Campaign

In 2007 Scion launched a new model into its lineup, the Scion xD. The recently acquired Dentsu subsidiary agency ATTIK assembled a vivid Cross Communication campaign in the United States targeted at youthful consumers that was consistent with the brand and the car itself. Understanding the Scion brand is key to under-standing ATTIK's marketing strategy and how the Cross Communication strategy fits the brand.

The Scion Brand

The Scion is a car in the subcompact category. The Scion brand was built from the ground up as a platform for its audience to express itself through customized, personalized features. Once an owner expresses his or her creativity, each Scion car becomes an expression of the owner's individuality. In keeping with the brand's spirit of experimentation and exploration, Scion's advertising pushes the boundaries of car advertising, associating the Scion brand with a lifestyle that respects the attitude and values of its audience.

Scion is a brand unique to the North American market (United States, Canada, and Puerto Rico), launched by Toyota in 2002. Toyota wanted Scion to speak to a youth market, offering unique cars that other manufacturers simply weren't producing. Up until the launch of Scion, the only cars aimed at young people were lower-priced vehicles. In contrast, Scion is dedicated to youth-oriented cars. Scion's unique position in the North American market is based on the phenomenon of "tuner culture," a youth movement dedicated to the customization of cars. No other manufacturer offers manufacturer-supported and dealer-delivered parts so that individual owners can customize their own Scion before it hits the streets. While other manufacturers offer vehicles that compete in size or price against Scion vehicles, these other vehicles don't have the ability to be turned into expressions of personal creativity.

Launching Scion xD: Brand Issue

ATTIK recognized the brand issues as follows:

> Clearly communicate the powerful attitude and identity of the Scion xD, which has the unique ability to be customized and personalized freely, and capture the interest of young people who make the trends others follow on the launch of the new brand in the compact car market.

In 2007 Scion launched the all-new model xD as the successor to the xA, one of the original launch vehicles for the Scion brand.

The Scion xD replaced the xA in the Scion lineup as a five-door car with a small footprint. The challenge was to ensure that the xD had a different attitude from the xA, so that the xD didn't appear as simply a warmed-over xA. Adding to the challenge, the xD faced increased competitive pressure and noise in the marketplace, requiring a fresh and aggressive approach in launch marketing to allow its voice to be heard clearly.

Competitors in the subcompact category were often portrayed as "quirky" and "cute." To counter this, it was necessary to communicate the powerful attitude and identity of the new brand at the launch. The Scion audience is ahead of the curve in regard to trends in music, fashion, and urban style. It's adept at sorting out brands that are authentic and really deserving of respect, as opposed to those brands that are simply hiding behind a mask. Accordingly, any marketing efforts for Scion must be provocative and unique, demonstrating to Scion's audience that the brand stands for more than just cars; Scion is interested in supporting creative culture and showing that a car brand can also be a lifestyle brand.

The Core Idea

The creative idea was based on the tension between the xD's physical size and the size of its attitude, enhanced by Scion's unique ability to offer customization and personalization. ATTIK recognized that most small cars are bland and conform to a set of design traits that lead to a boring ownership experience; if your car is just like everyone else's car, is it really yours? The creative idea positioned the xD as out to prove that a small car can have a big attitude. It's ready to take on established rules and values, and to stand out as an alternative to small car conformity.

And from that, the following campaign Core Idea emerged:

> To underscore the aggressive, nonconformist personality of
> the Scion xD, create a bad-ass character using xD as a motif,

and develop a stimulating story that takes on established rules and values.

The Scion xD was given an edgy, aggressive personality, and a storyline came together. ATTIK developed a team of "Little Deviant" characters as a representation of the target audience and the xD itself. See Figure 6.10. The Deviants rebel against the common "Sheeple" of this world—"sheep people" who only follow the herd. Each Deviant shares a mischievous xD emoticon face, the common feature that binds them to the identity of the car.

The Scenario Idea

To ensure that the hip, younger target was hit in the right way and became more fully involved, ATTIK created the following Scenario Idea:

> Expose and draw attention to the character in keeping with the target Contact Points, and generate a buzz. Through games and virtual customization experience via online campaign sites, allow the targets to achieve a firsthand feeling of the entertainment value and worldview of the brand, to further increase interest.

Figure 6.10 "Little Deviant" characters. *Source: ATTIK.*

To achieve breadth, the campaign utilized a mix of traditional and newer media, presented in an edgy way. Communication components included 60-second cinema spots, 30-second television commercials, print magazine ads, outdoor advertising, "wild-postings" (street-level posters), transit vehicle placements, and "guerrilla" tactics on the street such as handout campaigns using

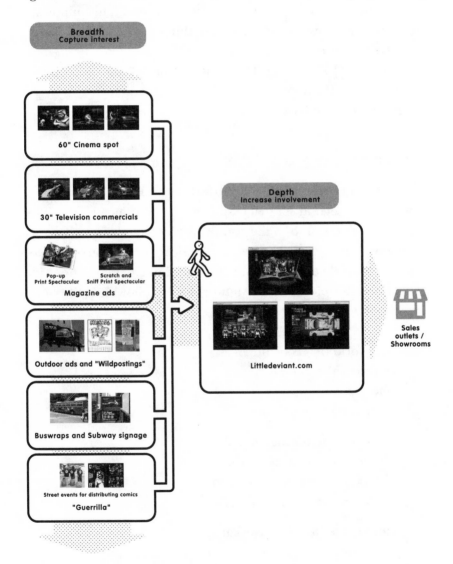

Figure 6.11 "Horizontal T model" depiction of the Scion xD campaign.

street teams staffed with youthful representatives. These media blasts all led to an elaborate microsite gaming experience in which xD Deviants fought off the hoards of hapless Sheeple. In this site, users would also be able to customize their own xD with the option of including images of the Deviants in their customizations. They would also be able to meet all the Deviants in nine different videos and create their own Deviant vacation photos. The important thing was to have developed everything according to young people's sensitive Contact Points.

Figure 6.11 shows the "Horizontal T model" for Breadth and Depth in the xD campaign.

From here, we'll explore the individual campaign elements.

The Fable and Television Spots

The prelaunch campaign started off with "Fable," a dark and dramatic 60-second cinema spot that introduced the little Deviants' relationship to the conformist Sheeple beings. It shook up many audiences and created a significant online buzz. "Fable" was a 60-second commercial that was aired in cinemas nationwide and on select cable television networks. The following is the voice-over for the "Fable of the Deviants":

> In a world that is bland,
> colorless and cold,
> where banality grows
> like a fungus or a mold;
>
> there live the boring Sheeple,
> who look just like each other.
> A darker force rides into town
> unleashing demon brothers.
>
> Here come the Little Deviants.
> They come from underground.

They're rising from the depths
to take those Sheeple down.

The Sheeple are compliant,
and make for fine ingredients
for customizing anything.
Here come the Little Deviants.

Figure 6.12 summarizes the cinema and television spots:

Magazine "Pop-Up" Ads

The Scion xD campaign went to market in a highly visible way with pop-up images and scratch and sniff materials (mostly pungent and unpleasant smells such as manure, body odor, smoke, dirty socks, and new-car smell for the car) in magazines. The theme was that those "who follow the herd will fall with the herd." The pop-up print spectacular ran in counterculture publications such as *Theme* and *Metropop*.

Figure 6.13 depicts these ads.

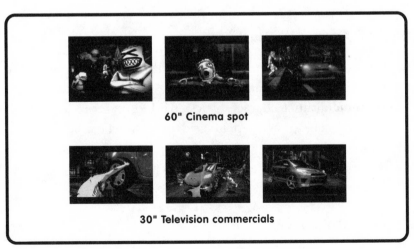

Figure 6.12 Scion xD cinema and television commercials. *Source: ATTIK.*

Pop-up Print Spectacular

Scratch and Sniff Print Spectacular

Figure 6.13 Magazine pop-up and scratch-and-sniff ads. *Source: ATTIK.*

Outdoor Ads and Wildpostings

Outdoor executions introduced the Little Deviant via traditional outdoor ads, transit placements, and "wildpostings" that established their distinct characteristics. Wildpostings are street-level posters that are pasted up in grids with a wheat-based paste. Buswraps are ads on the exterior sides of buses.

Figure 6.14 shows the outdoor ads and wildpostings. Figure 6.15 shows buswraps and subway signage.

"Guerrilla" Tactics

"Little Deviant Tales" comics, which told more Deviant versus Sheeple stories, were distributed by street teams. Life-size Deviants

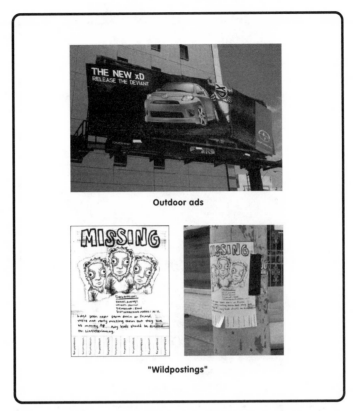

Figure 6.14 Outdoor ads and wildpostings. *Source: ATTIK.*

were found on streets bursting through air vents. These executions, in combination with other "guerrilla" tactics, drove the community to littledeviant.com, an online "pop-up book" experience where viewers could explore the Deviant mythology and play a series of xD games about fighting off the herds of Sheeple and returning vibrant life to the city.

Figure 6.16 depicts the "guerrilla" tactics.

Littledeviant.com

The Deviants resonated well with gaming youth. Some chose to use the Deviant characters and their messaging in the customization of their new cars. The launch campaign did away with the

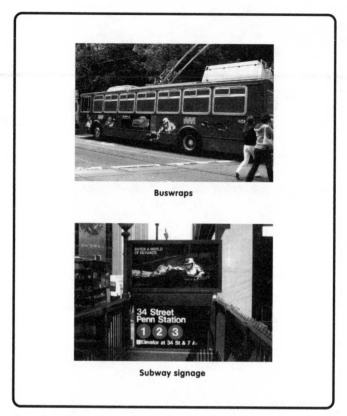

Buswraps

Subway signage

Figure 6.15 Buswraps and subway signage. *Source: ATTIK.*

Street events for distributing comics

Figure 6.16 Scion xD "guerilla" street campaigns. *Source: ATTIK.*

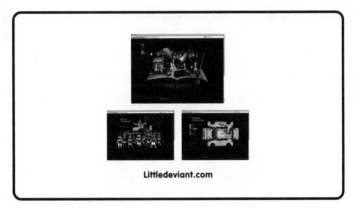

Littledeviant.com

Figure 6.17 Littledeviant.com: the Web site behind the Scion xD campaign. *Source: ATTIK.*

Sheeple to show how the xD released its inner Deviant. Little Deviants wreaked havoc on buswraps. The monsters were also seen ripping through billboards and a myriad of other media. Figure 6.17 shows examples of images from Littledeviant.com.

As you can see, the Scion xD was a rich and creative use of Cross Communication strategies and tactics. It achieved high levels of involvement in a manner congruent with the brand image, the brand issue, and the wants and needs of the consumer.

The total Web site page views (about six weeks after launch) were 3.5 million. The average time spent on site was 6 minutes and 50 seconds. This reflected the high level of engagement of the game play.

This campaign received the FWA Site of the Day award in July 2007 and was short-listed at both the 2008 Webby Awards and the 2008 Cannes Lions International Advertising Festival.

"Short" Cross Communication Scenarios

In our Cross Communication construct there are two types of Scenario Ideas: a long scenario and a short scenario. The adjectives are somewhat self-explanatory. Long scenarios are characterized by "a complete and comprehensive design throughout a single campaign," as in the three examples we looked at earlier in this chapter. Short scenarios, on the other hand, are "limited, individual scenarios rolled out over a comparatively short period of time, focusing on a specified target to achieve a specified goal." There are two main cases in which the client might consider using a short scenario.

1. *Individual short scenario.* Short scenarios can be used to break away from the flow of a long scenario and implement a separate smaller campaign component. Using an individual short scenario gives the brand more depth and more impact. For example, the main campaign aims to improve the brand image using several media over the course of a year. But as a separate component, a short scenario might be implemented, using a tie-in between radio and the Internet for a limited period of one month, as an independent sales promotion.

2. *Short scenarios used as a segment of the main campaign.* When the overall campaign is based on a long scenario, then short scenarios might be incorporated as separate segments of that campaign. For example, when a campaign is rolled out to stimulate purchases among the main buying group, then limited scenarios might be used to target surrounding individuals who might have an effect on buying behaviors (e.g., family members), aimed at promoting Word-of-Mouth recommendations that will eventually reach the main buyers.

Short scenarios are often designed to take maximum advantage of the unique characteristics of a given medium. But just as in the case of long scenarios, when developing the key mechanism that will capture the targets' hearts, it is important to consider the Contact Points, the Message, and the Psychological Approach. Here are some specific examples of both types of short scenarios.

Individual Short Scenario: Coca-Cola (Japan) Company Limited—"SOKENBICHA Beautiful Story: The Distance to Tomorrow"

"SOKENBICHA Beautiful Story: The Distance to Tomorrow"—a campaign implemented in 2005 by Coca-Cola (Japan) Company to promote its bottled tea product "SOKENBICHA"—was a short scenario in the form of a continuing drama.

This was the case of a beverage product that gained the sense of relevancy to young women by presenting the brand image to them. This case is a good reference when you create a campaign in a product category where women's emotions are important, such as fashion, cosmetics, and so on.

The brand concept for SOKENBICHA was "Beautiful from the inside." In 2005, to mark the tenth year of advertising activities, the company rolled out the "SOKENBICHA Beautiful Story: The Distance to Tomorrow" campaign as separate from the main sales promotion campaign. The idea was to create new opportunities to encourage empathy with the brand concept, "Beautiful from the inside," and to build its acceptance, as well as to increase the overall penetration of the brand image.

To write the story, the company selected Kei Yuikawa, an active writer, novelist, and essayist who received the Naoki Prize for Literature in 2002. The core of this campaign was a serialized story published in separate installments in two magazines, *CREA* and *FRaU*, over the course of three months.

Rather than being presented as the subject of an advertising campaign, the "SOKENBICHA" brand was presented as a sponsor for the campaign, which had the "Beautiful Story" at its core. In this way, it was possible to communicate the brand image naturally without drawing excessive attention.

The theme of the story was "The true beauty that lies within yourself." Two separate stories were run in parallel in *CREA* and *FRaU*, centering on two different main characters, both 27-year-old women who were true-to-life depictions of the main target consumers. The two stories told of the struggles faced by these women, focusing on the gap between one's true self and one's ideal self: difficulties at work, broken hearts, and the desire to run away and escape to somewhere. In the end, the two stories were synchronized, and the lives of the two heroines came together in a complex epilogue presented as a television drama on Tokyo Broadcasting System (TBS) titled "Summer Vacation at 27."

As a kind of "side program," the magazine *Da Vinci* simultaneously carried interviews with Ms. Yuikawa, along with reviews of books aimed at "finding the beauty inside yourself." A variety of other Contact Points were put in place through the course of the campaign to enable the target consumers to experience the brand image; for example, past installments of the story were posted on a Yahoo! tie-in page, so that targets who missed an earlier chapter could have a chance to catch up.

By the end of this campaign—which lasted for four months from March 2005 to June 2005—it had won the empathy of many women in this age group, and won over many new fans for "SOKENBICHA." Even women who might not have been reached by a regular advertising message showed increased interest and empathy as the story neared its conclusion, because they had a great deal in common with the main character. By following the paths, they were able to obtain new information, which allowed them to experience the brand image on repeated occasions over the course of more than three months. The central point of this scenario was a structure that captured the target consumers' hearts through a multilevel tie-up of various media, based around a continuing story published in magazines. Figure 6.18 summarizes the SOKENBICHA campaign.

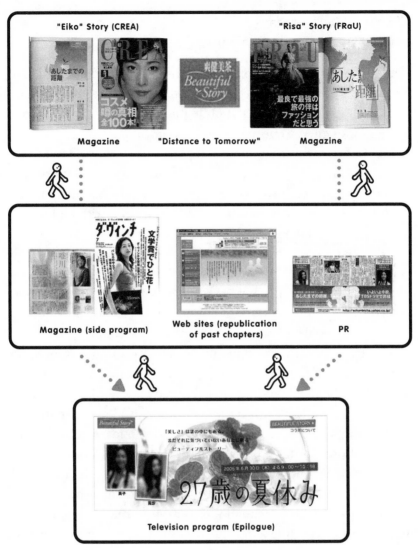

(Photos have been modified)

Figure 6.18 Coca-Cola (Japan) Company—"SOKENBICHA Beautiful Story: The Distance to Tomorrow" campaign.

"Partial" Short Scenario: East Japan Railway Company "Mobile Suica" Game Campaign

The next short scenario example comes from East Japan Railway Company's "Mobile Suica" game campaign. The short scenario campaign effectively used a mobile phone game as part of a long scenario designed to promote new subscriptions.

This was a case of a railway company that succeeded in attracting attention to its services by using mobile phones with mobile users. This case is a good reference for any kind of campaign since mobile phone services are offered in connection with all kinds of products and services.

East Japan Railway Company began offering the "Mobile Suica" service in 2006. "Mobile Suica" is a software application that runs on mobile phones; subscribers to the service are able to easily use public transportation, shop, buy tickets, and enjoy a variety of other functions with a single mobile phone.

East Japan Railway Company wanted to promote more subscriptions to the "Mobile Suica" service from among current mobile phone users, an important source of potential consumers. It had been studying a number of opportunities to secure new users using several ideas. One area receiving a lot of attention was mobile phone content, because games played on mobile phones were extremely popular among both male and female users of all ages, and could be played virtually anytime and anywhere.

The goal of the campaign was to capture the interest of these game users by creating a dedicated mobile phone game as part of the overall campaign. Users could choose one of two games, both of which focused on Suica's familiar penguin character. The first was "Penguin Reversi," a version of the board game "Othello." In the second game, "Guitar Penguin," the user could control the penguin as it plays the guitar along with a familiar theme song from the East Japan Railway Company television commercial.

The users felt a strong motivation to play the games, and as they played, they would naturally come to feel more familiar with

Suica. After they played the games, if they developed an interest in "Mobile Suica," they could jump to the site via a link. The site provided more detailed information and also offered tie-ins to user actions; for example, they could download related applications or actually subscribe to the service.

This campaign captured the interest of many mobile phone users and led them to subscribe to the "Mobile Suica" service. There were two key points to this campaign:

1. It eliminated the targets' psychological barrier to initially accessing the site, thereby securing large numbers of users. Mobile phone games have been used in the past for marketing purposes, but it was always necessary to access the client's site once and download the application. With this approach, it was only possible to capture users who were already close to the brand. In the case of "Mobile Suica," we secured a wide gateway by creating a framework in which multiple mobile sites were connected via a huge network; we used a mobile phone game portal called "Tsui-tsui," created as an original integrated mobile phone game distribution service from Dentsu, so that anyone who wanted to play the games could easily access the application from any site on the network. The "Tsui-tsui" portal enabled development of original games and also offered a wide range of game templates to choose from, so that companies could select and customize game templates that best suited their own brands and advertising messages.

2. The path skillfully and effectively moved the targets. In addition to mass advertising in newspapers and magazines, we drew out the targets using attractive game content and complex notices sent through Web sites, e-mail, and leaflets. We then increased involvement through actual game play and brought interested users

to the client's Web site to gather information and ultimately secure subscriptions.

Figure 6.19 illustrates the elements of the East Japan Railway
Company's short scenario campaign.

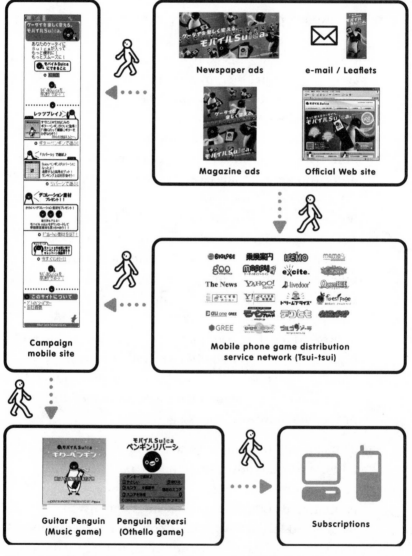

Figure 6.19 The East Japan Railway Company's "Mobile Suica" game campaign.

Hopefully these campaign examples gave a clearer picture of the Cross Switch application of Cross Communication solutions, including the recognition of brand issues, the creation of Core Ideas, Scenario Ideas, Scenario paths, and the assembly of other components in a creative and consumer-centric manner to deliver a client's message. Chapters 7 to 9 now give you a road map to creating your own Cross Communication, including a seven-step process for creating campaigns and explanations of a series of methods and tools created by Dentsu to assist in creating, running, and evaluating a Cross Communication strategy.

CHAPTER 7

THE CROSS SWITCH DESIGN PROCESS

In Chapter 6, we presented case studies using Cross Switch. At this point, it is time to learn how to design a Cross Communication of your own.

The goal of this and the next two chapters is really twofold. First, we will explain about the structure or recipe of Cross Communication planning that you should follow. In addition to a recipe or checklist, we will offer some tips and tricks for overcoming certain of the most challenging hurdles.

Second, at Dentsu we have developed a comprehensive set of tools to aid the Cross Communication planning process. While not all of these tools are currently available outside of Japan, knowing about the tools and how they assist in the planning and measurement of Cross Communication is important. Many of the tools may be available in various forms in different markets worldwide. The goal here is to understand how the tools fit into the Cross Communication planning process. The next step, which is beyond the scope of this book, is to assess what tools you have and what tools you need locally. We should note, however, that Dentsu is working to make as many of these tools as possible available in key markets worldwide.

Chapter 7, the first of the three chapters, will introduce the planning process used at Dentsu to put Cross Communication into practice. Chapters 8 and 9 will detail the planning and testing of Cross Communication elements and effects, including Dentsu's unique approaches to Scenario creation, scientific Scenario design, and verification of effects, using nine original Dentsu methods and tools, which we will describe.

Scenario Creation Meets the Conventional Planning Process

When putting Cross Communication into practice, as we have mentioned in previous chapters, it is important to create scenarios that will move the target consumers. Scenario creation thus becomes a key new element to add to the conventional planning process. Understanding the Dentsu approach to Cross Communication requires a working knowledge of Scenario creation and how it works together with conventional campaign planning processes.

A Review of Conventional Planning

To understand where we are going, it is helpful to review where we have been as advertisers and marketers. In that spirit, we will review an example of the total campaign planning process one might use in a conventional advertising campaign planning for a model change for an automobile brand. The major steps might be as follows:

1. Analyze the market, the social environment, the company's brand and competing brands, and the consumers and consumer segments.

2. Establish targets and goals of the communication.

3. Clarify the target's basic values with regard to the automobile, and create a Core Idea for the campaign.

4. Create a draft of the creative expression and language to be used in the advertisements, in keeping with the Core Idea.

5. Plan measures to be implemented in parallel in keeping with that central expression, for example, using mass media advertising, sales promotions, public relations (PR), events, and interactive media.

In conventional campaign planning, as shown in items 4 and 5, the common approach is to think of a plan based on the expressions used in mass advertising, and then to plan other measures in parallel, such as sales promotions, PR, events, and interactive media. With this type of planning, however, it requires a great deal of effort for the many team members involved to achieve "synergistic effects" through their work. Note that such a campaign is truly a "media mix," although it stops short of being "Cross Communication" in the sense that we advocate.

The work flow changes if we include a process to a Scenario Idea in between items 3 and 4. The Scenario Idea uses multiple Contact Points coherently to increase the "breadth" as well as the "depth" of involvement. When thinking this way, it becomes possible to think of extremely effective ideas from the consumer's perspective, transcending the boundaries of various communication methods like advertising, PR, sales promotions, events, and interactive media. As a result, the processes described in items 4 and 5 are integrated and coordinated, and more effective campaign tie-ups with greater synergy can be expected.

A Seven-Step "Planning Process Based on a Scenario Idea"

So the next question then is: "What is the specific device that allows us to plan Cross Communication without being limited by conventional approaches?" At this point we will introduce the Cross Communication planning process we have created and evolved based on our own experience. This process is designed to cover all the elements of Cross Communication effectively and with greatest efficiency for the marketing agency-client team. The process was created from the knowledge and experience of our Dentsu Cross Switch Team, in addition to information that we obtained through interviews with planners who have developed hit products at the front lines of the industry.

The Cross Switch planning process can be divided into seven main planning steps and includes not only the creation of the plan itself, but also the flow of the so-called "PDCA" (Plan-Do-Check-Act) cycle of implementation and evaluation of results. You may recognize PDCA from the lexicon of W. Edwards Deming and Japanese quality management; here Dentsu has applied PDCA, normally reserved for manufacturing and business process improvement, to the process of marketing.

Following is a basic outline of each element of the process.

Step 1. *Develop Insight and Strategy.* Gain deep insight into the target; then create ideas and form a set of communication goals and a basic communication strategy.

Step 2. *Create a Core Idea.* The Core Idea represents the central theme of the campaign and will be consistent throughout all communications.

Step 3. *Create a Scenario Idea.* The Scenario Idea gives a framework and form—a story—to the Core Idea.

Step 4. *Develop a "Holistic Creative."* Produce the creative work, including message and artwork, with a view toward the scenario as a whole.

Step 5. *Create a Structure Design.* This is a mostly quantitative design of the campaign plan using analysis from existing databases and new research. The output of this step is the identification of the "right" Contact Points and a plan to use them in an effective sequence; it is the nuts and bolts part of the Scenario Idea.

Step 6. *Negotiate and Implement.* Put the plan into play; this includes negotiations and coordination with media companies and collaboration partners toward implementation of the plan.

Step 7. *Evaluate Effects.* Test the results of the campaign, and use them as feedback for the next plan.

Figure 7.1 shows the seven-step planning process. Note the seven process steps and the connection to the PDCA cycle on the left. Also note the cyclical nature of Steps 3 to 6, running the Scenario Idea with the quantitative Structure Design and the qualitative Holistic Creative steps in parallel, with iterations through the implementation stage to verify that ideas are realistic and to put them into play. This is called the "Cross Communication Planning Cycle"—more on that shortly.

These steps provide a path and checklist to effective Cross Communication design. As you proceed through the steps, there are important considerations to take into account. At the risk of presenting too many lists; we have identified six considerations in particular to keep in mind when putting this planning process into practice.

Consideration 1: Incorporate a Perspective of Media Insight into the First Step, "Insight and Strategy"

It is said that true marketing insight has four component types of insight:

- Insight into the target
- Insight into the client
- Insight into society
- Insight into the media

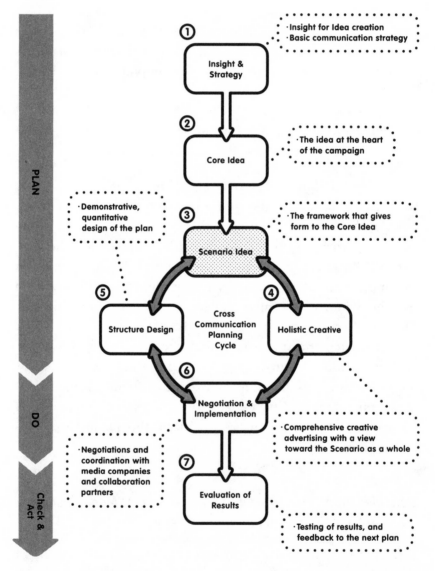

Figure 7.1 The seven-step process for Cross Communication planning.

When creating Cross Communication scenarios, it is particularly important to keep in mind the perspective of media insight and the relationship between the consumer and the media. It is also extremely important to keep abreast of new media and new technologies.

In addition, it is important to step back and establish effective goals of the campaign and communication before even embarking on developing strategies. Many campaigns have failed because clients or agencies, or both together, have failed to establish what they are really trying to accomplish. Everyone should agree on the goals before trying to apply insight and strategy to their achievement.

Consideration 2: Make Sure to Create a Scenario Idea in Addition to the Core Idea

This isn't a "consideration" so much as it is a necessity. A Core Idea without a Scenario Idea is like a movie without a plot—lots of scenes and characters, but no real message, script, or action to communicate anything. The Scenario Idea should flow naturally from the Core Idea. For example, in the case of the Cup Noodles "FREEDOM-PROJECT" introduced in Chapter 6, the Core Idea was to have consumers experience the *culture* of Cup Noodles through creating original Japanimation, and the Scenario Idea was to roll out a continuous story in real time through television commercials and DVD sales, thereby cultivating expectations in the targets. The Scenario Idea creates a sequence and flow of activities around the Core Idea, drawing consumers in and creating breadth and depth.

Consideration 3: The Holistic Creative and Structure Design Should Be Positioned as Two Sides of the Same Coin

At Dentsu, we refer to the creative expression that encompasses the entire scenario as the "Holistic Creative." When producing Holistic Creatives, it is essential to clarify the core Contact Points or combination of Contact Points, for example, advertising in a specialized magazine, a Web site, or street events. In some respects, Cross Communication is similar to a construction project. There can be many intricate connections that need to be planned out. With this in mind, we refer to the demonstrative and quantitative design of the scenario—namely, clarifying the core Contact Points or combination of Contact Points—as "Structure Design."

But one cannot forget about "Artistic Design." If a building's Artistic Design and Structure Design are both well defined, then the result will be an outstanding building. Similarly, in order to achieve effective Cross Communication, it is important to think about the strength and uniqueness of the advertising expression, as well as the structure, that is, "What effects will the expression bring about, and on what scale?"

Consideration 4. Negotiations Are Really Important

When securing a 15-second or 30-second television commercial spot or a quarter-page or full-page newspaper advertisement, there is a long-established business model involving the media company, the advertising company, and the client. In the case of Cross Communication, however, many plans cannot be handled by simply securing traditional media slots; for example, they might involve the use of new Contact Points or collaborations among various companies, like mobile phones and mobile phone service providers. Negotiations aimed at building win-win relationships between the companies and the media are an important process in bringing the plan and the ideas to fruition.

Consideration 5: Behavior Data Should Be Used to Verify the Effects of the Campaign

In the past, the most common way of verifying the effects of a campaign was to check for increases in sales or to use consumer surveys to check for changes in the brand image in terms of

THE CROSS SWITCH DESIGN PROCESS

recognition and preferences. With the proliferation of AISAS-driven purchasing behaviors and the evolution of information technology, it is now possible to capture consumers' behavioral data to verify results, for example, by analyzing point-of-sale (POS) data, blogs, and Web access logs. Using these data effectively to verify the effects of a campaign will also lead to meaningful learning and increased accuracy in subsequent campaigns.

Consideration 6: Steps 3 to 6 Are Really a Cycle: The "Cross Communication Planning Cycle"

The Cross Communication process is divided into seven steps, but four processes in particular—the "Scenario Idea," "Holistic Creative," "Structure Design," and "Negotiations and Implementation"—are not completely separate; rather, they are repeated and returned to over and over again. We therefore refer to these four steps as the Cross Communication Planning Cycle. In the course of actual planning, part of the work of the project team is to produce the Cross Communication Planning Cycle as a whole.

Another List: Nine "Methods and Tools"

Finally, now that we have covered the seven "dominant process steps" and the six "considerations" to set the context in background, we present a list of nine "methods and tools." These methods and tools are specific processes and/or databases designed to refine the scenario into an effective and convincing product, find and effectively utilize the right Contact Points, find out consumer insight, support creating ideas, and measure results.

The goal in planning Cross Communication based on this process is to maximize effect, and to quickly gain client understanding and present it in a convincing way. Dentsu brings to the table a set of methods and tools to achieve this goal. We will give a brief overview here, and then cover each process or tool in more detail as it fits into the process steps covered in Chapters 8 and 9.

Tools, Methods, and the Planning Process

To create an effective Cross Communication plan, it goes without saying that the skills and experience of those involved (the planners, the creators, the producers, etc.) are important. Like good quality tools and methods used in the construction trade, however, the Cross Communication solution can be delivered more effectively and more quickly with the right methods and toolsets. That said, having the right tools can go a long way to help even planners without much experience come up with effective plans more easily.

When we use the term "methods," we are referring to methodologies and frameworks for planning—essentially, processes. On the other hand, when we use the term "tools," we are referring to analysis methods and specific IT systems or databases created to make any marketing campaign effective. Dentsu has developed about 260 methods and tools to support marketing and communication planning in response to a wide range of issues and needs. Here we will introduce nine representative methods and tools that can be used in Cross Communication. We use all of these in our day-to-day planning activities.

Importantly, we should point out the four specific purposes served by the methods and tools:

1. *Support the development of consumer insight.* Greater insight into consumer behaviors and needs is gained through two tools: "d-camp" for quantitative insight and the Target Visualizer™ for a more qualitative sketch of and insight into the consumer. These two tools will be discussed in greater detail in Chapter 8.

2. *Support the creation of Scenario Ideas.* Here we have no specific data tools, but we have a method known as

"Scenario Idea sessions." This method is also described in Chapter 8.

3. *Make the Scenario Ideas effective.* Identify the right Contact Points and communication vehicles. We use the tool VALCON™ to select Contact Points and the tool DENTSU-CONNECT MEDIA™ to select communication vehicles. This part of the planning process is covered in greater detail in Chapter 9.

4. *Evaluate results.* Dentsu places a lot of emphasis on the scientific evaluation of campaign results. These results not only help the client determine how much value was gained from the campaign, but also give insight about what to do in subsequent campaigns; this is the "C" or "Check" in the PDCA cycle. Dentsu offers its "AISAS auditor," a tool designed specifically for Cross Communication to measure AISAS behaviors. There are also three tools set up to measure specific Internet activity in response to the campaign: x-AUDIT, which measures Web site logs; and the Dentsu Buzz Research™ and SHOOTI BUZZ REPORT, which together measure postings through blogs. The measurement of campaign results is also covered in Chapter 9.

The integration of the seven-step planning process, PDCA, and the tools is shown in Figure 7.2.

These tools are currently available in Japan. Most are available, under construction, or available through some other source in many other countries. In the United States some tools are systematized, just like in Japan; with others we have the methodology to achieve the same goals in a different way. The tools definitely help and are handy, but in many cases the thought process is the important thing, and much can be done by making some assumptions and testing where possible by sampling, surveying, or using other less robust methods. In the next two chapters, we dig

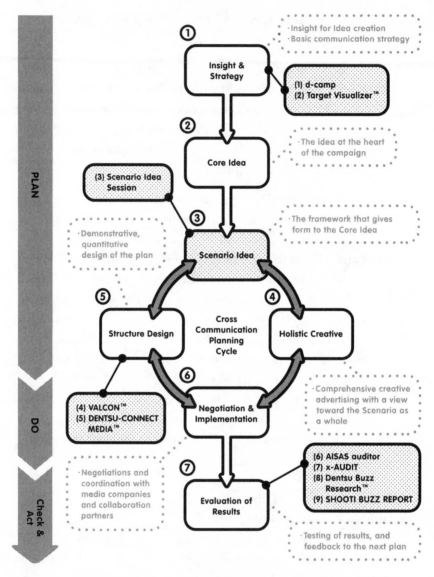

Figure 7.2 Dentsu's Cross Communication planning process: methods and tools.

deeper into consumer insight, media insight, and Scenario creation (Chapter 8) and into the Structure Design and measurement of Cross Communication (Chapter 9).

CHAPTER 8

FROM INSIGHT TO SCENARIO CREATION

No marketing campaign can be created in a vacuum. Instead, it is fundamentally important to understand as much as possible about the target audience (or audiences)—what they want, how they get information, what it takes to get their interest, and even more, what it takes to get their involvement. Likewise, it is important to understand the nature of and effects of different kinds of media in communicating a particular marketing message to an audience. Finally, especially for Cross Communication, it is critical to understand how the media can work together to get a message across. These three "understandings" are then essential to the development of a proper Scenario Idea.

Chapter 8 covers the processes, methods, and tools for gaining consumer and media insight. Then the chapter goes on to explain an established Dentsu process for creating Scenario Ideas.

The Importance of Insight

Campaigns have lived and died upon the effective (or ineffective) use of consumer and media insight. Insight is the starting point for all planning, and this process must be conducted carefully in the creation of Cross Communication scenarios as well.

In order to design effective Cross Communication, it is necessary to achieve a deep insight into the target from a variety of starting points, including gender, age, occupation, income, consumption, purchasing behavior, awareness, values, and lifestyles. At the same time, with regard to media insight, it is necessary to evaluate the media from neutral and broad perspectives, including the media and content that the target comes in contact with, as well as the characteristics, functions, and roles of each Contact Point. It is also important to have knowledge of new media and technologies.

The standard method for achieving insight is to use quantitative surveys (questionnaires, shop exit surveys, etc.) and qualitative surveys (group interviews, in-depth interviews, etc.). When doing quantitative and qualitative surveys, it is preferable to aim for both target insight and media insight using the same data source. Dentsu has developed original tools for gaining insight that meet the above requirements in terms of both quantitative and qualitative data. See Figure 8.1. Those tools are d-camp, which stands for "Dentsu Consumers and Audience Multi Panel" and the Target Visualizer. As we will see shortly, d-camp uses surveys to take a measured look at consumers and their interactions with media, while Target Visualizer helps to frame or group consumers by more qualitative means.

Studying the Target Quantitatively: "d-camp"

Dentsu has developed a quantitative database called d-camp, which, as mentioned above, stands for "Dentsu Consumers and

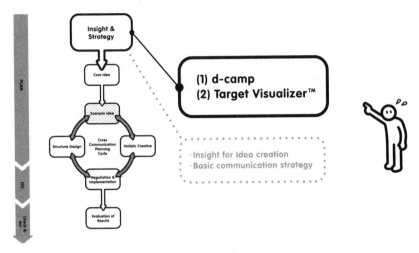

Figure 8.1 Methods and tools for insight and strategy.

Audience Multi Panel." In d-camp, surveys are conducted targeting consumer behaviors and media contact behaviors for the same survey subjects. The large volumes of single-source data obtained through these surveys can then be used to analyze consumption behaviors and media contacts simultaneously. The d-camp is an original Dentsu database and was created using continuous single-source panel surveys (surveys targeting the same subjects) over the course of one year. The subjects were male and female, ages 12–64; the sample size was approximately 4,800.

How to Gain Insight through Analysis

For example, let's assume that an airline company is designing communications to promote online reservations for individual travelers on international routes. Of course, the airline could assume that the targets are "people who travel overseas on their own," but undoubtedly, the number of people who make reservations directly with the airline company is more limited than that. If the condition "people who do not use package tours" is added, then the target becomes more specific.

Now, let's use d-camp to compare two groups of people who have made private trips overseas during the past year: "Individual travelers," who have not undertaken package tour vacations during the past year, and "package tour travelers," who have undertaken such vacations. Our first finding was that the ratio of women was higher among package tour travelers, but that among individual travelers, the number of male and female travelers was about the same. Looking at preferred destination countries, China and South America were slightly more popular among individual travelers than among package tour travelers. Under "hobbies and interests," we found that individual travelers were more likely to enjoy surfing the Internet, watching movies (and particularly Japanese anime), and reading manga. (Keep in mind, this example described a Japanese database; the travelers in this instance were Japanese.)

Based on this insight, to grow the consumer base, we could create a Core Idea along these lines: "target young men, establish a tie-in with an adventure movie, and promote routes to Central and South America."

One of the key features of d-camp is cross-tabulation between certain consumer attributes and their media behaviors. We've also collected those sorts of data from specific surveys, like the "Cross Communication Behavior Survey" introduced in Chapter 5. The d-camp panel is a larger and more generalized database and can be used to obtain these results as well. The panel enables detailed tabulation and analysis to gain target insight as well as media insight.

Figure 8.2 shows some of the kinds of attributes d-camp can collect and how they can be cross-tabulated.

A Second Example

As another example, we found that the behaviors of females in their teens in Japan showed greater contrast with those in their twenties than could be seen between most sets of adjacent 10-year

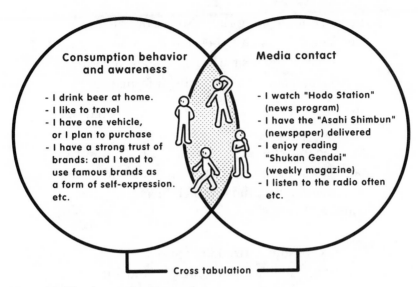

Figure 8.2 The d-camp database tool.

age brackets. From data sourced from the "Cross Communication Behavior Survey" and the d-camp system, we did an analysis and gained insight into how young women used the Internet and mobile phones. We found many differences in how the two adjacent age groups of "young women" used these devices. The two groups were females, ages 12–19, and females, ages 20–29.

From the analysis, we discovered the following:

- On the Internet, teenage girls often use video sites and diagnostic sites, and have a strong tendency to use the Internet as an entertainment tool. Women in their twenties, however, often use the Internet for online shopping or to gather information for future purchases, and have a strong tendency to use the Internet as an information tool.

- With regard to mobile phones, teenage girls are much more likely than women in their twenties to use their mobile phones for entertainment purposes, like reading novels, downloading ringer songs, or watching videos. Teenage girls also use their mobile phones for a variety of other purposes, such as communicating with friends and acquaintances or gathering information.

- In terms of consumption and purchase behaviors, teenage girls emphasize Word-of-Mouth information obtained from people close to them, such as friends and acquaintances, while women in their twenties tend to emphasize information from the Internet, fliers, and other media sources.

The results are summarized in Figure 8.3.

The target and media insight, thus, becomes the following:

When using the Internet or mobile phones as tools for communicating to the targets, it would be possible to design highly effective communications better suited to the target by using games and other entertainment contents as the starting point for targeting teenage girls, and focusing on

	Females aged 12-19	Females aged 20-29
Use of Internet (on PCs)	- Often views video sites Checks entertainment-based diagnostic sites	- Often uses portal sites - Often uses Internet shopping
Use of mobile phones	- Reads novels via mobile sites - Types e-mail with both hands	- Uses mobile coupons - Participates in net auctions via mobile phone
Consumption/ purchase behavior	- Emphasizes Word-of-Mouth information from close acquaintances - Goes with someone when buying clothing and accessories	- Checks prices via flyers or the Internet before going to buy - Often signs up for campaigns

Figure 8.3 Unique characteristics of females in their teens and their twenties, from d-camp. *Source: Dentsu d-camp Survey, Japan, 2008.*

products and campaign information that stimulates the sense of "savings" for targeting women in their twenties.

Next, we use a more qualitative approach to "storyboard" target consumers: the Target Visualizer.

The Target Visualizer™

Quantitative data are aggregated in the form of specific numbers. The advantage of this is that it is easier to grasp the overview, to get a sense of scale, and to share knowledge and conduct discussions based on the data. These numbers are real and defensible. However, there are disadvantages, too; for example, quantitative data alone do not assist in understanding the hidden needs of consumers, and it is difficult to form a concrete image of the target.

In order to grasp qualitative information that cannot be expressed as numbers, we must capture qualitative insights as well and combine them into a holistic, three-dimensional insight into our targets and their media interactions. Dentsu has developed a tool called the Target Visualizer for gaining qualitative insights and registered it as a trademark in Japan. The Target Visualizer is a database-based system that uses photographs and real feelings to visualize the status of consumers or contacts with Contact Points based on large-scale photographic diary surveys. In the same vein as the expression, "A picture is worth a thousand words," the Target Visualizer provides photographs of different types of consumers interacting with different types of media and Contact Points. It enables simultaneous monitoring of consumer insights and media insights from a qualitative perspective. The Target Visualizer enables the user to gain a real grasp of the status of targets and Contact Points that could not be determined using numbers alone.

For example, let's assume that an apparel manufacturer wanted to target women in their twenties and thirties. First, the manufacturer would have to find out what types of fashions are actually chosen by women in their twenties and thirties who are concerned about fashion trends. Using the Target Visualizer, the company would be able to see at a glance, along with live comments, which women are following the fashion trends and which are not. At the same time, it would also be possible to obtain information about the targets' values and information behaviors, the media that they often come in contact with, and the products and services that interest them.

In this way, we can see the characteristics of individual consumers, and we can create an image of a single ideal target or multiple targets. Visualizing the consumers—who they are, what they want, how they behave, and how they interact—provides valuable insight toward developing scenarios. It is similar to "storyboarding," a popular research technique, where consumer segments and consumer targets, their needs and behaviors, including information on gathering, buying, and using the product, are described using pictures, research results, and assumptions, in an effort to describe the "typical" consumer. The Target Visualizer both facilitates the storyboarding process and systematizes it into a database.

A Target Visualizer Example: "A Compact Automobile"

Suppose we define the target for a compact automobile brand as "a woman in her twenties, living in an outlying region." We would establish a hypothesis while maintaining an overview of several target groups narrowed down using these conditions, identify the representative target image, and create an ideal target. Through this process, we might arrive at an ideal target image such as this:

> A full-time housewife with one child. She is a hard worker
> who doesn't overdo things, and she surrounds herself with
> "little bits of happiness." She is slightly picky about fashion,
> but her basic style is casual denim . . .

Figure 8.4 shows an example of a "visualized" ideal target for a compact automobile.

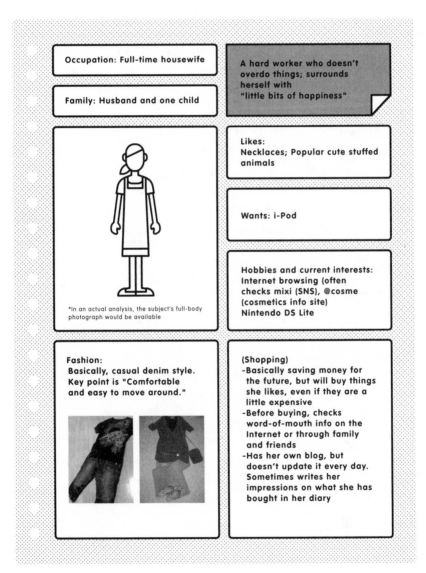

Figure 8.4 Target Visualizer ideal target image for a compact automobile.

Using the Target Visualizer to Gain Media Insight

The Target Visualizer can be used to gain "media insight" from the perspective of the consumer's lifestyle activities. More specifically, we can use the Target Visualizer to learn more about the quality, or value, of different Contact Points.

Recall from Chapter 5 the discussion of Contact Points and how the quality of Contact Points can vary throughout the day according to the time, place, circumstances, and feelings of the consumer—that is, the life cycle and lifestyle of the individual. A communication for a dinner restaurant works better, for example, on the radio or in a train station during an evening commute. This is all part of what we call "media insight."

At this point, we will introduce an example of media insight gained through the flow of a single day. In the Target Visualizer, this corresponds to an analysis framework we call the "One Day Board." As in the previous case study, we will analyze the Contact Points relevant to several women in their twenties who live in an outlying region of Japan.

If we look at an overview of contacts with Contact Points on an hourly timeline, we can see a number of overall trends:

- "She sees many television commercials on weekday evenings."
- "On days off, she reads newspapers and magazines through the morning and afternoon."
- "During the afternoon on days off, she goes to dealerships, where she sees catalogs, posters, and vehicles on display."

If we focus on the target's impressions of those Contact Points, it is notable that one target learned about an environmentally friendly vehicle from a television commercial on a weekday evening and thought, "It's good for the environment, and I would like to buy one if it's reasonably priced."

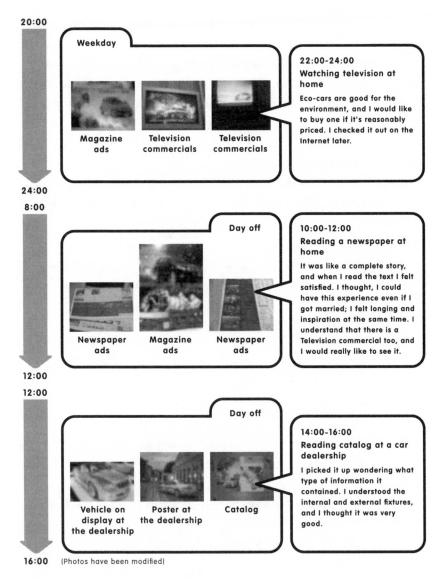

20:00

Weekday

Magazine ads

Television commercials

Television commercials

22:00-24:00
Watching television at home

Eco-cars are good for the environment, and I would like to buy one if it's reasonably priced. I checked it out on the Internet later.

24:00

8:00

Day off

Newspaper ads

Magazine ads

Newspaper ads

10:00-12:00
Reading a newspaper at home

It was like a complete story, and when I read the text I felt satisfied. I thought, I could have this experience even if I got married; I felt longing and inspiration at the same time. I understand that there is a Television commercial too, and I would really like to see it.

12:00

12:00

Day off

Vehicle on display at the dealership

Poster at the dealership

Catalog

14:00-16:00
Reading catalog at a car dealership

I picked it up wondering what type of information it contained. I understood the internal and external fixtures, and I thought it was very good.

16:00 (Photos have been modified)

Figure 8.5 Target Visualizer: "One Day Board" visualization of Contact Points and real feelings of the consumer.

Figure 8.5 shows how a timeline visualization of Contact Points and messages might work over the course of a day.

The target also said that she came in contact with a newspaper advertisement during the morning of a day off and felt, "It was like a complete story, and when I read the text, I felt satisfied," which indicated increased interest. In the afternoon of a day off, she stopped at a car dealership and received a catalog, which further increased her understanding and involvement: "I understood the internal and external features, and I thought it was very good." Looking at the flow over time in this way, we can gain a concrete image of how involvement increases, at what time of the day, and through which Contact Points.

Up to this point, we have described how to gain insight using two tools: the quantitative database d-camp and the qualitative database Target Visualizer. The important thing when gaining insight is to create a realistic, concrete image of the target, approaching that target from a variety of perspectives. The questions to be answered are not only the typical questions:

- "What type of person is the target?"

- "How does the target interact with which media?"

- "How are those media used?"

In Cross Communication, it is necessary to go a step further to secure a firm and actionable image:

- "What media does the target see, and in what situations?"

- "What psychological state is aroused?"

- "What behaviors are stimulated?"

Once we have this perspective in hand, the Core Idea for the campaign can be formulated.

Creating the Scenario Idea through Team Discussions

Step 3 in the seven-step campaign design process is to "create a Scenario Idea to give a framework and form—a story—to the Core Idea." This step is where the "rubber meets the road" in terms of connecting the brand issue, campaign goals, and the "Core Idea" of the campaign to the realities of consumer preference, lifestyle, and to the limitations and advantages of various media. Essentially, the challenge is to create the best "story" or scenario to break down Information Barriers, in order to get consumer attention, and better yet, consumer involvement.

As we have seen, the combinations of consumer preferences and behavior and media and message choices can be almost infinite, particularly with the growth of new digital media and new Contact Points. To create an effective Scenario Idea requires good analysis, but that isn't the end of the story (if so, it could be done on a computer!) Scenario Ideas are (or should be) based on facts, but there's enough qualitative intuition and judgment involved that it really takes a careful and well-thought-out and *human* approach to get the best results. Therefore, we advocate the use of "Scenario Idea Sessions"—dedicated group brainstorming and discussion sessions—to unlock creativity and match it to the structure and statistics of the situation. Figure 8.6 reviews where we are in the process.

So while we advocate a team approach, we recognize that it can be tricky to gain the best results from such a team. Challenges include the involvement of large numbers of people from both the client and the agency, and the "fractionalization" of plans. For example, team members may tend to concentrate only on the parts of the plan they are familiar with, such as creative. It's hard to get the "breadth and depth" of ideas together to put

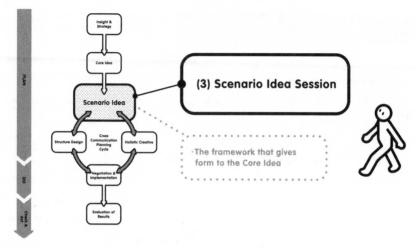

Figure 8.6 The method used for Scenario Idea creation.

together a good Scenario plan when such a plan must consider the multiple dimensions of Contact Points, Messages, Psychological Approaches, and media.

So at Dentsu, we use a process called "facilitation" as a method of creating ideas and forming consensus on projects involving many members. "Facilitation," for us, is "a set of activities and technologies designed to encourage comments from team members taking a neutral stance, and to support the resolution of issues in the context of knowledge creation activities by organizations and teams." Examples of facilitation activities include:

- Discovery and resolution of problems

- Creation of ideas

- Formation of consensus

The facilitation approach involves having large numbers of members gather in one place to discuss a given theme in order to effectively form a consensus. This approach is currently being used in a wide range of fields related to marketing communication as a new work approach and planning methodology.

Dentsu has developed a method called the Power Session™, which uses the facilitation approach in a workshop setting. The Power Session has actually been registered as a trademark in Japan.

We use the Power Session method in various fields, for example, to develop new products, to establish target images for brands, to develop campaign concepts, and to promote internal communications. In this case, we adapt the Power Session format to the creation of Scenario Ideas; the result, not surprisingly, is something we refer to as a Scenario Idea Session.

Using Facilitation to Create Scenario Ideas: Scenario Idea Sessions

Power Sessions demonstrate dramatic effects in the creation of Scenario Ideas. A Scenario Idea Session is illustrated in Figure 8.7.

In these sessions, several project members spend about one hour each day sharing ideas while conducting discussions from a variety of perspectives.

In Scenario Idea Sessions, it is important to make careful preparations in order to make it easier to create ideas. There are three key considerations:

1. Preparing a program for creating the Scenario Idea

2. Effectively bringing out the Scenario Idea, and preparing the facilitator

3. Putting in place an environment for creating the Scenario Idea

Here is a closer look at each of the three steps.

Figure 8.7 Image of a Scenario Idea Session.

Preparing a Program for Creating the Scenario Idea. Scenario Ideas must be considered from a number of perspectives, based on target insights and media insights, for example, Contact Points, Messages, Psychological Approaches, and budget limitations. While maintaining these perspectives, we have found that it works best to develop a program for creating Scenario Ideas during a concentrated period of about one day. The key is to gather as much information as possible that will be useful in the creation of the idea *before* the session. One approach is to use successful case studies from other companies. Earlier in this book, we introduced the successful examples *Jump Square* and Cup Noodles, both of which could act as effective stimulants in the creation of Scenario Ideas.

The tools and databases introduced in this chapter are also used, as they are helpful indexes for the Structure Design of Cross Communication in keeping with target insights, media insights, and the scope of the budget. The Communication Motivator (see Chapter 5) is a particularly effective tool for supporting the creation of ideas with a focus on human psychology.

It may be easier to visualize the Scenario Idea session by showing a typical agenda. Figure 8.8 is an example of a standard program. It can be customized to meet the requirements of the brand issues and circumstances to create an effective program.

Effectively Bringing Out the Scenario Idea and Preparing the Facilitator. The individual facilitator is a key presence in terms of effectively creating Scenario Ideas using a facilitation format. The facilitator is "the person who oversees the proceedings in the session where the project members have gathered, and keeps track of the status and thoughts of the participants." The facilitator must have the skills to manage all aspects of the session processes from a neutral standpoint, encourage the participants to engage in active discussions, and increase the quality of the output. The facilitator plays an important role that influences the atmosphere and the outcome of the meeting, so it is preferable for that person to have a certain level of experience and training with Cross Communication applications.

Putting in Place an Environment for Creating the Scenario Idea. As with any effective meeting, you also want to have an appropriate environment for the Scenario Idea Sessions. Conducting these

Time-line		Work	Content
9:30	10 min	Opening Remarks	Confirmations Goal & Objectives
9:40	40 min	Work 1:Reviewing past campaigns	Session with tool 1
10:20	30 min	Work 2:Clarify target image	Session with tool 2
10:50		Break	
11:00	60 min	Work 3:Identify Communication Motivator	Find the target's desire/motivation that will bring him/her close to the brand with tool 3,"Communication Motivator".
12:00		Lunch	
13:00	40 min	Work 4:Choose Contact Points	Session with tool 4
13:40	60 min	Work 5:Consider case studies	Session with tool 5
14:40		Break	
14:50	110 min	Work 6: Cross Communication Scenario Planning	Create Cross Communication Scenarios using "Horizontal T model"
16:40	20 min	Wrap-up	/
17:00	/	/	/

Figure 8.8 Agenda for a standard Scenario Idea Session.

sessions in a different location and atmosphere from regular meetings makes it easier to create ideas freely. For example, you might use one of the following approaches that we have used in Japan:

- Conduct the sessions in an open meeting place, with large windows.

- Play music to create a comfortable atmosphere.

- Use aromas to make the space more relaxing.

- Use large cushions and massage chairs.

- Prepare large sticky notes for sharing and expanding on ideas, and to promote understanding.

While not all of these ideas will work in all places, the idea of getting "off-site" and doing what is necessary to stimulate thinking holds up.

Summary

Scenario Ideas can be created using the individual skills of planners and creators, but those ideas will improve exponentially if the knowledge of the project team members is used to its greatest potential. It is the job of the facilitator to draw as much as possible out of each team member and to prevent the session from getting too "locked" on one or two ideas. It should be noted that Scenario Idea Sessions work for all kinds of campaigns, including "long" and "short" Scenario campaigns; a Cross Communication team should not hesitate to call a Scenario Idea Session together to resolve any brand issue, create a campaign, or even to modify a campaign once it has started.

Once the Scenario Idea is created, the next step is to supply the details of Contact Points and the messaging used. This is the beginning of the "Cross Communication Planning Cycle," mentioned earlier, an iterative movement—through "Holistic Creatives," "Structure Design," and "Negotiations and Implementation"—necessary to bring the Scenario Idea and the campaign as a whole to market. Chapter 9 examines the next stage and the stage that follows after: Structure Design and measuring the effects of the campaign.

CHAPTER 9

STRUCTURE DESIGN AND MEASUREMENT FOR CROSS SWITCH

Chapter 7 outlined the overall design process for Cross Switch, Dentsu's application of Cross Communication. Chapter 8 got us as far as consumer and media insight, that is, what consumers wanted, when and under what circumstances, and what media approaches worked best. With that knowledge, we went on to build a Scenario Idea using facilitated Scenario Idea Sessions. Now we approach the nuts and bolts of campaign development, namely, scientific evaluation and selection of Contact Points. The analysis behind these nuts and bolts comes mainly through two Dentsu tools: VALCON™ and DENTSU-CONNECT MEDIA™. Figure 9.1 shows where we are in the process later on.

The "scientific" approach is continued through the measurement of campaign results, where we will discuss three more important Dentsu tools to accomplish that task. At this point, we will have discussed all "seven steps" of the Cross Communication planning process, although it is a process that never really ends. Why? Because after we analyze the results from the Step 7 evaluation, we will start all over again; perhaps not in this campaign, but certainly in campaigns to come. PDCA—Plan-Do-Check-Act.

Structure Design and the Analysis of Contact Points

In order to achieve highly effective Cross Communication, it is important to have a demonstrative, quantitative design in relation to the breadth and depth of the scenario. As we mentioned earlier, we borrowed an architectural term and called this "structure design." Structure design is as important a planning process as "Holistic Creative" (the comprehensive creative expression covering the scenario) when implementing Cross Communication based on a Scenario Idea.

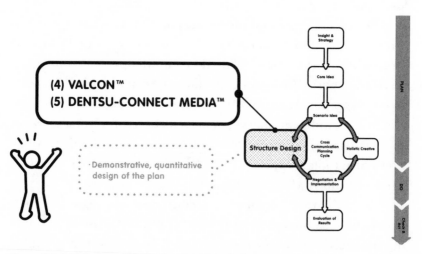

Figure 9.1 Methods and tools for structure design.

There are two main levels of Dentsu's Structure Design. The "top" level covers the Contact Point or communication medium *in general,* for example, television commercials, newspaper articles, company Web sites, and POP displays. The other, which we call "vehicles," covers very *specific* contacts and media —such as specific media selections or even specific issues among those selections, specific magazines, specific advertising locations, specific events, and so forth where specific target audiences and even timing become critical factors. Examples include TV Asahi's *Hodo Station* news program, the *Nikkei Shimbun* newspaper, or a Yahoo! placement done on a particular day or targeted to a particular locale; a similar placement program in the United States might include *NBC Nightly News, USA Today,* or a targeted page in Yahoo! We will now look at analysis methods on each of these two levels: Contact Points and "vehicles."

Selecting Effective Contact Points with VALCON™

When creating Cross Communication scenarios, it is important to select Contact Points that are effective for the target based on a quantitative understanding of the connectivity between the Contact Point and that target. When creating the scenario, the concept of "Contact Point Management" is essential. This means taking a neutral view of the various Contact Points that connect the target and the brand, and seeking out the combinations that are truly effective for the brand.

The "VALCON" Approach

"VALCON" stands for "Value Contact Point Tracer," and is a proprietary Dentsu tool registered as a trademark in Japan, China, Taiwan, Indonesia, and Thailand for achieving Structure Design at the Contact Point level. VALCON enables quantitative selection of highly effective Contact Points in keeping with the issues faced by the brand, and can be used in diverse situations both in Japan and elsewhere.

VALCON helps with two decisions in the Structure Design process:

1. Identify all Contact Points that could potentially be used in the campaign.

2. Investigate the most effective Contact Points for the brand and analyze them quantitatively.

Identifying Potential Contact Points

In addition to the Contact Points that are common to all categories—such as television commercials and programs, or corporate home pages—it is also important to identify those that are unique to the categories and brands in question.

For example, in the case of automobiles, unique Contact Points would include car dealerships and other sales outlets, specialized automobile magazines, motor shows, and other related events. Even car dealerships should not be seen as a single Contact Point; rather, they must be broken down to include the external view of the dealership, the signs around the building, the cars on display, the salespersons, and even the test drives.

There are two main methods of identifying Contact Points in this way:

1. Conduct studies involving project members from the client company and the advertising company.

2, Directly ask the consumers, for example, through group interviews and questionnaires.

If the company and the brand have sufficient experience, then the project members will likely be successful in identifying the main Contact Points through their own studies. If the company has never done an analysis from the perspective of Contact Points or if the campaign involves a category or brand in a new industry or one where it is difficult to grasp the actual conditions, then it is probably best to conduct a consumer survey at least once.

Figure 9.2 gives an idea of the variety of available Contact Points for designing campaigns. Obviously, these Contact Points will vary according to geography, type of audience, and type of product being advertised.

Quantitative Contact Point Analysis

Once the Contact Points have been identified, we can conduct consumer surveys or apply data already collected to determine which Contact Points will be most effective. Which of the two approaches we choose depends obviously on how much data we have and the uniqueness of the product category.

VALCON emphasizes three perspectives when conducting quantitative analyses based on consumer surveys of Contact Points. Even the same Contact Point may demonstrate very different effects depending on (1) the target, (2) the category, and (3) the goal of communications and the message to be communicated.

The best way to explain is by illustration. In Figure 9.3, we will introduce the results of an analysis conducted on digital camera categories. We analyzed which Contact Points would be effective in achieving two communication goals—generating interest and promoting understanding—when targeting men and women in their twenties and thirties.

The left- and right-hand columns show the two different communications goals: generating interest and promoting understanding (in this case, an understanding of features.) The different goals are a key part of the analysis; it is a mistake to assume that a given Contact Point will work the same way for each stage of the consumer buying process.

In this case, there was no significant difference in the effective Contact Points for men and women in terms of generating interest

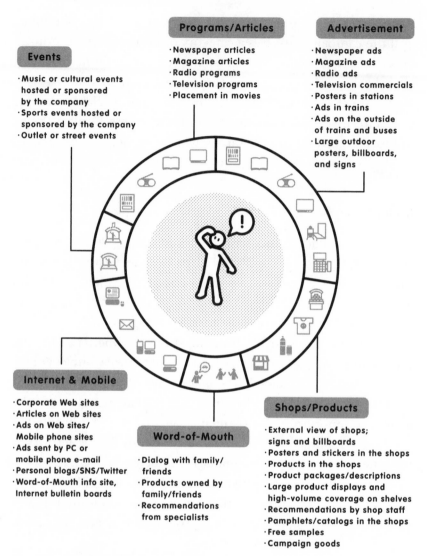

Events
· Music or cultural events
 hosted or sponsored
 by the company
· Sports events hosted or
 sponsored by the company
· Outlet or street events

Programs/Articles
· Newspaper articles
· Magazine articles
· Radio programs
· Television programs
· Placement in movies

Advertisement
· Newspaper ads
· Magazine ads
· Radio ads
· Television commercials
· Posters in stations
· Ads in trains
· Ads on the outside
 of trains and buses
· Large outdoor
 posters, billboards,
 and signs

Internet & Mobile
· Corporate Web sites
· Articles on Web sites
· Ads on Web sites/
 Mobile phone sites
· Ads sent by PC or
 mobile phone e-mail
· Personal blogs/SNS/Twitter
· Word-of-Mouth info site,
 Internet bulletin boards

Word-of-Mouth
· Dialog with family/
 friends
· Products owned by
 family/friends
· Recommendations
 from specialists

Shops/Products
· External view of shops;
 signs and billboards
· Posters and stickers in the shops
· Products in the shops
· Product packages/descriptions
· Large product displays and
 high-volume coverage on shelves
· Recommendations by shop staff
· Pamphlets/catalogs in the shops
· Free samples
· Campaign goods

Figure 9.2 Identifying Contact Points.

in digital cameras; television commercials were extremely effective, as were products on display at the shops. The results showed, however, that it would probably be more efficient to use advertising in trains to target male consumers, and to use Word-of-Mouth information to target females.

Interested			Understands features		
	1	Television commercials	31.6	1	Manufacturer's Web sites	34.8
	2	Products on display in shops	24.2	2	Products on display in shops	30.7
Males aged 20-39	3	Advertisements inside trains	22.1	3	Pamphlets/ catalogs in shops	28.7
	1	Television commercials	36.9	1	Pamphlets/ catalogs in shops	22.1
	2	Products on display in shops	20.5	2	Products on display in shops	21.3
Females aged 20-39	3	E-mail and dialog with friends	19.7	3	Television commercials	20.1

Figure 9.3 An analysis of Contact Points in the digital camera category.

We also saw significant differences among the Contact Points for promoting understanding of the product features. In the case of males in their twenties and thirties, the manufacturer's Web site, products on display, pamphlets, and catalogs scored high marks, suggesting that only Contact Points that offer detailed information are effective for this group. In the case of women in their twenties and thirties, however, in addition to pamphlets and catalogs, we saw that television commercials were also highly effective, suggesting that television commercials can function as a medium for promoting greater understanding of product features to women. By conducting such analyses, we can efficiently and effectively select the Contact Points that should be used strategically in a scenario from the consumer's perspective.

Measuring Strength of Connectivity to Specific Media Vehicles: DENTSU-CONNECT MEDIA™

Once the Contact Points have been selected—for example, television commercials and magazine articles—it is time to think more specifically about which vehicles—that is, television shows, publications, Web sites, events, advertising space, etc.—to use, or which vehicles should be combined to create the path.

Dentsu has developed a system called "DENTSU-CONNECT MEDIA" as a tool to support Structure Design at the vehicle level. This tool is also trademarked in Japan.

Again, we utilize two functions for working through this analysis:

1. Visualize the strength of connections between "vehicles."

2. Further categorize targets based on media contact volumes.

Visualizing the Strength of Connections between "Vehicles"

Even today, as media contacts become increasingly diverse, consumers come in contact with the media in set combinations, depending on their personal interests and tastes. Our database tool, DENTSU-CONNECT MEDIA, allows you to diagram the strength of connections between individual vehicles from the consumer's perspective by quantifying the contents of a high-volume database using Dentsu's original computation logic. This additional level of granularity can be quite useful, as we will see.

Suppose that the target is "people who are interested in golf." There is a high probability that people who read Golf Magazine A also read Golf Magazine B. It is also highly likely that people who read Golf Magazine A and Golf Magazine B watch the satellite broadcast channel dedicated to golf, or check Web sites for making reservations at golf courses. Furthermore, given that many people who play golf are relatively comfortable economically, there is also a strong possibility that the same people also read lifestyle magazines and business magazines, watch news programs, and view Internet news sites.

By gaining a clear grasp of the strength of connections between "vehicles" in this way, you can make complex selections regarding highly effective "vehicles" that would not be possible simply by evaluating each individual "vehicle," for example, by using television program viewer ratings, or readership figures for newspapers and magazines.

Figure 9.4 shows visually how this strength of connection analysis might look. The numbers on the lines show the "correlation factor" between two communication "vehicles." When the number is close to "1," the relationship is strong.

For example, in the digital camera category, in order to communicate a scenario based around "travel," you could use DENTSU-CONNECT MEDIA to analyze the strength of connections between "vehicles" related to travel—such as Travel Magazine C, Travel Information Program D, and the travel information page on Portal Site E—and obtain data required to select the most effective combination of "vehicles." This analysis data could also provide stimulation for ideas that can be applied to new planning proposals.

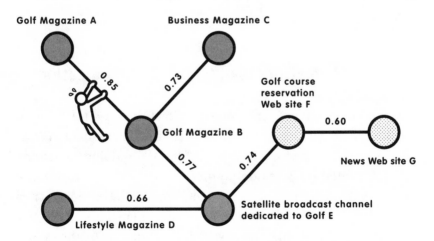

Figure 9.4 Quantitatively visualizing the strength of connections between "vehicles."

Further Categorizing Structure Design Targets Based on Media Contact Volumes

In addition to targeting of consumers subject to analysis using demographics like "males in their thirties," you could also implement effective Structure Design by categorizing targets from the perspective of the "type" and "volume" of media contact.

For example, even among "males in their thirties who are potential buyers of digital cameras," there are consumers who are steeped in digital media, and consumers who watch television and read newspapers, but rarely browse the Internet. By using DENTSU-CONNECT MEDIA, you can further categorize the targets according to the volume of media contact and then design the structure of connections between "vehicles."

In Figure 9.5, each point in the 3-D space represents individual targets. Media contact times (heavy → light) can be used to represent three axes, and the targets can be plotted in three dimensions. For example, in the case of television, the Internet, and mobile phones, the result is as shown in Figure 9.5. By dividing this distribution into groups, we can conduct an analysis between "vehicles" representing the unique characteristics of diverse media contacts.

Measuring the Effects of Cross Communication

It is a good principle to measure the effects of any advertising or communications campaign to capture return on investment (ROI) and to learn for the future. In particular, when doing something as sophisticated as Cross Communication, campaign performance measurement is particularly important because the lessons learned are more fruitful for future campaigns. Furthermore, measurement and learning can give more validation to the AISAS

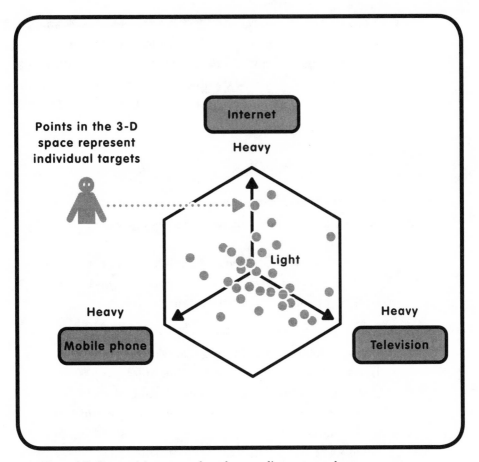

Figure 9.5 Categorizing targets based on media contact volumes.

consumer behavior model. So the question becomes: "How can we measure the effects after proposing and implementing Cross Communication?"

The first step to answering this question is to have all members share an image of the goal when proposing the communication strategy, and to set objectives accordingly. When the team is setting the goal of communications, it is preferable to first discuss and decide upon the measurement of effects. Since Cross Communication planning involves a diverse combination of Contact Points, there are many things to measure, and measurement can be challenging.

How to Evaluate Cross Communication Results

Key considerations to keep in mind when establishing measures for the effects of Cross Communication are the following:

- *Decide on the time frame.* Decide whether the objectives will be set based on a short-term campaign, or over a longer period (e.g., in order to achieve branding effects).

- *Establish the objectives.* Set the objectives to be achieved, based on the target, the Message, and the Contact Points to be used, and measure against those objectives.

    Cross Communication planners should separate communication goals (generally, psychological and attitude changes such as recognition, understanding, or purchase intent) and marketing goals (direct effects on sales, such as sales volumes or market share), and if necessary, set goals for both. Also, decide on policies. For example, make broad judgments using a single measure, set several intermediate measures, or look at multiple measures. For instance, you might want to look not just at consumer purchase or brand acceptance, an end measure, but also search activity, share activity, number of "touches" at different Contact Points, and other intermediate measures.

- *Incorporate goals unique to Cross Communication.* Incorporate goals to verify, for example, whether the consumers moved according to the scenarios, and the types of responses that were derived. Measures should capture both psychological and attitudinal changes and how the consumer actively interacts with the brand.

Specifically, this means making a more comprehensive evaluation of the overall effects of Cross Communication, and selecting measures such as the number of Internet hits, the number of people who sampled a product, and the number of comments posted on blogs. In some cases, however, we may not be measuring the results of actual behaviors, but rather the behaviors themselves in the form of a questionnaire in which the consumers indicate that they did something or experienced something. By watching the same measure continuously and using fixed-point observations, it becomes possible to make comparisons along the campaign timeline, and to ensure independence and breadth in the analysis.

To manage the campaign, we use a process similar to the familiar "PDCA" (Plan-Do-Check-Act) cycle. There is one difference. Depending on the timing deemed appropriate, rather than immediately evaluating the results or the "Check" step *after* the "Do" step is completed, we might conduct that evaluation while the campaign is being implemented (the "Do" and "Check" steps at the same time). The timing of the evaluation should be based on the company's marketing plan, and should be determined, taking into consideration the established goals and the schedule of planning (the "Plan" step) and execution (the "Do" step) after the evaluations have been completed.

Four Tools for Cross Communication Evaluation

Here we will introduce four original tools that Dentsu uses to evaluate the results of Cross Communication. As a point of reference, Figure 9.6 shows the tools and where they fit into the seven-step Cross Communication planning process.

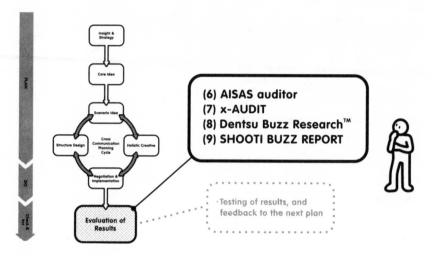

Figure 9.6 Methods and tools for the evaluation of results.

The first of the four tools is the AISAS auditor, which prepares the survey design and index of effects in advance in the form of an analysis package, based on the AISAS framework ideally suited to Cross Communication. Next is x-AUDIT, a tool for analyzing logs integrated with questionnaires to enable complex evaluations of perception and behavior data. The final two tools are Dentsu Buzz Research Powered by hottolink and SHOOTI BUZZ REPORT, which enable monitoring of the number of comments posted on blogs.

Evaluating Results Quickly through the AISAS Auditor

A variety of survey methods and items are used in the advertising industry to measure the effects of Cross Communication. Dentsu's offering is a survey package called the AISAS auditor. The purpose of this package is to conduct consumer surveys based on the AISAS framework.

Specifically, the AISAS auditor is first composed of indexes for psychology/attitude changes, which correspond to the "Attention" and "Interest" stages. Then there are behavior indexes which correspond to the "Search," "Action," and "Share" stages. It also includes related indexes required for each process. For example, in the "Share" process, in addition to indexes or "spoke to people" (or "posted comments"), there are indexes for "recommended to others."

Because the AISAS auditor incorporates general-purpose survey items based on Dentsu's past databases and analysis know-how, it is able to measure effects quickly. The indexes can also be customized freely to accommodate the communication issues being faced at the time.

Figure 9.7 shows the survey results for a campaign designed to notify consumers of the release of new core food products. It provides a quantitative measurement of the types of effects that were achieved at each stage of AISAS. In this diagram, we can see that more than 60 percent of consumers surveyed searched for information, indicating that many consumers gathered information, particularly through Word-of-Mouth communications from friends and acquaintances, before purchasing the product.

The behavior of gathering information is largely thought of as occurring in categories such as durable consumer goods or involvement products—higher-cost, longer-lasting, and more expensive products—but in this campaign, it became clear that consumers were gathering information on a level that compares favorably with those kinds of products.

The AISAS auditor is thus effective in that it enables a wide range of discoveries through tracking design that follows up on the details of each goal, and in that it allows comparisons with standard values derived from past surveys conducted using the same framework. The AISAS auditor also opens the way for multi-faceted testing; for example, one could determine the differences between groups that were aware of the campaign and groups that were not.

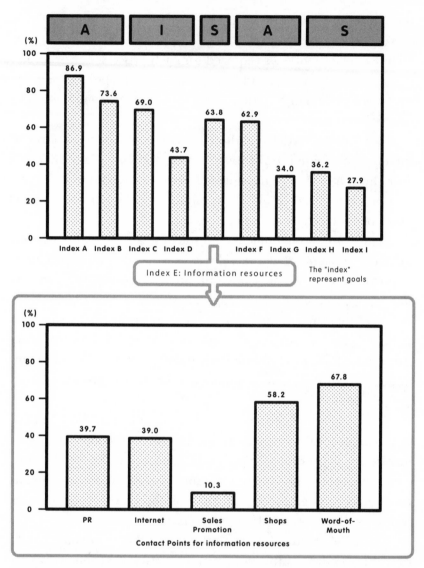

Figure 9.7 Evaluation of campaign results from an AISAS perspective: New food product launch campaign.

Measuring Combined Psychology/Attitude and Behavior Changes: x-AUDIT

x-AUDIT is a tool for analyzing Web logs integrated with questionnaires and is used in situations involving complex evaluations of psychology/attitude changes and behavior data. See Figure 9.8. There are many opportunities to use this tool in "Go to Web" campaigns that lead consumers from mass media advertisements to Internet Web sites, as in the case of television commercials that tell viewers, "Please search for XXX on the Internet."

Log analysis systems are incorporated into Web sites and can be tied into systems that display simple questionnaires. It is thus possible to link and analyze the access logs for people who visited and toured the Web site, and the data on questionnaire responses, for example, regarding awareness and personal attributes.

Figure 9.9 is an example of the flow from the moment a consumer becomes aware of Internet securities accounts to the moment that a consumer opens an account, and how that flow

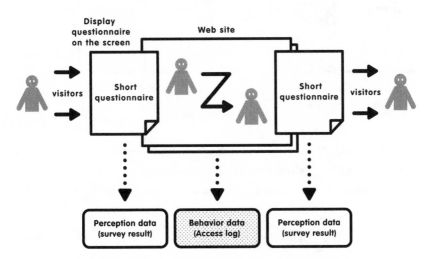

Figure 9.8 Structure of the "x-AUDIT" integrated questionnaire/log analysis tool.

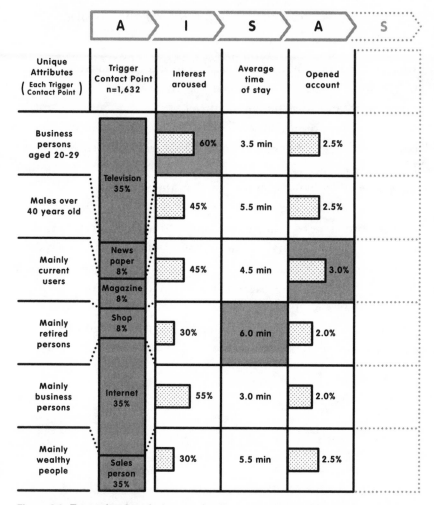

Figure 9.9 Example of analyzing results: From awareness of Internet securities accounts to opening an account.

might be measured: Those data come from Web access logs and questionnaires, as shown in Figure 9.8.

Based on the AISAS framework, we analyzed visitors to the Web site from various perspectives:

- Contact Point that triggered the visit

- Interest aroused

- Average time of stay

- Ratio of accounts opened

Because it was possible to combine questionnaire response data with actual behavior data derived from access logs, we were able to make a number of discoveries:

- "Television commercials are useful in attracting initial interest."

- "People who learned about the campaign at the sales outlet tend to spend more time at the Web site."

- "Most of the people who learned about the campaign through magazines are current users and are the most likely to eventually open an account."

If the questionnaire is adapted to the Internet, then when an Internet advertisement is used, it is possible to link questionnaire response data for each individual advertisement. This would yield analysis results like: "X percent of people who visited the Web site after clicking on a certain banner advertisement knew about the product beforehand through a television commercial."

The results of data tabulations and analyses can be quickly grasped and shared among team members, including members from the client company, by using data mining tools and basic tabulation systems provided via the Internet. Figure 9.9 shows a rather elaborate example of such a cross tabulation.

Getting the "Buzz": Analyzing Word-of-Mouth Information on the Internet

Next is an attempt to analyze "share" activity; that is, the tendency for consumers to post Word-of-Mouth information on the Internet. The tools we use to do that are called "Dentsu

Buzz Research Powered by hottolink" and "SHOOTI BUZZ REPORT."

The number of users of Japan's major social networking services (SNS) including "mixi" and "Mobage-Town" (a mobile phone Internet portal site) has exceeded 10 million. The number of blogs and SNS participants is increasing steadily worldwide. SNS systems, in general, and Facebook, in particular, have seen huge increases in membership. Amid an increase in Cross Communication aimed at stimulating Word-of-Mouth communication, analyzing real-world comments on consumer blogs and bulletin boards is essential to verifying the effects of campaigns. Are people talking about what we're selling?

Dentsu Buzz Research Powered by hottolink and SHOOTI BUZZ REPORT (provided by Blogwatcher Inc.) are Word-of-Mouth analysis systems used by Dentsu to gain a quantitative and qualitative grasp of the content of comments posted on the Internet. With Dentsu Buzz Research Powered by hottolink, if you set the brand name, company name, or product name that you want to survey, then the search engine will "crawl" major blog and bulletin board sites and display the number of related comments posted each day. This tool was used to analyze the results of Word-of-Mouth effects in the *Jump Square* inaugural issue campaign, first discussed in Chapter 3.

Dentsu Buzz Research Powered by hottolink gives a count of the number of postings over a period of time for a given keyword or search word. In addition to the number of postings, SHOOTI BUZZ REPORT allows you to monitor whether the contents of the posting are positive or negative, using a dictionary function incorporated into the system. It can also display words posted along with the keyword searched in the form of "related word rankings." The tool links certain words or phrases with positive or negative or even male or female responses, not with absolute certainty, but within statistical significance. Extracts of actual postings can also be displayed to enable qualitative analyses. This service provides an analysis system in a Web-based

Application Service Provider (ASP) format, and there is also an optional report service.

Blogwatcher Inc., which was established in April 2007 by Recruit Co., Ltd., and Dentsu, offers an analysis system using a similar ASP format, along with "SHOOTI BUZZ REPORT," another Word-of-Mouth analysis service conducted by specialized researchers.

Figure 9.10 shows an example of Word-of-Mouth analysis for a PC-related company. About 500 million Word-of-Mouth comments related only to the company in question were picked up from blogs and Question and Answer (Q&A) sites; the results were then plotted according to the attributes of male and female posters, along with analyses of the meanings of the posted comments on three levels: positive, neutral, and negative.

An analysis of the SHOOTI BUZZ REPORT for this PC-related product shows that males tended to post contents related to "commercials," "technologies," "sales location," "events," and "performance," while females tended to post words related to usage situations, such as "use" or "ease of use."

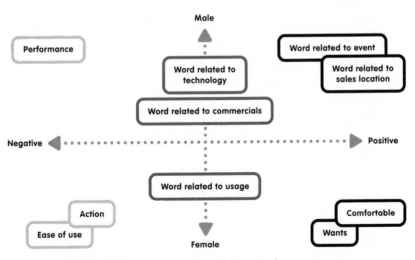

Figure 9.10 SHOOTI BUZZ REPORT analysis example.

Summary

In review, Chapters 7, 8, and 9 have introduced methods for actually designing Cross Communication, along with an outline of nine key methods and tools for each planning process. There are three main reasons for planning campaigns using these methods and tools:

- Tacit, or intuitive, knowledge becomes formal knowledge. This helps beginners and others not familiar with the Cross Communication framework to plan campaigns effectively.

- Using such planning processes is faster than planning from scratch.

- Databases and data tools not only allow for campaign and return on investment (ROI) measurement, but they also make it easy to compare current campaigns to past examples.

Dentsu has a wide range of methods and tools in addition to those outlined in this book, in order to increase the effectiveness and efficiency of Cross Communication. The company is working to evolve these methods and tools on a daily basis, and to make them widely available outside of Japan.

EPILOGUE

We hope that *The Dentsu Way* has been an enlightening and enjoyable reading experience.

By now, you have a good overview of what The Dentsu Way is and how it evolved. You understand the concept and context of "Good Innovation.," and how it applies to "Integrated Communication Design." You understand how the Cross Switch platform evolved out of the imperative to gain broader and deeper consumer involvement and to cut through the overabundance of media in today's consumer markets.

You understand why the AISAS model has become the fundamental consumer response model of the day. You understand how all of these factors have become the foundation of the Cross Switch model. And you understand how we at Dentsu integrate Cross Switch strategies, tactics, and tools to design and implement a

Cross Switch campaign, from the recognition of the brand issue to the inception of the Core Idea to the creation of the Scenario Idea, all the way through measuring the actual performance of the campaign.

Admittedly, there have been a lot of lists presented in *The Dentsu Way*. But with that in mind, as well as the "understandings" just outlined as background, we wish to close with another list: "The Ten Principles for Success in Cross Communication." These rules are handy to keep in mind as you consider, design, and implement Cross Switch. Here they are, one at a time:

1. *Think carefully, from the individual consumer's perspective.* The starting point for planning is creating ideas from the consumer's perspective. In order for the Scenario Idea you have created to be broadly accepted, it must have an element of reality for each individual consumer. You must walk in the target's shoes. You must think about:

   - "What does he or she want?"
   - "How will he or she behave?"
   - "What does he or she feel?"

   Then you must create a clear image of that consumer's actions. To achieve this, you must apply analysis and deep insight into the consumer's preferences, awareness, and lifestyle views, as well as related media and social trends.

2. *Create new ideas. Have the courage to say, "If it isn't new, it isn't Cross Communication."* That may sound profound, but you will not be able to attract the consumers' attention using campaigns like those that have appeared in the past. You must always emphasize the innovativeness of ideas. Thinking outside the framework of conventional advertising will provide hints for encouraging the consumer to act independently. Maintain an awareness of creating

something truly innovative—something that has never been seen before.

3. *Gather diverse team members, and actively "encroach on airspace."* Cross Communication requires specialization in a variety of fields, so it is essential to bring together the knowledge and wisdom of specialists. When diverse team members exchange opinions, the result is a chemical reaction of unexpected ideas, and members will often notice things exactly because those things are outside their fields of specialization. It is important to create a flexible atmosphere in which each individual team member can express ideas without being confined by the boundaries of his or her own field, transcending the barriers of divisions or titles. A structure in which members can create together while demonstrating their individual specialties will result in good, refined scenarios.

4. *Continue to share the goal among the entire team throughout the planning process.* Right from the outset, create a structure in which the team members share the goals to be achieved. In order to cooperate in seeing the project through to the end with the same goals, team members must always aim to share awareness and information. It is important for the team to work as a close-knit unit, for example, by incorporating "consensus" as a core element of processes, or forming smaller work units composed of key members.

5. *Make it easy to explain.* Sometimes, during the course of repeated trial and error while creating scenarios, the ideas can become quite complex. The ideas that stick in people's minds the most, however, are the simplest ones. The ability to explain the fundamental concept in simple terms is the first step in moving the targets once the campaign is implemented. If you feel that the idea or structure is complex and difficult to explain, then you may be headed

in the wrong direction. You must have the courage to scrap an idea that you have created and start again from scratch.

6. *Always maintain an image of the scale of communication.* Cross Communication is defined by both breadth and depth. Because "breadth" corresponds with "reach," it is fairly easy to predict the number of people who will be aware of the campaign and show interest in it. "Depth," however, has a more qualitative focus—how to increase the consumers' involvement, and how to motivate the consumers to take action—so we must remember not to overlook the issue of "volume." Even if the scenario is unique, perhaps the "triggers" or Contact Points are limited, which would mean that a smaller number of people would actually have the opportunity to experience the brand. In order to ensure success, it is important to always maintain an awareness of scale, in terms of both breadth and depth.

7. *Be persistent in negotiations, and don't give up until the plan becomes reality.* Innovative Cross Communication campaigns often include new media activities or collaborations with content holders. In this context, a determination to take on challenges without giving up is essential to making the plan a reality. You need the ability to be persistent in negotiations, and to create win-win relationships. In this new era of advertising, planners must also have the qualifications of a producer. Campaigns only have value when the idea becomes a reality. Take responsibility for following through until the campaign has taken a concrete form in the real world.

8. *Reexamine the plan once more, to ensure that it truly solves the issue at hand.* The scenario should be created so as to resolve an issue being faced by the brand. Does your plan to draw the consumers out from within their Information Barriers and actively experience the brand truly reduce

the distance between the consumer and the brand? Look at your scenario closely once more, and be sure that it truly resolves the issue at hand.

9. *Thoroughly review the campaign, and tie this into the next campaign.* After one campaign has been rolled out, conduct a thorough review, and identify both the good and bad points. To what degree were the goals set in advance achieved? If they were not achieved, what got in the way? Was it a problem in the planning, the budget, or the operations? Quickly correct the problem points, strengthen the successful points, and reflect these results in the next campaign. Reviews have a tendency to be neglected, but it is important to conduct reviews from a "PDCA" perspective and thoroughly incorporate them into the daily cycle.

10. *Have fun with Cross Communication!* The creation of Cross Communication scenarios requires free thinking that is not confined to past experiences of success. Create something that you honestly think is interesting and encourages the consumers to feel the same way. Thinking of changes as opportunities, and enjoying those opportunities, is the starting point for the creation of ideas that will move the consumers. The project will achieve the best results if the planners and the team members genuinely enjoy themselves.

Ten Principles for Success in Cross Communication

. . . .

1
Think carefully, from
the individual consumer's perspective.

2
Create new ideas.
Have the courage to say, "If it isn't new, it
isn't Cross Communication".

3
Gather diverse team members,
and actively "encroach on airspace"

4
Continue to share the goal
among the entire team throughout the planning process.

5
Make it easy to explain.

6
Always maintain an image of
the scale of communication.

7
Be persistent in negotiations, and don't
give up until the plan becomes reality.

8
Reexamine the plan once more, to ensure
that it truly solves the issue at hand.

9
Thoroughly review the campaign,
and tie this into the next campaign.

10
Have fun with Cross Communication!

APPENDIX 1

OUTLINE OF CROSS COMMUNICATION BEHAVIOR SURVEY

Cross Communication Behavior Survey, Japan

- *Subjects:* Individual males and females, ages 12–64
- *Sample size: n* = 2,090
- *Areas:* Kanto region (cities and wards with populations of 150,000 or more in Tokyo and six prefectures: Kanagawa, Chiba, Saitama, Ibaraki, Tochigi, and Gunma)
- *Survey method:* Internet survey
- *The Internet Panel Survey used:* A segment of the Survey Panel from Dentsu's original database d-camp.
- *Survey period:* Feb. 22 (Fri.) to Feb. 29 (Fri.), 2008

Cross Communication Behavior Survey, Japan

	Total	12–19	20–29	30–39	40–49	50–59	60–64
Total	2,090	118	527	682	377	291	95
Male	1,217	62	278	374	242	190	71
Female	873	56	249	308	135	101	24

Cross Communication Behavior Survey, United States

- *Subjects:* Individual males and females, aged 18–59
- *Sample size:* n = 982
- *Areas:* United States (all over the country)
- *Survey method:* Internet survey
- *Survey period:* May 18 (Thurs.) to May 23 (Tues.), 2010

Cross Communication Behavior Survey, United States

	Total	18–19	20–29	30–39	40–49	50–59
Total	982	13	151	233	292	293
Male	439	4	62	104	137	132
Female	543	9	89	129	155	161

APPENDIX 2

DENTSU GROUP TROPHY CASE

Cannes Lions International Advertising Festival				
	Section	Client	Product	Title	Agency
2007					
Gold Lion	Media Lions	HITACHI	WASHING MACHINES	A TIME MACHINE? A WASHING MACHINE?	DENTSU
Silver Lion	Media Lions	SHOGAKU-KAN	COMIC BOOKS	COMIC SHOGAKU-KAN BOOKS	DENTSU
Bronze Lion	Media Lions	HITACHI	WASHING MACHINES	A TIME MACHINE? A WASHING MACHINE	DENTSU
Silver Lion	Cyber Lions	SHOGAKU-KAN	COMIC SHOGAKU-KAN BOOKS	COMIC SHOGAKU-KAN BOOKS	DENTSU
Promo Lion	Promo Lions	GOLDWIN	THE NORTH FACE	NO PAIN, NO GAIN	DENTSU Y&R
2008					
Silver Lion	Film Lions	SECOM CO.	HOME SECURITY SERVICE	THE BIG TEST	DENTSU/ SHINGATA
Bronze Lion	Film Lions	MORINAGA & CO.	CARRÉ DE CHOCO-LAT CHOCO-LATE BOX	NON-BLINKING WOMAN	DENTSU
Grand Prix	Radio Lions	CANON MARKETING JAPAN	EOS KISS DIGITAL CAMERA	SHUTTER CHANCE	DENTSU
Gold Lion	Media Lions	THE ASAHI SHIMBUN	NEWS-PAPER	THE ASAHI NEWS-PAPER MOVES	DENTSU Kansai
Silver Lion	Media Lions	TOKYO METROPOLI-TAN	2016 OLYMPIC HOST BID	TOEI STATION STADIUM	DENTSU
Bronze Lion	Media Lions	SHUEISHA	JUMP-SQUARE MAGAZINE	HIDE-AND-SEEK ADVERTIS-ING	DENTSU

	Section	Client	Product	Title	Agency
Gold Lion	Cyber Lions	SONY MARKETING (JAPAN)	SONY WALKMAN PORTABLE AUDIO PLAYER	REC YOU	GT/DENTSU
Silver Lion	Cyber Lions	HONDA MOTOR CO.	CAR NAVIGA-TION SYSTEM	ZOOM IN/OUT	DENTSU
Silver Lion	Cyber Lions	JAPAN ADVERTIS-ING COUNCIL	CAMPAIGN AGAINST DOMESTIC VIOLENCE	RELIEF	DENTSU
Bronze Lion	Cyber Lions	SONY MARKETING (JAPAN)	FOOTBALL SPONSOR-SHIP	ZIKKYO GENERA-TOR	GT/DENTSU
Gold Lion	Promo Lions	WILD BIRD SOCIETY OF JAPAN	BIRD PROTEC-TION	VOICE OF ENDAN-GERED BIRDS	BEACON COMMUNI-CATIONS
Silver Lion	Design Lions	TROPICAL PLANT-RESOURCES RESEARCH INSTITUTE	HEALTH SUPPLE-MENT DRINK	THE DEW OF LONGEV-ITY	DENTSU
Bronze Lion	Design Lions	KYURYUDO ART-PUB-LISHING CO.	EVENT	IWAI	DENTSU Kansai
Silver Lion	Press Lions	Canon Marketing (Thailand)	Canon IXUS 75	Cheetah/Baseball/Rock Concert	DENTSU THAILAND
2009					
Grand Prix	Promo Lions	YUBARI RESORT	RESORT FACILITIES	YUBARI	BEACON COMMUNI-CATIONS
Gold Lion	Design Lions	YOSHIDA HIDEO MEMORIAL FOUNDA-TION	2008 ONE SHOW EXHIBI-TION	2008 ONE SHOW EXHIBI-TION	DENTSU
Gold Lion	Design Lions	MITSUBISHI ESTATE CO & IDEE CO	HAIKU EVENT	COMING MOON	DENTSU Kansai
Silver Lion	Design Lions	MITSUBISHI ESTATE CO & IDEE CO	HAIKU EVENT	COMING MOON	DENTSU Kansai

	Section	Client	Product	Title	Agency
Silver Lion	Design Lions	NICHIREI FOODS	ACEROLA FRUIT DRINK	FROM THE COUNTRY OF PASSION	DRILL/DENTSU
Bronze Lion	Design Lions	ICHIDA GARDEN	WRAPPING PAPER	NEWSPAPER TO NEW PAPER PROJECT	DENTSU Kansai
Gold Lion	Media Lions	SONY MUSIC ASSOCIATED RECORDS	JUJU FEAT. SPONTANIA	WISH I COULD BE TRUE TO MYSELF	DENTSU
Bronze Lion	Media Lions	JAPAN TOBACCO	CANNED COFFEE	"ROOTS" CANNED COFFEE BOOK	DENTSU
Bronze Lion	Media Lions	UNIQLO CO.	VARIATED PARKA SERIES	TOKYO FASHION MAP	DENTSU
Gold Lion	Cyber Lions	UNIQLO CO.	VARIATED PARKA SERIES	TOKYO FASHION MAP	DENTSU
Bronze Lion	Cyber Lions	SONY MUSIC ASSOCIATED RECORDS	JUJU FEAT SPONTANIA	WISH I COULD BE TRUE TO MYSELF	DENTSU
Bronze Lion	Cyber Lions	KDDI	iida	iida Calling	DENTSU/ground
Gold Lion	Outdoor Lions	DUNLOP FALKEN TYRES	SAFETY AWARENESS CAMPAIGN	MELODY ROAD	DENTSU
ADFEST					
	Section	Client	Product	Title	Agency
2007					
Gold	360 Lotus	NapsterJapan	Napster	Open Your Ears Campaign	DENTSU
Gold	Cyber Lotus	Japan Advertising Council	Smoking Manner	Specified Area	DENTSU
Silver	TV Lotus	Shizuoka Broadcasting	Shizuoka Broadcasting	Fishermen	DENTSU
Silver	Radio Lotus	Otsuka Pharmaceutical	NEMU	Previous Life-Queen of France	DENTSU

	Section	Client	Product	Title	Agency
Silver	Radio Lotus	Suntory	Bird Protection Campaign	Bird Theater	DENTSU
Silver	Cyber Lotus	Madre: X Co., Ltd.	Ex-Beaute	The Beauty Ex:press	DENTSU
Silver	Cyber Lotus	Japan Advertising Council	Don't Drink and Drive	The Wiper	DENTSU
Silver	Cyber Lotus	Honda Motor	Honda Automobile	Enjoy/Live Drive	DENTSU
2008					
Grand Prix	Innova Lotus Grand Innova	NISSIN FOODS HOLDINGS	Nissin Cup Noodles	"FREEDOM-PROJECT"	ground/DENTSU
Grand Prix	Cyber Lotus	Sony Marketing Inc.	Sony Walkman	Rec You	GT/DENTSU
Gold	TV Lotus	Recruit Co., Ltd.	Rikunavi	Ms. Yuko Yamada Looks For Her First Job	DENTSU
Gold	Cyber Lotus	Sony Marketing Inc.	Sony Walkman	Rec You	GT/DENTSU
Gold	360 Lotus	NISSIN FOODS HOLDINGS	Nissin Cup Noodles	"FREEDOM-PROJECT"	ground/DENTSU
Gold	360 Lotus	Yurakucho Marui Ne	Yurakucho Marui Ne	Fashion Therapy	Drill/DENTSU
Gold	Innova Lotus	NISSIN FOODS HOLDINGS	Nissin Cup Noodles	"FREEDOM-PROJECT"	ground/DENTSU
Silver	TV Lotus	MORINAGA & CO., LTD.	Carré de Chocolat	Non-blinking Woman	DENTSU
Silver	Radio Lotus	CANON MARKETING JAPAN	EOS KISS DIGITAL CAMERA	SHUTTER CHANCE	DENTSU
Silver	Outdoor Lotus	Tokyo Metropolitan	Subway Station Stadium Project	TOEI Station Stadium	DENTSU
Silver	Direct Lotus	Japan Tobacco inc.	Canned Coffee	Go with Roots!	DENTSU

	Section	Client	Product	Title	Agency
Silver	Cyber Lotus	DENTSU INC.	Dentsu Creative And Planning School	Dentsu CR&P School 2007	DENTSU
Bronze	TV Lotus	CALPIS Co.	Calpico Soda	The Kind Boy	DENTSU
Bronze	Design Lotus	KANSAI PAPER CO., LTD.	Tissue Box	Lace Queen	DENTSU
Bronze	Poster Lotus	Monceau Fleurs	Monceau Fleurs (Flower Shop)	Flower Magic (Hug/ Entry/ Surprise/ Pee)	DENTSU
Bronze	Outdoor Lotus	Asics	Asics Shoes	No More Branding Campaign	DENTSU
Bronze	Direct Lotus	SHUEISHA	JUMP-SQUARE MAGAZINE	HIDE-AND-SEEK ADVERTIS-ING	DENTSU
Bronze	Cyber Lotus	Honda Motor Co., Ltd.	Corporate	Honda Website Weekend Top Page	DENTSU
Bronze	Cyber Lotus	Honda Motor Co., Ltd.	Car Navigation System	Viewpoint/ Trans-former/ Zoom In/ Out/The Ten Command	DENTSU
2009					
Grand Prix	Innova Lotus	DUNLOP FALKEN TYRES	SAFETY AWARE-NESS CAMPAIGN	MELODY ROAD	DENTSU
Gold	Cyber Lotus	UNIQLO Co.,Ltd.	UNIQLO BRA TOP	UNIQLO TRY	DENTSU
Gold	Film Craft Lotus	Honda Motor Co., Ltd.	Corporate	Music	DENTSU
Silver	Cyber Lotus	SONY MUSIC ASSOCIATED RECORDS	JUJU FEAT SPONTA-NIA	WISH I COULD BE TRUE TO MYSELF	DENTSU

	Section	Client	Product	Title	Agency
Silver	TV Lotus	Toyota Motor Corporation	iQ	Parking/ Clean Up/ Catch/ Heading	DENTSU
Silver	TV Lotus	Yamaguchi Chiropractic	Yamaguchi Chiropractic	Crossing/ Cockroach/ Delivery	DENTSU
Bronze	Design Lotus	DENTSU INC.	Dentsu Recruitment Book Maru-Ru	Dentsu Recruitment Book Maru-Ru	DENTSU
Bronze	Design Lotus	NTT Docomo	Docomo-dake Art Exhibition: How to Cook Doco-modake?	Docomo-dake Art Exhibition: How to Cook Doco-modake?	DENTSU
Bronze	Design Lotus	Yoshida Hideo Memorial Foundation	2008 One Show Exhibition	2008 One Show Exhibition	DENTSU
Bronze	Cyber Lotus	Intel	Intel (R) Processor	Intel GASSAKU	DENTSU
Bronze	TV Lotus	The Yomiuri Newspaper	Yomiuri Newspaper	Olympic Ping Pong	DENTSU

APPENDIX 3

BIOGRAPHIES OF KEY DENTSU CONTRIBUTORS

SO YAMADA

Planner; Strategic Planning Office, Dentsu Inc.
"No Matter the Era, Concept Is the Key"

Entered Dentsu Inc. in 1993. Worked in the Marketing Supervision and Account Executive Offices and the IMC Planning Center before being assigned to his current position in the Strategic Planning Office in July 2008.

He has worked on numerous campaigns, creating outstanding concepts and developing ideas that always show great imagination. He has drawn attention by developing new Contact Points and creating new triggers for Word-of-Mouth communications.

He has received several major advertising awards, including the Promo Lion (equivalent to the current Gold Award) at the 53rd Cannes Lions International Advertising Festival in 2006, the Bronze Award in the "Direct Lotus" category at the 11th ADFEST in 2008, and the Bronze Award in the "Media Lions" category at the 56th Cannes Lions International Advertising Festival in 2009. He also served as a jury member of the "Media Lions" category at the 56th Cannes Lions International Advertising Festival in 2009.

YUKI KISHI
Communication Designer; Communication Design Center, Dentsu Inc.
"Don't Design the Mechanism—Design Consumers' Feelings Instead"

Graduated from the Waseda University Graduate School of Information and Telecommunication Studies. Entered Dentsu Inc. in 2004, after working as a full-time researcher at the Chuo University Research and Development Initiative. Worked in the Central Branch Magazine Division, the Media and Marketing Division, and the Interactive Communication Department. Assigned to the Communication Design Center in July 2008.

He has worked on numerous innovative campaigns and "viral" campaigns using approaches that are not limited by conventional advertising wisdom and has gained attention for developing communications that involve the consumer. He is also recognized as a Media Researcher, and his many activities include writing and lectures at universities. His latest book, *A Book for Designing Communications*, was published in Japan in 2008.

He has received many awards, including the Gold Award in the "Media Lions" category at the 56th Cannes Lions International Advertising Festival in 2009, Grand Prix in the "Digital" category at the Spikes Asia Advertising Festival in 2009, London International Awards, ADFEST, the One Show, the Tokyo Interactive Ad Awards (TIAA), and the Good Design Award. He also served as a jury member of the "Cyber Lions" category at the 57th Cannes Lions International Advertising Festival in 2010.

SATOSHI TAKAMATSU
Creative Agency "ground" Representative/Chief Creative Director
The Starting Point "How to Create Ideas as Freely as Possible"

Born in 1963. After entering Dentsu Inc., he worked in Sales and later in the Creative Division. In 2005, he established the Creative Agency "ground." His main projects include the Nissin Cup Noodles "NO BORDER" and "FREEDOM" campaigns, Meiji Milk Chocolate, NTT Resonant "goo," Olympus "Digital Single-Lens," "PEN," KDDI "iida," and UNIQLO "Heat tech," "UT," and "UJ."

He has won numerous awards, including the Asahi Advertising Award and the TCC Award, as well as a Gold Award at the Cannes Lions International Advertising Festival; the Clio Awards Grand Prix; a Gold Award from the London International Awards; and a Gold Award of the ADC Hybrid from the New York Art Directors Club.

He has gained international attention for projects that transcend traditional boundaries. The "Outer Space" commercial for the beverage Pocari Sweat was the world's first commercial to be filmed on a space station. He established "SPACE FILMS," a company dedicated to creating an infrastructure to enable filming in outer space on a regular basis. The production of Nissin Cup Noodles' "NO BORDER: Outer Space Version" was a successful example. Recently he has been expanding his work to consulting in corporate strategy, business models, and product development.

KOJI HIRAYAMA
Senior Creative Director; Communication Design Center, Dentsu Inc.
"Cross" Is Not Just About Media, but Also Creativity

Entered Dentsu Inc. in 1986. After working in the Account Division, he transferred to the Creative Division in 1988 on an experimental basis. Since then, he has been active as a copywriter and Creative Director.

He is constantly seeking out new expressions for a broad range of creative elements, without being limited by existing media and approaches to presentation.

His major projects have included Asahi Kasei Corporation's "Creating things that didn't exist until yesterday" series (winner of the Asahi Advertising Awards Top Prize, the Mainichi Advertising Awards Top Prize, the Nikkei Advertising Awards Top Prize, the Fuji Sankei Group Advertising Awards Top Prize for a newspaper advertisement, the TCC Award, the ADC Award, and the Dentsu Newspaper Advertisement Award, among others), and Hitachi, Ltd.'s "Next MADE IN JAPAN" campaign (which won the Asahi Advertising Award Silver Prize, ACC Division Award). Other awards include: The New York Festival Gold Prize, the Japan Newspaper Publishers & Editors Association Top Prize, and the "Advertisement for the Consumers" Award.

REFERENCES

Advertising Economy Research Institute (Japan). *Advertising and Economy* (April 1, 2010).

Akiyama, Ryuhei. *Information Explosion.* Sendenkaigi Co., Ltd. (October 2007).

Akiyama, Ryuhei, and Kotaro Sugiyama. *Holistic Communications.* Sendenkaigi Co., Ltd. (January 2004).

Crain Communications Inc. *Advertising Age* (April 26, 2010).

Dentsu Inc. S.P.A.T. Team. *How to Create a "Want to Buy" Atmosphere.* Diamond Inc. (June 2007).

Dentsu Inc. "Special Theme: Campaign Management." *Advertising* 8 (February 2003).

Dentsu Inc. "Special Theme: Evolving IMC." *Advertising* 14 (September 2006).

Gunn, Donald, and Emma Wilkie. *The Gunn Report 2009.* Flaxman Wilkie (2009).

Ishigai, Satoshi, So Ninomiya, and Hisashi Matsunaga. "IMC Strategies from a Contact Point Perspective." Nikkei Advertising Research Institute. *Nikkei Advertising Research Institute Report* 217 (October 2004).

Japan Ministry of Internal Affairs and Communications. *2006 Information Distribution Census Report* (March 2008).

Kobayashi, Norio, and Takaharu Tokunaga. "Advertising Communication in the Broadband Era." Dentsu Inc. *Dentsu Advertising Yearbook '06–'07* (November 2006).

Kobayashi, Norio, and Takaharu Tokunaga. "AISAS® Campaign Planning That Captures Consumers' Hearts in an Era of Excess Information." Japan Advertising Federation. *Monthly Zenkoren* (December 2007).

Morioka, Shinji, So Hasegawa, and Shigetaka Yamakawa. "Proposal for Planning Methods in the Process of Forming Word-of-Mouth Communications, as Seen from the AISAS® Model." Japan Marketing Association. *Marketing Journal* 101 (June 2006).

Morita, Masataka, Naohiko Oikawa, and Yasushi Hidaka. "New Cross Media Effects Brought About by Digital Interactive Media." Japan Marketing Association. *Marketing Journal* 105 (June 2007).

INDEX

INDEX

ABOUT THE AUTHORS

Kotaro Sugiyama: Senior Vice President and Chief Creative Officer, Dentsu Inc.

Kotaro Sugiyama studied in the Department of Economics at Rikkyo University and graduated in 1971. He joined Dentsu Inc. in 1974.

At Dentsu, he was promoted to Creative Director in 1988. In 1997, he became Deputy Director of the Interactive Solution Center, then the Digital Business Design Division, and later the Internet Business Division. From the early days, he initiated the development and cultivation of Dentsu's interactive and new media businesses, making Dentsu the first in the field among traditional advertising agencies. In May 2000, he was promoted to Director of the Internet Business Division. In June 2004, he was appointed as Executive Officer, and Deputy Managing Director of the Media & Contents Business Headquarters. Sugiyama continues to be a leading figure in Dentsu's new and innovative communication-related businesses. His unique strength and ability is backed by his extensive experience and expertise in both traditional venues as well as in modern/interactive creative and media work. His leading efforts and interest in combining the traditional and the new have allowed Dentsu to become a leader of the advertising industry in Japan for the provision of advanced integrated solutions for clients.

Creative Works and Activities

Sugiyama is an internationally renowned Creative Director who has received worldwide attention. He served as a jury member at the Cannes Lion International Advertising Festival for two years and Cyber Lion for one year. He was featured in the English periodical *Campaign*. Major creative campaigns include those for Shogakukan (the publisher), Seven-Eleven, Suntory, Toyota, and Sony, among many others. He is also an author of a number of published books. His current activities include professorships at Rikkyo University and Tokyo Geijutsu Daigaku (Tokyo National University of Fine Arts and Music), specializing in areas of communication. He played an important role in the foundation of the Tokyo Interactive Ad Awards where he served as chairman from 2003 to 2007.

Achievements and Awards

Some of his awards include:

2006 Cannes Lions/International Advertising Festival Cyber, Silver Prize

New York ADC, CLIO Awards Gold Prize

"Honda Sweet Mission," Honda

2004 International Advertising Festival, Cyber Lions Gold Prize

"Toshiba Presents FM Tokyo Festival 2004" Toshiba/ Tokyo FM

1999 Cannes Lions/International Advertising Festival Cyber, Short List

London International Awards, Cyber, Educational Section Prize

NewMedia Magazine INVISION Awards,

Best Graphics and Animation Grand Prix

Educational Section Silver Prize, Grand Prix

Ministry of International Trade and Industry

Multimedia Grand Prix Edutainment Prize

www.Willing-to-try.com Web site, "Try Group"

1998   Cannes Lions/International Advertising Festival Silver Prize

New York Festivals Gold Prize

"Delight" campaign, JT (Japan Tobacco)

1997   IAA International Advertising Awards Grand Prix, New York Festivals Gold Prize, and other international awards

"WATER MAN' campaign, AC (The Japan Ad Council) London International Advertising Award

Asia Advertising Awards Grand Prix, and other international awards

"Tosui" advertisement, Suntory Hall

Books

Holistic Communication (co-author), Sendenkaigi Co., Ltd. (January 2004).

Japan Presentation (author), Kadokawa Shoten Publishing Co., Ltd. (June 2003).

Oriental Boy (author), Kawade Shobo Shinsha Publishers Inc. (June 1989),

. . . and others.

Tim Andree: Executive Officer, Dentsu Inc., President and CEO, Dentsu Network West

With his trio of executive management and leadership roles in the Dentsu organization, you might assume that Tim Andree's first love was advertising.

Not quite.

After graduating from Notre Dame and then playing in the NBA and overseas, Tim's life was all basketball. That is, until he hung up his sneakers and decided to pursue the next stage of his life off the court.

Joining Toyota headquarters in Tokyo, Tim quickly rose through the ranks—eventually leading External Affairs for Toyota Motor Corporate North America. After 13 years at Toyota, Tim joined Canon U.S.A. to head up Marketing and Corporate Communications. His unparalleled track record of success landed him the top marketing spot at BASF and ultimately returned him to the NBA as Senior Vice President, Marketing and Communications.

Tim came to Dentsu America in 2006, and in two short years moved the agency to its new state-of-the art headquarters in TriBeCa, acquired the leading-edge digital/design group ATTIK, and made Dentsu the fastest-growing agency in the United States per *Ad Age*'s 2008 Agency Report rankings.

In June 2008, Tim was named the first non-Japanese Executive Officer of Dentsu Inc. Later that November, he was appointed President & CEO, Dentsu Holdings USA, Inc., expanding his role to lead all operations in North and South America, and at the same time, he acquired celebrated New York-based advertising agency, McGarryBowen (*Ad Age*'s 2009 Agency of the Year). Tim's role expanded again in April 2009, when Dentsu's European operations were added to his responsibilities, which now includes a total of 29 offices in 9 countries. Most recently, in January 2010, he announced the acquisition of Innovation Interactive, a leading provider of global services and technology for search marketing, social media, and audience targeting.

Now Tim's greatest passions are ensuring that Dentsu delivers fresh, breakthrough thinking to all of our clients in the Americas and Europe who rely on his unique experience as a former client and offering them true 360-degree global resources by building a Dentsu Network West the size and scope of Dentsu Inc. Tim is leading the charge to garner talent in the Western region through new hires and M&A.

During his time away from the office, Tim and his wife (and college sweetheart) Laureen, enjoy chasing their six children around the basketball court at their home in Colts Neck, New Jersey.

The Dentsu Cross Switch Team

This is a cross-functional team comprised of Dentsu employees with experience and specializations in fields such as marketing, media, promotions, interactive media, and R&D. The team was formed to develop and implement Cross Communication.

The team is currently involved in various activities, including the development of new key concepts, methods, and analytical approaches that will be useful in planning and idea creation, and in accumulating know-how and successful case studies. It also provides planning support to client companies in a wide range of industries.

Team Members

Shun-ichi Akai: Planning Director, Division Manager, Planning Office 4, Strategic Planning Division

Shin-ichi Akai joined Dentsu Inc. in 1995 after working in a large distribution company. He worked in the Brand Creation Center, the MP Management Office, and the IMC Planning Center before taking up his current position in July 2008. He now works in client services, including strategic planning, product development, and brand consulting. He loves cats.

Hideaki Haruta: Marketing Supervisor, Business Strategy Planning Division

Hideaki Haruta joined Dentsu Inc. in 1994. He worked in the Magazine Office, the Media Marketing Office, and the Communication Design Center before taking up his current position in January 2010. For more than twelve years, he has provided media planning services to many clients and media companies; he is currently working on the development of tools and on consumer analysis from a Cross Communication perspective.

Yasushi Hidaka: Supervisor, Public Account Division
Yasushi Hidaka joined Dentsu Inc. in 2005, after working at a large advertising agency. He coauthored "Internet Marketing Basics (Nikkei BP):The Progress of Advertising (Dentsu)" and acted as coordinator for the Japan Marketing Association's e-Marketing Study Group, whose work was based on the theme of Cross Communication. His interests include playing golf, taking walks in the city, and collecting music CDs.

Naoto Ichimaru: Chief Planner, Business Strategy Planning Division
Naoto Ichimaru joined Dentsu Inc. in 2003. He worked in the Account Management Office and the Communication Design Center before taking up his current position in January 2010. He worked on media planning and creative for the client as a member of the account team. Recently he has been working on client support using the Cross Communication methodology and on the popularization of the Cross Communication method for the overseas market.

Satoshi Ishigai: Chief Planner, Business Strategy Planning Division
Satoshi Ishigai joined Dentsu Inc. in 1997. He worked in the Corporate Communication Office and the Communication Design Center before taking up his current position in January 2010. He developed "Contact Point Management." He initiated and continued to work on the Cross Communication Development Project and works on client services for a variety of industries. His hobby is visiting temples throughout Japan.

Mamoru Nishiyama: Chief Planner, Business Strategy Planning Division
Mamoru Nishiyama joined the Dentsu Communication Institute Inc. in 1998. He transferred to Dentsu Inc. in 1999 as a result of a merger. He later worked in the Sales Office, MP Management Office, and Communication Design Center before taking up his current position in January 2010. He worked on the Cross

Communication Development Project and the development of tools (Target Visualizer and VALCON). His interests include street dancing and traveling overseas.

Kenzo Setoguchi: Senior Director, Media and Marketing, Dentsu Network West

Kenzo Setoguchi joined Dentsu Inc. in 2000 after working for the world's leading beverage company as an advertising manager. His responsibilities at Dentsu Headquarters included media planning and research direction, not only for the Japanese market, but also for other Asian countries as well. Following his transfer to the U.S. office in 2008, he now pursues global media planning and advanced research.

Takaharu Tokunaga: Planning Supervisor, Business Strategy Planning Division

Takaharu Tokunaga joined Dentsu Inc. in 1996 after working in a large printing company. He worked in the First Marketing Promotion Office and the IMC Planning Center; and has been involved in creating brand strategies for various industries, including beverages, financial products, and government agencies, and in the popularization of the AISAS model. He also worked in the Communication Design Center before taking up his current position in January 2010. His favorite movie is *The Remains of the Day.*

Supervisors:
Hiroshi Nakahara
Kazumichi Iwagami
Masakazu Okano
Naoto Kawai

Special thanks to:
Chigusa Amano
Yuzaburo Amemiya

The ATTIK Scion team
David Cameron
Eugine Chung
Scott Daly
Junko Fujii
Shohei Hara
Keita Hashiguchi
Kyu Honjo
Midori Ikeda
Shusaku Kannan
Stephen Kentwell
Fuyuhiko Kiso
Koji Kobayashi
Norio Kobayashi
Takaaki Koshiba
Kazuya Kusumoto
Satoru Makino
Akira Maruyama
Sheryn Gaye Mason
Mitsuyoshi Matsuda
Toyoko Mori
Ryutaro Nagasawa
Koichi Ohno
Norihisa Ozawa
Teruhiko Sakuraya
Hiroaki Sano
Kyoko Shioda
Yuko Shiromizu
Masahiro Takeshita
Shin Takeshita
Tina Toda
Yasumasa Uemura
Masahiro Watanabe

Writer: Peter Sander
Illustrations: groovisions